G Roger Knight

Born in deeply rural Shropshire (UK), G Roger Knight has been living and teaching in Adelaide since the late 1960s. He gained his PhD from London University's School of Oriental and African Studies, where his mentors included John Bastin and CD Cowan. He is an internationally recognised authority on the sugar industry of colonial Indonesia, with many publications to his name. Among the latest is *Commodities and Colonialism: The Story of Big Sugar in Indonesia, 1880-1940*, published by Brill in Leiden and Boston in 2013. He is currently working on a 'business biography' — based on scores of his newly discovered letters back home — of Gillian Maclaine, a young Scot who was active as a planter and merchant in colonial Java during the 1820s and 1830s. For a change, it has almost nothing to do with sugar.

This book is available as a free fully-searchable ebook from

www.adelaide.edu.au/press

Sugar, Steam and Steel:
The Industrial Project in Colonial Java, 1830-1885

by

G Roger Knight

School of History and Politics
The University of Adelaide

UNIVERSITY OF
ADELAIDE PRESS

Published in Adelaide by

University of Adelaide Press
The University of Adelaide
Level 14, 115 Grenfell Street
South Australia 5005
press@adelaide.edu.au
www.adelaide.edu.au/press

The University of Adelaide Press publishes externally refereed scholarly books by staff of the University of Adelaide. It aims to maximise access to the University's best research by publishing works through the internet as free downloads and for sale as high quality printed volumes.

© 2014 G Roger Knight

This work is licenced under the Creative Commons Attribution-NonCommercial-NoDerivatives 4.0 International (CC BY-NC-ND 4.0) License. To view a copy of this licence, visit http://creativecommons.org/licenses/by-nc-nd/4.0 or send a letter to Creative Commons, 444 Castro Street, Suite 900, Mountain View, California, 94041, USA. This licence allows for the copying, distribution, display and performance of this work for non-commercial purposes providing the work is clearly attributed to the copyright holders. Address all inquiries to the Director at the above address.

For the full Cataloguing-in-Publication data please contact the National Library of Australia: cip@nla.gov.au

ISBN (paperback) 978-1-922064-98-1
ISBN (ebook: pdf) 978-1-922064-99-8
ISBN (ebook: epub) 978-1-925261-00-4
ISBN (ebook: kindle) 978-1-925261-01-1

Editor: Rebecca Burton
Editorial support: Julia Keller
Book design: Zoë Stokes
Cover design: Emma Spoehr
Cover image: *De suikerfabriek 'Kedawong' bij Pasoeroean op Java* by H Th Hesselaar (1849), courtesy of Rijksmuseum, the Netherlands

Contents

Abbreviations and Glossary	vii
Acknowledgements	xi
Introduction Java Sugar, an Industrial Project and the 'Oriental Cuba', 1830-85	1
Part I — The 'Industrial Revolution' in Sugar Manufacture	
1 Java's Singular Trajectory: Steam, Steel and the Industrial Project in Sugar	11
2 A Creole Prometheus: Steam, Paddle Boats and Sugar Factories	33
3 The Industrial Sugar Factory: Wonopringgo, Thomas Edwards and the Nederlandsche Handel-Maatschappij (NHM)	63
Part II — The 'Peasant' Economy, the Money Trail and the Bourgeoisie	
4 Sugar without Slaves: The Agrarian Basis for the Industrial Project	95
5 The Money Trail: State, *Suikerlords* and Bourgeoisie	133
Part III — Metamorphosis	
6 Metamorphosis: Machinery, Science and the Manufacture of Sugar in Java on the Eve of the Crisis of the Mid-1880s	177
Conclusion The Future of an Industrial Project: The 1880s and Beyond	203
Archival Sources	213
Bibliography	225

Abbreviations and Glossary

AD	Arsip Daerah (Local Archive), ANRI
ANRI	Arsip Nasional Republik Indonesia, Jakarta
ASNI	Archief voor de Suikerindustrie in Nederlandsch-Indië
AV	Algemeen Verslag (General Report)
BC	*Bataviasche Courant*
Bij	*Bijlage* [Appendix]
Bouw	0.709 65 hectares
Bupati	High ranking Javanese provincial official (see also *Regent*)
Cacah	Unit of taxation
Cultuurstelsel	System of (State) Cultivations inaugurated in 1830 to secure the expanded production of export commodities in Java, primarily coffee, sugar and indigo
Desa	Village
DNB	*Dictionary of National Biography*
DNL	*De Nederlandsche Leeuw*
Exh.	Exhibitum (Agenda item), NA, MK
f.	guilder
Factorij to A'dam	Letters from the NHM Batavia Factorij to NHM Head-Office located in Amsterdam, unless otherwise stated, in Tweede Afdeeling/B, NA, NHMA
JV	Jaarverslag [Annual Report]

JVFB	Jaarverslag Factorij Batavia NHM [Batavia Branch Office NHM], NA, NHMA
GG	Governeur-Generaal
HCHO	*Handboek voor Cultuur-en-Handelsondernemingen* in Nederlandsch-Indië, Amsterdam, De Bussy, 1888-1940
IB	Indische Besluit [Indies Government Decision]
IN	*De Indische Navorscher*
JV	Jaarverslag [Annual Report]
JVFB	Jaarverslag Factorij Batavia NHM [Batavia Branch Office NHM], NA, NHMA
JC	*Javaasche Courant*
Kring (Beschikkingskring)	Area of land assigned to each sugar factory for the cultivation of cane and commandeering of labour
KV	*Koloniale Verslag* (Bijlage bij de Handelingen van de Tweede Kamer der Staten Generaal), The Hague, Landsdrukkerij
Lurah	Javanese village headman
Menumpang	Landless, dependent peasant
MT	Metric tonne
MK	Archief Ministerie van Kolonien, NA
NA	Nationaal Archief, The Hague
NAB	*Nederlands Adelsboek*
NFB	Notulen [Minutes] Factorij Batavia, NA, NHMA
NHM	Nederlandsche Handel-Maatschappij
NHMA	Archief Hoofdkantor [Head Office] Nederlandsche Handel-Maatschappij, NA
NHM	*Factorij* Branch Office of the NHM in Batavia
NHMR	Registers houdende inschrijjvingen van overeenkomsten met diverse Suikerfabrieken …, [Registers recording agreements with Sugar Factories …] 1858-1879, 7 vols, NA, NHMA

NP	*Nederland's Patriciaat*
Oosthoek	Java's eastern salient
Paal	1.507 kilometres
Pangeran	High ranking Javanese aristocrat
Pasisir	Java's Northeast Coast
Picul	61.72 kilograms
Priyayi	Elite Javanese official
PV	Politiek Verslag [Political Report]
Regent	Dutch term for Bupati (see above)
Resident	Dutch official in charge of a Residency
Sawah	Irrigated (rice) field
Sf.	*Suiker Fabriek* [Sugar Factory]
SU	*Stukken Betreffende het Onderzoek de Benoemde Commissie [Umbgrove Commissie] voor de opname der verschillende suikerfabrieken op Java*, Batavia, 1857. The copy cited here is a separately bound version in the library of the Koninklijk Instituut voor de Tropen in Amsterdam, but the compilation forms part of Appendix C to *Handelingen van de Tweede Kamer der Staten-Generuul* 1862-1863
VMK	Verbaal Ministerie van Kolonien, NA, MK
VOC	Vereenigde Oostindische Campanie [Dutch East India Company]

Acknowledgements

Over more years than I care to remember, scores of fellow academics, librarians, archivists and friends have greatly facilitated the research that produced this book. I would like, however, to specifically acknowledge five people: Dr Margaret Leidelmeijer, Dutch scholar extraordinaire, for sage advice and vital information; Peter Christiaans of the Centraal Bureau voor Genealogie in The Hague for his invariably generous assistance and vast knowledge of 'Indies People'; Professor Ulbe Bosma of the IISH and the Vrij Universitiet in Amsterdam for his invaluable support and encouragement; and, here in Adelaide, Margaret Hosking of the Barr Smith Library for her unwavering assistance over many years in tracking down and obtaining research materials close to home, and Rebecca Burton, Senior Editor at the University of Adelaide Press.

Introduction

Java Sugar, an Industrial Project and the 'Oriental Cuba', 1830-85

This is a book about cane sugar and the transformation of an Indonesian island into the 'Oriental Cuba' during the middle decades of the nineteenth century. Between the 1830s and the 1880s, sweetener manufacture in Dutch-controlled Java — the crown jewel of the erstwhile Netherlands Indies — drew decisively away in matters of technology and sugar science from other Asian centres of production which had once equaled or, more often, surpassed it in terms of both output and know-how. Along with its larger and altogether more famous Caribbean counterpart, Java's industry came to occupy a position at the apex of the trade in what had become by this date a key global commodity. Along with the beet sugar producers of (post-1870) Imperial Germany, Cuba and Java accounted for a little over one-third of the world's recorded output of the industrially manufactured kind of sugar usually referred to as 'centrifugal'.

'Industrially manufactured' is the key phrase here, since during the third quarter of the nineteenth century, it was these two island producers that became the prime centres of industrialised manufacture of cane sugar in their respective hemispheres. In neither case has this fact always been grasped. Cuba, along with the United States, was the nineteenth century's greatest holdout of slave-based commodity production, and the institution of slavery there outlasted its American counterpart for the better part of two decades, only coming to a (de facto) end in the 1880s. As a result, the industrial dimension of the Cuban 'project' in sugar has been obscured by notions — now largely exploded — that slavery and technological advance were incompatible.

In respect to Java, the focus of the present discussion, the parallel development of industrialised sugar manufacture has been obfuscated for reasons not dissimilar to those operating with regard to its Caribbean antipode. At least until recently, a parallel historiography charting a different kind of servility likewise had the effect of obscuring the industrial evolution of sugar. This occurred due to a near-exclusive concentration on the role played in the expansion of its production by commandeered inputs of land and labour under the aegis of the so-called *Cultuurstelsel* or System of [State] Cultivations. Inaugurated by the Indies Government in 1830, enduring — albeit in modified and reduced form — for some fifty years thereafter, and notorious for its brutality and compulsion, the *Cultuurstelsel* put its stamp not only on the people of Java but also on our understanding of the sugar industry that grew up under its mantle. As will be argued in the pages that follow, this 'understanding' is in need of a far-reaching overhaul.

The Industrial Project in Sugar in Java in the Mid-Nineteenth Century: Preliminary Facts and Explanations

Java had begun the nineteenth century as one of a number of centres — in fact, a rather minor one — of pre-industrial, artisan sugar production located in tropical and sub-tropical Asia from the Indian subcontinent through to the China Sea. It ended the century not only as the largest by far of Asia's producer-exporters of sugar, but also as the sole example of the large-scale sustained industrialisation of sugar manufacture anywhere in the East. On the face of it, the island was not a likely place for an 'industrial project' in sugar to take hold. Java was far away from the commodity's main markets in Europe and North America (markets ostensibly far better served by New World producers). It also had a rural economy and social formation so heavily dominated by a rice-growing peasantry that the 'plantations' generally thought vital for the successful raising of cane stood little chance of being established. Moreover, as if that was not enough, the island was under the control of a small, poverty-stricken European state that seemed incapable of providing the necessary capital for any such venture.

Yet the project not only took hold there during the middle decades of the nineteenth century, but also flourished to an extent not yet fully reflected in the relevant literature. In line with the view that the *Cultuurstelsel* was more incubus than incubator with respect to modern economic growth, literature has often assumed that the 'real' modernisation of Java sugar only began toward the very end of the century, reflecting a new wave of metropolitan interest and investment. As this book will demonstrate, however, key developments began much earlier. Beginning rather slowly in the 1830s and accelerating fairly rapidly in the decades that followed, Java's long-established place in the history of Asian sugar manufacture was totally transformed during the third quarter of the nineteenth century.

Globally, sugar stood on the cutting edge of the 'first' industrial revolution in metallurgy, technology and the science that accompanied it, and these developments formed the vital context for what happened on Java. By 1885 — the date of a crisis in the international sugar economy which shook the industry to its foundations (and the end-point for the present study) — the island could boast scores of sugar factories. Continuous, fully industrialised production took place in these factories in tandem with most of the major technological advances and appurtenances of contemporary, state-of-the-art manufacture. Already well before that, by the late 1850s, a substantial number of the colony's one hundred or so factories had taken on board many of the key contemporary advances in the technology and science of sugar manufacture.

In setting out to explain how this came about, the book falls into three main parts. The first three chapters deal with what can properly be called an 'industrial revolution' in sugar manufacture worldwide which took place during a 'long' nineteenth century extending from the French Revolution to the outbreak of the First World War. Using a variety of settings, these chapters discuss the impact of that 'revolution' on Java and the way in which sugar was made on the island. In the second part, the book first sets out to analyse the agrarian basis for that project, and, in particular, the unique configuration of an industrial sugar complex that was embedded in a much larger rice-based 'peasant' economy and society. The agrarian base for the production of raw material forged over the mid-century decades did much to explain why an industrial project in sugar was feasible in Java, but does not account for why it actually happened. For that, both finance and entrepreneurs were necessary. The second part then attempts to elucidate both the 'money trail' itself and how a colonial (and to an extent cosmopolitan) bourgeoisie of sugar manufacturers and merchants came to be located along that trail. The third and final section of the book concludes with a summary of the state of the sugar industry in Java — in respect, above all, to the technology of manufacture — in the decade or so prior to the international sugar crisis of 1884.

Chapter One begins by discussing the significance for Java of an industrial revolution in sugar manufacture which began around 1780 and culminated shortly before the outbreak of the First World War. This revolution had the potential for impacting on cane sugar manufacture throughout Asia, just as it did in the Atlantic Zone, which has been more widely written about. Indeed, a number of industrial projects in sugar made their appearance at various locations in the East from the 1820s onward. The Dutch colony of Java was one of these. In total, these ventures in the industrial manufacture of sugar had the capacity to radically alter the entire international sugar economy by introducing bulk supplies of Asian-made sugar into commodity circuits that had depended hitherto almost exclusively on supplies from the Americas. In fact, however, most of the ventures proved over time either abortive or, after enjoying some initial success, sank into obsolescence, not to be revived until the next century. This left Java very much on its own as the sole Asian centre of production in which the industrial project was sustained and ongoing from the mid-nineteenth century through to the century's end.

Chapters Two and Three set out to describe the rise of the industrial project in Java sugar in terms, first and foremost, of the men and machines that came to define it with regards to technology, science and expertise. 'Creole' seems an appropriate term here, since it is contended that the 'diffusion' of technology which underlay the progress of the industrial project in Java was a matter of local *adaptation* as well as simple adoption. The critical argument here, however, is that the degree of progress made in the manufacture of sugar in Java between the 1830s and the mid-1880s was such as to place the industry roughly on par with the 'best practice' internationally. In other words, earlier representations of Java sugar manufacture in the mid-nineteenth century as both wanting in expertise and technologically backward are substantially incorrect. The weakness of such representations stems both from a misunderstanding of the real character of the advance of the machinery in contemporary sugar production worldwide, and from an uncritical acceptance of a polemical contemporary literature hostile to the *Cultuurstelsel* and its every manifestation.

Chapter Four discusses the agrarian basis for the industrial project. That project would have been impossible without the supplies of raw material and labour that were underwritten by a colonial Government anxious to ensure that commodity production flourished — and that the profits of the Indies flowed back to Holland. In terms of the cultivation of cane and factory labour, mid-century Cuba owed its ascent in the international sugar economy to the plantation slavery of captive Africans. Contemporary developments in Java, however, eschewed both plantations and the slave or indentured workforces that were their usual concomitant. Instead, they were predicated on a different kind of servility based on the requisitioning of peasant fields — on which sugar cane was planted in rotation with peasant crops — and a commandeering of locally available peasant labour on the basis of its purported corvée obligations to the state.

As has long been recognised, this requisition and commandeering was feasible because of the colonial Government's ability to harness a labour-service regime of some antiquity which it inherited from the pre-colonial state. In turn, as is emphasised here, the effectiveness of that regime was dependent — to a degree at least — on the presence among the rural working population not only of myriad petty landholders but also of significant numbers of largely or totally landless households, which were dependent on their labour power alone for their subsistence. An important part of the present argument, however, concerns what may be termed 'peasantisation'. During the mid-century decades, in great swathes of rural Java — on the book's reading of the situation — people became more 'peasant-like' to an extent that clearly advantaged the industrial project. In sum, the agrarian basis for sugar production was a mixture of the new and the old, one in which the exploitation of long-standing ways of mobilising rural resources took place in tandem with fairly far-reaching changes in the way in which rural society was structured.

Yet, as we will see in Chapter Five, the industrial project was dependent for its success on substantially more than a unique agrarian base. Indeed, a key factor — one without which it is difficult to imagine that the project would have been sustained over time — was the emergence over the mid-century decades of an 'Indies bourgeoisie' from within the bowels of the Indies state's *Cultuurstelsel*. To be sure, the relation between the industrial project in sugar and the various institutions of the state in Java in the mid-nineteenth century is a problematic one. Not least of the difficulties is that even the formal distinction between industry and 'state' was ill-defined. State officials in the Residencies — both Dutch and Javanese — were themselves in charge of the cultivation of cane and were often directly involved in the supervision of its production. They were also responsible for providing the industry with much of the labour that it required during the manufacturing season or 'Campaign'. Moreover, the state was initially the main financier of sugar production and the major market for the Contractors' output. In this respect, as we shall see, some of the tensions between 'industry' and 'state' might be more accurately delineated as tensions between various production sectors of an industry in which the industry/state dichotomy was itself largely meaningless.

Nonetheless, within this framework, recent scholarly work has heavily qualified lingering but fanciful notions of mid-century Java as being in the thrall of a colonial 'bureaucratic state' whose 'monopolistic' practices and outlook effectively blocked the emergence of 'private' entrepreneurial capital. Taking up and developing this critique, the argument presented here is that — in however contingent a fashion — the *Cultuurstelsel* nurtured the presence in Java of an influential group of colonial sugar factory owners and top managers. Together with their close and essential associates in the colony's more substantial mercantile houses, and their friends and relatives in the Indies Government service, they constituted a bourgeoisie that maintained close ties with its metropolitan counterparts. Always potent, these ties significantly underpinned the local bourgeoisie's base on the colonial 'periphery' and were of vital importance when the suddenly plummeting world price of sugar threatened the industrial project with financial disaster in the mid-1880s.

Chapter Six takes up the history of the advance of steam and steel in sugar manufacture in Java in the mid-nineteenth century and reviews the state of technology and science in the industry in the decade prior to the crisis of the mid-1880s. In essence, this chapter argues that by the early 1880s the Java industry was, in most important respects, fully on a par with other major sectors of the international sugar economy. By the same token, in respect to the technology and science of manufacture, it had drawn away decisively from its erstwhile counterparts elsewhere in Asia.

The chapter sets out to sustain this argument through an analysis of contemporary information relating to the appearance, during the 1870s and early 1880s, of significant quantities of new, up-to-the-minute equipment, including larger, more powerful mills for grinding the cane and, above all, various forms of Multiple Effect apparatus, which transformed operations in the boiling house from about 1870 onward even more than the Vacuum Pan had done some decades earlier. (Both of these forms of apparatus will be described in more detail in this chapter.) Of necessity, moreover, technological advance went hand-in-hand with advance in the chemistry of manufacture, such that the 'sugar chemist' and the factory laboratory began to make their appearance, in however embryonic a fashion, alongside the new machines. There were strong influences here from the German beet sugar industry, yet Java also had its own 'tradition' of sugar science that dated from initiatives taken by the Dutch Colonial Office and the Indies Government in the 1840s and 1850s.

In an important sense, however, neither advanced technology nor its accompanying science could have been so smoothly — or effectively — incorporated into the Java sugar industry had it not been for the unique metamorphosis that the colony's sugar factories underwent during the period between the 1850s and the 1880s. In most major sectors of the international sugar economy during the second half of the nineteenth century, the great strides made in sugar milling and in the subsequent processing of cane-juice needed, if they were to be successfully implemented, to be accompanied by a whole-scale reconstruction of the industry. Existing units of production — particularly the mill-cum-plantation — often proved too small to sustain the scale, let alone the expense, of what was now required of sugar manufacturers.

In Java, however, this was not the case, for reasons to do first and foremost with the flexible matrix set up (in however contingent a fashion) for proto-industrial sugar production under the aegis of the *Cultuurstelsel*. This matrix allowed for expansion without the necessity for reconstruction. As a result, the Java industry was able to benefit from a history of continuous — and continuously evolving — sugar manufacture dating in some cases back to the 1830s. To an extent that was highly unusual globally, the new systems of manufacture — from the Vacuum Pan through to the Multiple Effect and beyond — could be grafted effectively onto the existing units of production. The upshot was that when crisis came in the mid-1880s, in the form of the collapse of the world price for industrially manufactured sugar, the industry was quite literally well-equipped to meet it.

The book's conclusion takes up the industry's story from this potentially terminating event through to the period of the project's late colonial heyday — and beyond. In explaining how the industrial project rode the crisis of the mid-1880s and entered on a period of unprecedented expansion, it draws attention to four main factors. The first and most necessary of these related to markets, where the key development was the prospect of mass sales for Java sugar elsewhere in Asia itself — sales that compensated for the loss of most of the markets in the West, which had sustained Java during the middle decades of the nineteenth century. A second factor related to the industry's ability — in the wake of the dismantlement of the

Cultuurstelsel — to hold down or depress the cost of its access to both the rural resources and the factory workforce on which it depended for its supplies of raw material. On this basis it created a super-efficient 'agro-industry' that was uniquely productive in the field in global terms. This was bolstered by an equally exceptional programme of Research and Development that drew many of its (initial) strengths from metropolitan Holland's own proximity to the great beet sugar industry of Imperial Germany.

A third factor in explaining the industrial project's survival is linked to this exceptional productivity, in so far as it helped account for profits that could be reinvested in expanding the industry's operations. This was a point of critical importance in allowing the project to continue, because the inflow of metropolitan (or other overseas) capital into Java sugar was fairly minimal in contrast to the situation prevailing in other major sectors of colonial commodity production in the Indies. In consequence — and this is the fourth and final factor — the industrial project was able to continue the 'tradition' it had established in the mid-century decades of constantly updating its factories (and building new ones) in line with global advances in the technology of manufacture.

The upshot of these developments post-1880 was that in terms of productivity and total output, the industrial project continued (with some interruptions) on an upward trajectory until the very eve of the inter-war depression that began in 1930. Thereafter, things began to fall apart, as is briefly narrated in the book's final pages. The focus of the present volume, however, is on the formation of the industrial project rather than on its eventual fate — which is another story.

Part I

The 'Industrial Revolution' in Sugar Manufacture

1 Java's Singular Trajectory: Steam, Steel and the Industrial Project in Sugar

During the course of the 'long' nineteenth century, sugar reinvented itself as an industrially manufactured product. Together with the applied sciences that sustained them, steam and steel — beginning, initially, as iron — characterised a sugar 'revolution' that took place globally during a period that began around 1780 and reached its apogee circa 1914.

The term 'revolution' seems appropriate even though the time span was lengthy. Much has been written about this revolution in the context of cane sugar in the Caribbean and the New World in general (the production areas, that is to say, which since the sixteenth century had supplied the commodity to the Atlantic Zone and its hinterland). Nonetheless, the revolution also had a significant impact throughout Asia and the Indian Ocean, in areas as diverse as Mauritius, the Indian subcontinent and South-East Asia (and in the neighbouring north-east of Australia).

In Dutch controlled Java, however, the impact was particularly pronounced and sustained. There, a singular industrial project — singular in respect to its combination of scale, output and technological-scientific advance — took shape during the middle decades of the nineteenth century and reached a precocious florescence toward the century's end. Indeed, by the 1880s the developed state of manufacturing on Java placed the island well ahead of any of its erstwhile counterparts elsewhere in Asia or its Indian Ocean counterparts and roughly on par with the most advanced sugar industries of the New World. The Dutch colony had become, in effect, the 'Oriental Cuba', with an exported output of cane sugar that was only exceeded by that of its Caribbean antipode.

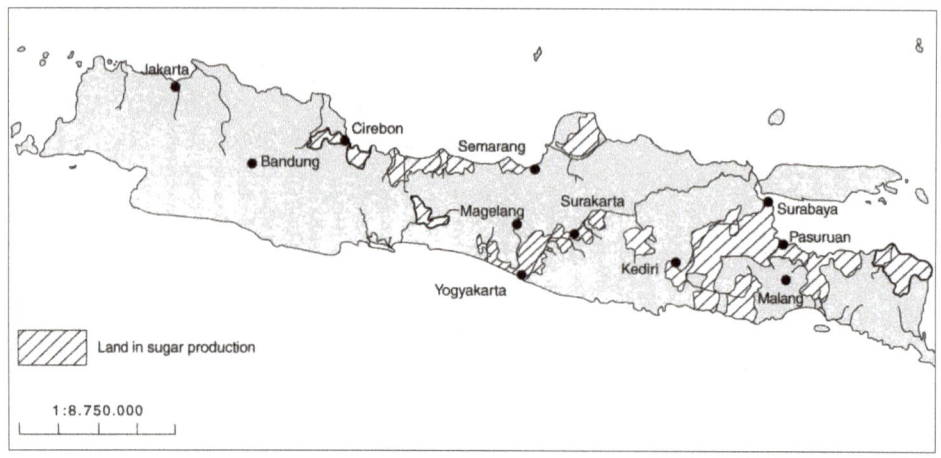

Figure 1: Java in the colonial era: showing the main sugar-growing areas.
Source: Courtesy of the author

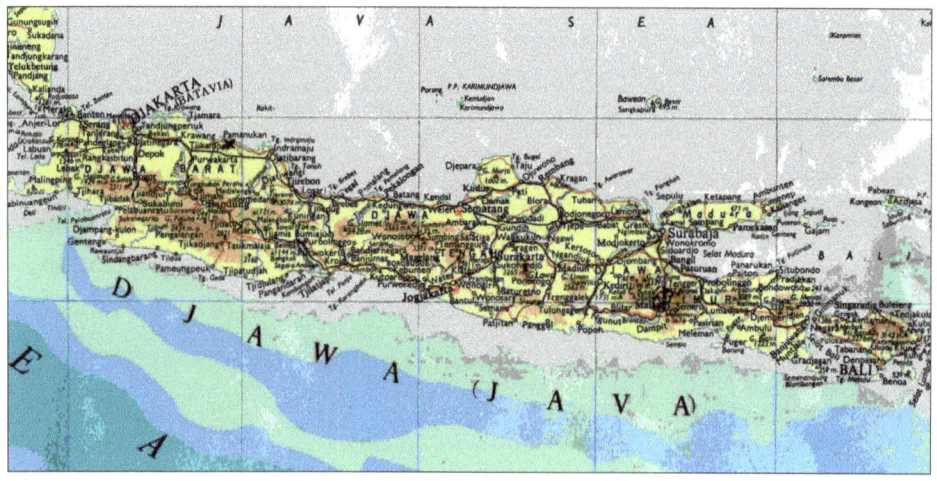

Figure 2: Java: the Garden of the East.
Source: Courtesy of the author

Sugar's Reinvention as an Industrially Manufactured Commodity

Until the nineteenth century, the commodity we know as 'sugar' was derived exclusively from the sugar cane, which in turn was selectively bred from grasses found, it seems most likely, on the south-eastern fringes of Asia, possibly New Guinea.[1] The use of cane to make sugar appears to have originated in various regions of Asia in pre-modern times, and to have been transmitted from there to the Middle East, then into the Mediterranean and eventually from there into the New World.

For centuries, sugar was manufactured worldwide by artisans using essentially handicraft techniques. In some places, it still is. Though these techniques varied considerably from place to place as well as over time, there were some essential similarities. The sucrose content of sugar cane — the part vital for making sugar — was extracted by devices that crushed the cane, either through some variation of the pestle-and-mortar principle or through combinations of rollers between which the cane was ground, utilising manual labour, animals (horses, oxen and so on) or water power as the motive force. The resultant juice, thin and full of impurities that would adversely affect its conversion into sugar, had then to be cleansed and reduced through a combination of boiling it and then adding substances that would cause impurities to rise to the surface (or sink to the bottom) of the cauldrons or pans in which these processes took place. Only then could the thickened cane-juice be brought to near 'setting' point, again over the same direct heat source — a fire or a furnace — which had been used to cleanse and reduce the juice. It could then be poured off into casks, hogsheads, pots or other containers, where it was drained of extraneous liquid and allowed to set (to some degree at least) into a transportable, saleable form.

In some of the more advanced forms of handicraft production (as in parts of East Asia, for example), settling took place in conical pots covered at the top in wet clay, the water from which percolated down through the setting sugar, in so doing purging the upper layers of the sugar of the molasses (the part of the sugar that would not 'set'). When the pot was smashed and the sugar cone revealed, its upper layers were white ('clayed'), its lower layers brown. Whatever methods of manufacture were

---

[1] For substantiation, elaboration and qualification of the information in this and the following two paragraphs, see Jock H Galloway, *The Cane Sugar Industry: An Historical Geography from its Origins to 1914*, Cambridge, Cambridge University Press, 1989, pp. 11-18; and Peter Griggs, *Global Industry, Local Innovation: The History of Cane Sugar Production in Australia, 1820-1995*, Bern, Peter Lang, 2011, pp. 15-17.

used, they were all immensely time-consuming, highly labour-intensive, and very heavily dependent on the individual skill and experience of the artisans in charge. No wonder that sugar, in the early modern era, was a relatively rare and distinctly expensive commodity.

Beginning sometime in the late 1700s, however, this began to change. It did so in the context of what is often referred to as the 'first' industrial revolution, predicated on steam power, new forms of metallurgy and their accompanying sciences. The resultant radical change to the way in which sugar was manufactured had three major dimensions. One dimension related to far-reaching improvements in the grinding of cane. The second concerned revolutionary advances in cleansing and reducing cane-juice and processing it into 'sugar'. The third dimension, which was very importantly and closely allied to these developments, resided in the transformation of sugar manufacture from an art into a science.

We can begin with the appearance of steam-driven mills with iron or steel crushers; these achieved an unprecedented increase in extraction rates. The first stationary steam engine to be used in 'the colonies' was erected in Cuba in 1797, and a little over a decade later, steam-operated sugar-mill engines began to appear, eventually in rather large numbers, in both Cuba and the British Caribbean. These were exported mainly by the British engineering firms of Boulton and Watt (119 engines between 1803 and 1825) and the predecessor of Fawcett Preston, Fawcett and Littledale (148 engines between 1813 and 1825). The export of such apparatus meant that in the Caribbean 'by the mid-nineteenth century steam-power was an embedded technology in the more advanced sugar producing islands'.[2] From the 1820s onward, moreover, the stationary steam engine was also making its appearance in the Indian subcontinent, though not initially in the context of sugar production.[3] That development dated from the 1830s and 1840s[4], and was subsequently paralleled

---

[2] Jennifer Tann, 'Steam and Sugar: The Diffusion of the Stationary Steam Engine to the Caribbean Sugar Industry, 1770-1840', *History of Technology*, vol. 19, 1997, pp. 63-84, here pp. 71-5; Galloway, *Cane Sugar Industry*, pp. 135-41.

[3] Jennifer Tann & John Aitkin, The Diffusion of the Stationary Steam Engine from Britain to India, 1790-1830, *Indian Economic and Social History Review*, vol. 29, no. 2, 1992, pp. 199-214.

[4] Andrew Ratledge, *Competing for the British Sugar Bowl: East India Sugar 1792-1865: Politics, Trade and Sugar Consumption*, Saarbrücken, VDM Verlag Dr Müller, 2009.

elsewhere in Asia. As we shall see, in Java itself stationary steam engines to power the grinding mills for cane only became common at a somewhat later date.

Nonetheless, equally crucial advances took place in the boiling house as well as in the mill. Indeed, substantial improvements in the process of cleansing cane-juice and concentrating it to a quasi-solid state were at least as important as the initial business of extracting juice from cane itself. Most of these advances in the boiling house originated from inventions designed to solve the problems of sugar refineries, rather than having been invented by the producers of the raw form of the commodity. That is to say, much of the original stimulus for the sugar revolution came from metropolitan businesses that melted down raw sugar and reconstituted it in a commercially more convenient and palatable form. These businesses were found, by the early nineteenth century, in numerous locations in Western Europe — London and Amsterdam and Hamburg, for example — and subsequently in North America, where New York became the key centre.

Even so, colonial producers of raw sugar — the kind that was bought by refineries — were not slow to take up the new technologies of manufacture. The same or very similar methods to those used in sugar refining could be appropriated by the plantation sugar industries in the 'peripheries' of the New World and of Asia.

In addition to supplying the refineries with an improved product, however, there was a further and eventually crucial dynamic at work here. During the course of the nineteenth century, sugar, unique among global commodities in this respect, began to be manufactured to similar standards and appearance from two totally different forms of raw material: cane and beet. Beet was a latecomer on the scene. Scarcely heard of as a commercially viable source of sucrose at the beginning of the century, it started to gain a substantial market share from the 1850s onward.

In northern Europe, beet sugar manufacture took off on a grand scale, and (post-1870) Imperial Germany emerged as the largest singular producer-exporter of this form of the commodity. There were global forces at work here. During the second half of the nineteenth century, northern European grain farmers found themselves drawn into the vortex of a world market increasingly fed by the production of the vast and newly 'opened-up' North American plains (and their lesser counterparts in the Antipodes). One of the upshots was that European farmers increasingly turned to sugar beet as one form of economic salvation.

In turn, this had major consequences for the international sugar economy. Colonial producers of cane sugar had begun to find themselves in increasing competition from sugar made from beet. Moreover, competition was not limited to markets. It extended, equally critically, into the sphere of manufacture, since the nascent beet sugar industries of Germany, the Low Countries and northern France sought to secure an edge over their colonial cane sugar rivals by utilising all the latest inventions that the first industrial revolution had placed in their way.[5] In consequence, colonial producers of cane sugar were forced to follow suit — or were driven into the backwoods of the international sugar economy.

The combined result of these several developments, in both the manufacture of raw sugar and its subsequent refining, placed sugar on the very cutting edge of global industrialisation. What had been a technologically somewhat retrograde industry, one that relied on crude methods predicated on heavy inputs of manual labour, was transformed in the more advanced sectors into an exemplar of ever-improving technological achievement on par with virtually anything that the industrial revolution might create in relation to any other major commodity.

At the risk of some oversimplification, three complementary major inventions were involved. Chronologically speaking, the first was the Vacuum Pan, a piece of equipment designed to obviate the danger of liquid sugar scorching over direct heat during the final stages of its conversion into a semi-solid mass — a problem inherent to varying degrees in the forms of 'open-pan' manufacture which preceded it. The Pan took the form of

> a slightly flattened sphere of copper, provided inside at the lower part with a coil of steam pipe, and also a vacuum jacket. An air-pump creates a partial

---

[5] For the discussion in the following paragraphs, see Margaret Leidelmeijer, *Van Suikermolen tot Grootbedrijf: Technische Vernieuwing in de Java-Suikerindustrie in de Negentiende Eeuw*, Amsterdam, NEHA, 1997, pp. 39-68; Bill Albert & Adrian Graves (eds), *Crisis and Change in the International Sugar Economy, 1860-1914*, Norwich, ISC Press, 1984, especially pp. 1-8; Noel Deerr, *The History of Sugar*, vol. 2, London, Chapman and Hall, 1950, pp. 534-95; Jon Curry-Machado, *Cuban Sugar Industry: Transnational Networks and Engineering Migrants in Mid-Nineteenth Century Cuba*, New York, Palgrave Macmillan, 2011, pp. 23-47; Curry-Machado, '"Rich Flames and Hired Tears": Sugar, Sub-Imperial Agents and the Cuban Phoenix of Empire', *Journal of Global History*, vol. 4, no. 1, 2009, pp. 33-56; Martijn Bakker, *Ondernemerschap en Vernieuwing: De Nederlandse Bietsuikerindustrie 1858-1919*, Amsterdam, Stichting Het Nederlandsch Economisch-Historisch Archief, 1989, pp. 15-26, 135-63; Roger Munting & John Perkins, 'The Cane-Beet Sugar Rivalry in the 19th Century', in Roger Munting & Tamas Szmrecsanyi (eds), *Competing for the Sugar Bowl*, St. Katharinen, Scripta Mercaturae Verlag, 2000, pp. 1-15; Galloway, *Cane Sugar Industry*, pp. 120-42.

Figure 3: The heart of the industrial sugar factory: the Vacuum Pan.
Source: Courtesy of the author

vacuum, and a condenser, through which the steam from the boiling juice passes on its way to the air pump, by rapidly condensing the vapour, greatly helps to increase the vacuum.[6]

The Vacuum Pan enabled the final stages of 'cooking' the sugar to take place at a significantly lower temperature than was the case in the old open-pan method. When all went well, the new apparatus not only afforded significant savings in fuel costs but also produced more sugar of a better quality than previously by virtue of the fact that it increased the proportion of crystalisable sugar in relation to the quantity of molasses.[7] Early versions of the Vacuum Pan first appeared in European sugar refineries around 1820 — and within less than a decade were taken up by progressive raw sugar manufacturers worldwide.

Almost contemporaneously, moreover, further technological progess began to be made, along with a steadily evolving chemistry of sugar manufacture, in respect to the process of cleansing ('defecating') and partially evaporating cane-juice before it reached the Vacuum Pan for the penultimate stage of its transformation into sugar.[8]

---

[6] George Martineau, *Sugar*, London, Pitman, c. 1910, p. 66.

[7] See e.g. AH Adamson, *Sugar Without Slaves: The Political Economy of British Guiana, 1838-1904*, New Haven, Yale University Press, 1972, pp. 171-2; HC Prinsen Geerligs, *Cane Sugar and the Process of its Manufacture in Java*, Manchester, Roberts, 1898, pp. 39-40; Griggs, *Global Industry, Local Innovation*, pp. 182-3.

[8] I would like to thank Dr Margaret Leidelmeijer for her sage advice on the importance of

For the most part, during the middle decades of the century, this vital stage of the manufacturing process took place (in the industry's more advances sectors, at least) in steam-heated open pans of one kind or another, in a process that remained more an art than a science.

Other possibilities, however, were being actively explored from the 1820s onward. In particular, a further sophistication of advances in 'boiling house' technology in the mid-nineteenth century was the provision of an external serpentine or rack of copper pipes which utilised the heated vapour coming off the boiling sugar inside the Vacuum Pan in order to condense juice prior to the final stages of processing. This 'double effect' process was most closely associated with the French firm of Derosne et Cail. It was not without its operational problems, however, particularly when used in cane sugar manufacture, where the juice was more viscous and hence more easily burnt than beet. Moreover, its other disadvantages — as expounded upon by one Dutch authority circa 1860 — were several-fold, not least the need for singularly skilled workmen, and the presence of a knowledgeable engineer in case things went wrong. (The writer advised his readers to opt instead for 'simple' Vacuum Pans coupled with 'orthodox' open-pan cleansing and concentration of the juice in the preceding stages of manufacture.)[9]

Even so, the principle the Double Effect utilised — that is, the taking of steam generated in one part of the process and using it to heat the juice at another — had a great future. Indeed, the prototypes of earlier decades evolved into the full-fledged Multiple Effect, the second great advance in the technology of sugar manufacture in the mid-nineteenth century. Noel Deerr, whose pioneering *History of Sugar* has stood the test of time, categorised the Multiple Effect as having 'a place among the world's great inventions'.[10] When it finally came into its own in the 1860s — its evolution had taken place over the better part of twenty years — the Multiple Effect, variously known as 'Double Effet', 'Triple Effet' or 'Quadruple Effet' (or in English as Double Effect, Triple Effect and Quadruple Effect), conquered the world. Described succinctly:

---

mid-century developments — both technological and scientific — in cleansing and reducing cane-juice *prior* to its arrival at the Vacuum Pan. For her discussion of these and related issues, see Leidelmeijer, *Grootbedrijf*, pp. 147-230.

[9] WL de Sturler, *Handboek voor den landbouw in Nederlandsch Oost-Indië*, Leiden, Sythoff, 1863, p. 1134.

[10] Deerr, vol. 2, p. 562.

> [i]t replaced the old set of open pans with a set of closed vessels ... Steam heating was used throughout, and as the atmospheric pressure was reduced in succeeding cylinders, the steam from the first was used to boil the sugar in the second [and so on] ... Because boiling under vacuum now permitted a lower temperature throughout the entire process of evaporation, the formation of molasses was minimalized and a much greater quantity of crystallisable sugar produced.[11]

In a nutshell, the Multiple Effect offered huge savings in fuel costs, greatly simplified the operation of the production line (thereby reducing labour costs) and, above all, perhaps, confirmed — through the level of control over the production process it conferred on a skilled operator — that sugar-making was indeed now a science rather than an art.

Initially designed, like the Vacuum Pan before it, for operation in refineries, the Multiple Effect was at first considered far too bulky and expensive for use in raw sugar production.[12] By the late 1860s, however, that was precisely where it began to be found, in rapidly increasing numbers. As was also the case with the Vacuum Pan, the Multiple Effect presupposed a familiarity with steam/vacuum technology and the presence of a sufficient supply of experientially trained technicians. In Java, at least, this appears (as we shall see in subsequent chapters) not to have been a major problem, thanks to a global 'diaspora' of the requisite personnel — and to the adaptive capacities of elements of the skilled local workforce.

Along with the Vacuum Pan and the Multiple Effect came a third major advance in the technology of manufacture in the mid-nineteenth century, one which gave its name to the type of sugar that industrialised factories began to produce

---

[11] Adamson, *Sugar Without Slaves*, p. 187.

[12] According to the noted sugar expert Noel Deerr, while the apparatus began to evolve in the 1840s, 'for the next twenty years progress was slow' and it was only from around 1870 onward that the Multiple Effect began to become wide-spread in either beet or cane sugar production (vol. 2, pp. 562-72). This view is supported by reliable contemporary testimony. Peter Soames knew about this apparatus, but in relation to cane sugar regarded it as applicable only in 'very large works' and so left it out of his account (*Treatise on the Manufacture of Sugar from Sugar Cane*, London & New York, Spon, 1872, pp. 58ff.). A decade later, Lock et al. regarded the introduction of fully-fledged Multiple Effect procedures as recent: '... [I]t is not long since that the French house of Cail & Cie introduced a great improvement in the economy of the Vacuum Pans, by working them in sets of 2 or 3, known as "double effet" and "triple effet" respectively'. See CGW Lock, GW Wigner & RH Harland, *Sugar Growing and Refining*, London & New York, Spon, 1882, pp. 269-73.

worldwide. This advance took the form of the Centrifuge, a device for spinning the sugar crystals free of the remaining molasses at the very end of the production line.[13] Invented in the 1840s and rapidly taken up throughout the industry, the Centrifuge resembled nothing so much as a modern top-loading washing machine. Usually, there was a set of Centrifuges in each factory. They revolutionised the final stages of sugar manufacture and refining by doing away with cumbersome and often wasteful, highly labour-intensive methods for separating sugar crystals from the residue of the boiled-down and clarified juices. Thereafter, sugar produced by this means was ubiquitously referred to as 'centrifugal'.

In short, the Centrifuge rendered redundant — or drove into the backwoods of the international sugar economy — a wide variety of 'pre-industrial' methods for 'setting' sugar into a commercially viable, transportable and convenient form. Prior to that, even in the most advanced of 'industrial' factories, sugar had generally been laboriously and slowly drained of its molasses, after which it needed to be further dried. The Centrifuge not only did a better job but also a speedier one, cutting down considerably on the number of workers required. Those workers who were required, however, had to be singularly adept: in Java, they were mostly women.

Industrialised Sugar Manufacture in Nineteenth-century Asia

Though the Vacuum Pan, the various forms of Multiple Effect apparatus and the Centrifuge eventually came to characterise the large-scale, commercially oriented production of cane (and beet) sugar worldwide during the course of the nineteenth century, they did not do so at an internationally consistent pace. As far as the manufacture of cane sugar was concerned in the West, Cuba developed as the standout industry during the middle decades of the nineteenth century. Cuba was followed by a number of other producers elsewhere in the Caribbean area and on the North American mainland. In Asia, however, it was Java that evolved quite uniquely in this respect. Among Asia's other long-established sugar industries, the Dutch colony was by no means the only one in which the industrial project was essayed during the period between the 1840s and 1880s. Nonetheless, as things transpired, it emerged as the one most able to adopt, adapt and — above all — sustain the project. The upshot was to put the island's industry in the position of a world leader in the technologically

---

[13] For a detailed history of its mid-century evolution, see Deerr, vol. 2, pp. 573-7.

industrialised manufacture of the commodity, decades ahead of any of its erstwhile counterparts in its own and adjacent regions.

Sugar manufacture in Asia had a fundamentally pre-industrial character prior to the nineteenth century. In the Indian subcontinent, Siam, the Philippines, southern China, Formosa and elsewhere, cane sugar was manufactured by methods that demanded high inputs of labour and a great deal of experiential, 'rule-of-thumb' knowledge. To be sure, machines of a kind played some part. Throughout East and South-East Asia, cane was ground in simple mills comprised of two (or three) vertically set rollers, generally made of wood or stone, and set in motion by cattle roped to an overhead beam. As mentioned earlier, this technology had worldwide currency in one form or another, having most probably originated in Southern China in the course of the sixteenth century.[14]

By the late eighteenth century, however, Asia as a whole lagged behind the Caribbean in proto-industrial innovation.[15] There were some scattered exceptions. In Ryukyu — a remote and relatively minor production area immediately to the south of Japan — water power was apparently harnessed to an innovative three-roller mill early in the eighteenth century.[16] In Java, a solitary mill 'constructed in

---

[14] The development (in southern China) and rapid dissemination early in the sixteenth century of a new style of geared, vertical two-roller mill which considerably improved the efficiency with which cane was expressed is discussed in J & C Daniels, 'The Origin of the Sugar Cane Roller Mill', *Technology and Culture*, vol. 29, no. 3, 1988, pp. 493-535. Roller milling of this kind does not appear, however, to have extended beyond East and South-East Asia. Early modern sugar production in India was dominated by the (generally less efficient) mortar press or *kohlu*, usually worked by oxen, while in some parts of the subcontinent the more usual method was for cane to be milled with hand-operated rollers. See Shahid Amin, *Sugar Cane and Sugar in Gorakphur*, Delhi, Oxford University Press, 1984, pp. 53-6.

[15] The major technological advances in the New World industry prior to the mid-nineteenth century can be summarised as follows: (a) a more efficient vertical metal or metal-clad three-cylinder mill was in common use by the early eighteenth century; (b) an improved system of open-pan sugar boiling, which saved on fuel and gave a greater degree of control over heat (the Jamaica or Spanish 'Train'), had been widely though not universally adopted by the late eighteenth century; (c) by the early nineteenth century, a very much more efficient milling system based on horizontal metal rollers set in a triangular configuration was coming into use (and appears to have had eighteenth-century prototypes in the more advanced sectors of New World sugar production). See Dale W Tomich, *Slavery in the Circuit of Sugar: Martinique and the World Economy 1830-1848*, Baltimore, Johns Hopkins University Press, 1990, pp. 150-88; Galloway, *Cane Sugar Industry*, pp. 84-119.

[16] Sucheta Mazumdar, *Sugar and Society in China: Peasants, Technology, and the World Market*,

the West Indian manner, with brass cylinders and put into motion by water' was a novelty when installed in one of the long-established production areas of the island's Northeast Coast late in the same century.[17] Generally speaking, however, it looks as if neither the water-driven mill nor any equivalent of the 'Jamaica' or 'Spanish' train — that is to say, 'a series of semi-hemispherical vessels placed in line in a masonry flue with a furnace at one end' — had made their appearance in Asia on any scale prior to the nineteenth century.[18]

During the first half of the new century, however, progress was both rapid and fairly wide-spread. Like their counterparts in the New World, beginning around 1830 sugar producers in South and South-East Asia — though not apparently in East Asia — set about implementing the industrial project in manufacture. They undertook such ventures in the subcontinent and on the Indian Ocean island of Mauritius — and in various other scattered locations between the Bay of Bengal and the South China Sea, including Siam, the Malay Peninsula, the Philippines and, of course, Java itself. They did this, moreover, at a time when Asian sugar production was being integrated increasingly into a world market for the commodity.

Asian sugar, it is true, had reached Western markets in intermittent and varying quantities since at least the early seventeenth century. Together with the output of Mesopotamia, it may have constituted the first manufactured sugar known in the ancient civilisations around the Mediterranean. Nonetheless, it was only in the nineteenth century that sugar from Asian producers began to play a significant part in world trade. It was only then, and initially in the Occident, that the commodity

---

Cambridge, MA, Harvard University Asia Centre, 1998, pp. 174-5; Robert LeRoy Innes, 'The Door Ajar: Japan's Foreign Trade in the Seventeenth Century', PhD Diss, University of Michigan, 1980, p. 511. Innes records both the invention in Okinawa of a three-roller mill (1669) and the successful connection of the rollers to a water-wheel (1717).

[17] It was built at Jepara on Java's Northeast Coast in the 1790s, on the orders of the 'progressive' Dutch Resident Dirk van Hogendorp. See E du Perron-de Roos, 'Correspondentie tussen Dirk van Hogendorp en Zijn Broeder Gijsbert Karl van Hogendorp', *Bijdragen tot de Taal-, Land- en Volkenkunde*, vol. 102, nos. 1 & 2, 1943, pp. 125-273, here p. 199; 'Resident Doornik's Replies …', 28.10.1812, India Office Library, London, Mackenzie Collection (Private), vol. 7, p. 173. This mill may have had an equally rare counterpart in the West Java production area around Batavia, where a stone triple-roller mill, built in the 'American Style', was recorded by de Haan as having existed on the Tanjung-West estate circa 1785. See F de Haan, *Oud Batavia*, 2nd edn, vol. 1, Bandoeng, AC Nix & Co., 1935, pp. 325-6.

[18] Deerr, vol. 2, p. 556. As Deerr's discussion makes clear, there is no absolute certainty on the point.

in general became an item of mass consumption, due to the rapidly increasing penetration of sucrose into the diet of the industrial populations of Western Europe — above all, those of the United Kingdom. As a result, sugar from all over the world, Asia included, began to be drawn into European and North American commodity circuits on a hitherto unprecedented scale. In turn, this development stimulated attempts to foster the industrial project in sugar well beyond the confines of the Atlantic Zone.

Indeed, in the Indian subcontinent as early as the 1770s (and reflecting the precocity of the British market to which it was connected) Bengal was the scene of attempts to emulate the best of contemporary production in the New World. An even more significant development took place some sixty years later when, beginning in the mid-1830s, a further influx of British and local Indian capital occurred, as a result of a determination to take advantage of the recent equalisation of colonial sugar duties in the metropolis to realise the subcontinent's potential as the 'sugar bowl' of the United Kingdom. Extensive attempts to industrialise Indian sugar production with Vacuum Pans, steam mills and other state-of-the art manufacturing equipment got underway in Bengal, Madras and other prospectively favourable locations using the skills of some former slave-masters from the British Caribbean.[19]

A parallel development, on a smaller scale and at a somewhat later date, and involving both British and local Chinese capital, took place in Siam during the 1860s.[20] Later still, the ubiquitous Vacuum Pan was said to have reached Province Wellesley on the Malay Peninsula, where a moderate-sized sugar industry existed

---

[19] For sugar production in the Indian subcontinent during this period, see Ulbe Bosma, *The Asian Sugar Plantation in India and Indonesia: Industrial Production 1770-2010*, Cambridge, Cambridge University Press, 2013, pp. 44-87; Amin, *Gorakhpur*, pp. 32-80; PJ Marshall, 'The Bengal Commercial Society of 1775', *Bulletin of the Institute of Historical Research*, vol. 42, 1969, pp. 173-87; PJ Marshall, *East Indian Fortunes*, Oxford, Oxford University Press, 1976; PJ Marshall, *Bengal: The British Bridgehead, Eastern India 1740-1828*, The New Cambridge History of India II, vol. 2, Cambridge, Cambridge University Press, 1987, pp. 5-22, 34-9; Ratledge, *British Sugar Bowl*, passim.

[20] On sugar in nineteenth-century Siam, see Suehiro Akira, *Capital Accumulation in Thailand, 1855-1985*, Tokyo, Centre for East Asian Cultural Studies, 1989; David Bruce Johnson, 'Rural Society and the Rice Economy in Thailand, 1880-1930', Yale University, PhD Diss, 1975, pp. 26-31; Sarasin Viraphol, *Tribute and Profit: Sino-Siamese Trade 1652-1853*, Cambridge, Mass, Council for East Asian Studies, Harvard University, 1977, pp. 177-9, 201-6, 331-4.

from around 1870 onward.[21] Contemporaneously, in the maritime zone of South-East Asia, a new production area for sugar was created in the western districts of the Philippine island of Negros, equipped with steam mills, Vacuum Pans and Centrifuges — and financed, at least initially, by British mercantile capital. One contemporary source from the 1850s, for example, noted the importation into the island of iron cattle mills, and also of a large steam-driven mill, 'with corresponding evaporating pans and "centrifugals" for curing'. The source reported that it could be

> confidently state[d] that in the course of three years at least three other large steam mills will be erected … These improvements, though limited if compared with those of the great centres of sugar cultivation in other colonies, are what no one would have ventured to anticipate a few years ago as attainable in this quarter where the introduction of the steam mill … was looked upon as quite chimerical.[22]

At around the same time but further north, an already-established industry expanded considerably in the Pampanga districts of Luzon.[23]

---

[21] See Soames, *Treatise*, p. 59, for the claim that there were Vacuum Pans in 'Province Wellesley opposite Penang', from where sugar went to the Chinese market. According to a recent study, the British-owned Penang Sugar Estates Limited 'from its beginnings … was one of the largest, most technologically sophisticated of the European-owned sugar producers in Malaya. Its original landholdings dwarfed the typical Chinese-owned sugar estate of 500 acres or less, and they were several times the size of competing European firms, which usually worked only one plantation. A European visitor in the 1880s remarked that six of the nine large sugar estates in Province Wellesley were owned by the PSE [Penang Sugar Estates], making them the largest single producer of sugar in the region. PSE refineries, touted as "the last word in modernity", also processed the canes of smaller producers'. See Lynn Hollen Lees, 'International Management in a Free-Standing Company: The Penang Sugar Estates, Ltd., and the Malayan Sugar Industry, 1851-1914', *Business History Review*, vol. 81, spring 2007, pp. 27-57. Unfortunately, the author (whose prime concern is with the organisation of the business) elides the making of raw sugar with the subsequent *refining* of such sugar. (Refineries do not — as her account implies — process cane.) It is extremely unlikely that the PSE would have had refineries on each of its estates, and quite possible that it did not possess a refinery at all. Professor Lees nonetheless provides the most detailed and authoritative account to date (pp. 42-7) of sugar production in nineteenth-century Malaya.

[22] Robert MacMicking, *Recollections of Manilla and the Philippines during 1848, 1849, and 1850*, edited and annotated by Morton J Netzorg, with an Appendix, 'Trade in Panay, 1857-67, Four Letters by Nicholas Loney', Manila, Filipiniana Book Guild Inc., 1967, pp. 246-9.

[23] On developments in sugar production in the Philippines during the course of the nineteenth century, see Filomeno V Aguilar, Jnr, *Clash of Spirits: The History of Power and Sugar Planter Hegemony on a Visayan Island*, Honolulu, University of Hawai'i Press, 1998;

Most significant of all, however, was the development that took place on the island of Mauritius during the mid-century decades.[24] Beginning in the 1840s, almost contemporaneous with developments in the Indian subcontinent (and, as we shall see, in Java itself), a well-equipped sugar industry evolved on the island. It was well provided with Vacuum Pans and the other appurtenances of industrial production — and with supplies of 'cheap' indentured labour from India. Some Dutch colonial contemporaries wrote enviously of the fact that around 1860 'little' Mauritius was producing as much sugar as Java.[25] Its industry was destined to be one of the very few in Asia, apart from the Dutch colony, which had a continuous history of (semi-)industrialised sugar manufacture running through into the twentieth century.

John A Larkin, *The Pampangans: Colonial Society in a Philippine Province*, Berkeley & Los Angeles, University of California Press, 1972; Larkin, *Sugar and the Origins of Modern Philippine Society*, Berkeley and Los Angeles, University of California Press, 1993; VB Lopez-Varga, *The Socio-Politics of Sugar: Wealth, Power Formation and Change in Negros 1899-1985*, Bacolod, University of St La Salle Press, 1989; Alfred W McCoy, 'A Queen Dies Slowly: The Rise and Decline of Iloilo City', in Alfred W McCoy & Ed C de Jesus, *Philippine Social History*, Quezon City, Ateneo de Manila University Press, 1982, pp. 297-360; McCoy, 'Sugar Barons: Formation of a Native Planter Class in the Colonial Philippines', *Journal of Peasant Studies*, vol. 19, no. 3, 1992, pp. 106-41.

[24] According to A North Coombes (*The Evolution of Sugarcane Culture in Mauritius with a Chapter on the Evolution of the Mauritian Sugar Factory*, Mauritius, Department of Agriculture, 1937, p. 124), in 1862 some 56 of the island's 300 factories had installed Vacuum Pans, and most of them operated with Centrifuges. The majority of the factories without Vacuum Pans had installed steam-heated evaporating pans, and 277 of the factories had steam mills installed. Noel Deerr reported that the first Vacuum Pan was installed there in 1844 (vol. 2, pp. 561-2). JA Leon (*On Sugar Cultivation in Louisiana, Cuba &c. and the British Possessions by an European and Colonial Sugar Manufacturer*, London, Ollivier, 1848) remarked that Mauritius was the only British colonial plantation known to him 'where the modern process of making sugar has tolerably succeeded'. He cited 'Darruty's plantation', which was equipped with a Vacuum Pan, five double bottom clarifiers, five oblong steam evaporators, three cylindrical steam boilers, filters, Monte-jus, etc. For Mauritius in general, see Richard Allen, 'The Slender, Sweet Thread: Sugar, Capital and Dependency in Mauritius, 1860-1936', *The Journal of Imperial and Commonwealth History*, vol. 16, 1981, pp. 177-200; William Kelleher Storey, *Science and Power in Colonial Mauritius*, Rochester, NY, University of Rochester Press, 1997; and the series of articles by Ronald Lamousse, under the general title of 'The Economic Development of the Mauritius Sugar Industry', *Revue Agricole et Sucrière de L'île Maurice*, vol. 43, nos. 1, 2 & 4, 1964, pp. 23-38, 113-27, 354-72; and also vol. 44, no. 1, 1965, pp. 11-36.

[25] That is, in 1860 Mauritius produced around 130 000 MT. See DC Steijn Parve, 'Nieuwe Uitvindingen Betreffende de Koloniale Suikerbereiding', *Tijdschrijft voor Nederlandsch-Indië* (Nieuwe Reeks), vol. 1, no. 2, 1867, pp. 392-408.

In the event, however, none of these ventures achieved their full potential. The attempts to restructure cane production in the Indian subcontinent to suit the requirements of the industrial project had largely collapsed by 1850, not to be reinvigorated on any scale until the 1920s. Those entrepreneurs and investors who survived the debacle transferred their attentions to the production of indigo (which required very modest capital investment in its essentially pre-industrial technology).

By the 1870s, the Mauritius industry had entered a long period of stagnation and Mauritius had ceased to be a major producer in world terms, though it continued to supply substantial quantities of the commodity to the specialised Indian market. Indeed, by the century's end, its factories were authoritatively described as antiquated museum pieces.[26] One key factor here was that the Mauritius manufacturers lacked the intimate contacts with bourgeois capital in the British metropolis which (as we shall see) characterised their Indies-Dutch counterparts in Java, while Indian capitalists seem to have been unwilling to fill in the gap.[27] In the same decade, industrialised manufacture was largely abandoned in Siam, not to appear there again until the 1930s, while attempts to produce sugar on any scale on the Malay Peninsula petered out around 1900, in consequence of the better prospects of rubber and of competition from cheap imports from Java.[28]

A similar, though not identical, picture also held good for the Philippines. It would appear that the advance there of industrial technology was largely restricted to the milling of cane by steam-operated equipment and some few Vacuum Pans. The Multiple Effect looks to have made no appearance there — in what had become a cash-starved industry — prior to the American makeover in the early decades of the twentieth century after America's conquest of the ex-Spanish territory.[29] In the

---

[26] Noel Deerr, as quoted in HC Prinsen Geerligs, 'Invoer en Fabrikatie 1904', *ASNI*, vol. 12, no. 2, 1904, pp. 13-28.

[27] Richard B Allen, *Slaves, Freedmen and Indentured Labourers in Colonial Mauritius*, Cambridge, Cambridge University Press, 1999, pp. 22-3.

[28] Lees, 'The Penang Sugar Estates', pp. 28, 54.

[29] According to Deerr, a couple of Vacuum Pans were first installed in the Philippines in 1879 (vol. 2, p. 562). Other sources, while indicating steam mills, have nothing to say about Vacuum Pans or the Multiple Effect before the early twentieth century. 'It is an astonishing fact', remarked an early twentieth-century American investigator, 'that so little attention is paid in Negros to the importance of skill and care in the manufacture of sugar, even by the present crude methods'. He estimated that not more than one plantation-owner in twenty was fully conversant with the sugar-manufacturing process. See Herbert S Walker, *The Sugar*

1890s, for example, the Negros industry's foremost apologist lamented that a system of industrialised *centrales* had yet to appear, arguing that it was 'because of his lack of capital' that the planter-manufacturer of Negros was forced to adopt 'quick and simple methods' which produced only a low-grade sugar from the excellent raw material available to the mills.[30] Shortage of capital may also have been the chief factor in holding back the advance of industrialised manufacture in East Asia's main production areas in southern China and Formosa.[31] As was the case in the Philippines, the fully-fledged industrial project in sugar had to wait until the twentieth century. This left Java very much on its own.

The Rise of Java Sugar on the World Market 1780-1885

The commodity production of sugar had a long history in Java. Indeed, it appears to have begun there around the beginning of the seventeenth century, or perhaps somewhat earlier. From the start, it had been directed toward overseas markets. The local taste for sweeteners was mainly catered for by the manufacture of sugar from the sap of the palm tree[32], and sugar made from cane was largely an export

---

Industry on the Island of Negros, Manila, Department of the Interior, Bureau of Science, 1910, pp. 111-12.

[30] Robustiano Echauz, *Sketches of the Island of Negros*, 1894, translated and annotated by DV Hart, with an Introduction by John Larkin, Ohio, Ohio University, Centre for International Studies, Papers in International Studies, Southeast Asia Series, no. 50, 1978, p. 61.

[31] Mazumdar, *Sugar and Society in China*, pp. 338-86. For Formosa, see Christopher M Isett, 'Sugar Manufacture and the Agrarian Economy of Nineteenth-Century Taiwan', *Modern China*, vol. 21, no. 2, April 1995, pp. 233-59. The sugar entering world markets from Formosa/Taiwan in significant quantities, especially by the 1880s, was 'pre-industrial' sugar, manufactured by 'traditional means'.

[32] MAP Meilink-Roelofz, *Asian Trade and European Influence in the Indonesian Archipelago between 1500 and about 1630*, The Hague, Nijhoff, 1962, pp. 14, 242; K Glamann, *Dutch-Asiatic Trade, 1620-1740*, The Hague, Nijhoff, 1958, pp. 155-6; Paul Wheatley, *The Golden Khersonese: Studies in the Historical Geography of the Malay Peninsula before A.D. 1500*, Kuala Lumpur, University of Malaya Press, 1961, pp. 66-8; Anthony Reid, *Southeast Asia in the Age of Commerce*, vol. 1: *The Lands below the Winds*, New Haven, Yale University Press, 1988, p. 31. Reid remarks of the situation in the region in the fifteenth to seventeenth centuries that 'as a sweetening ... Southeast Asians themselves made greater use of brown sugar derived from boiling the sap of the Arenga or sugar palm, also native to the region and a prolific source of liquid sugar'. This still appears to have been substantially true at the beginning of the nineteenth century. TS Raffles (*The History of Java*, vol. 1, London, Black, Parbury and Allen, 1817, p. 97) says of Java that 'the sugar used by the natives is not prepared from the sugar cane, but from the aren and other palms'. According to H Deinum ('Bevolkingssuiker',

commodity, which was shipped out either via the Chinese junk trade on Batavia (or more rarely) on vessels owned by the VOC (the Dutch East India Company, or Verenigde Oostindische Compagnie). The China market was evidently of great importance. Like contemporary Formosa, Java functioned as an (albeit rather distant) 'off-shore island': one that supplied the mainland with a commodity that was cheaper and quite possibly tastier than that produced in southern China itself.[33] Along with China, the great ports of the Indian subcontinent and the Persian Gulf figured in the eighteenth-century destinations for the island's exports. In Europe, Java sugar generally competed only intermittently and often ineffectually with the output of the New World.[34]

Information on the output and export of cane sugar in eighteenth-century Java is sketchy and none-too-reliable. It is also necessary to distinguish between developments that took place in western parts of Java, particularly in the so-called *Ommelanden* [hinterlands] around the VOC's base at Batavia, and those that took place elsewhere on the island, notably on the *Pasisir* [shore], effectively Java's Northeast Coast from Cirebon to Surabaya and beyond. Manufacture in the *Ommelanden* (and commensurate exports) is generally reckoned — the evidence is

---

in CJJ van Hall & C van de Koppel, *De Landbouw in de Indische Archipel*, vol. 2A, The Hague, van Hoeve, 1948, p. 419) there are in Indonesia/South-East Asia three kinds of palm tree from which sugar is produced on a commercial scale. These are the Arenga Palm (*Arenga saccharifera*), the Siwilan or Lontar Palm (*Borassus flabillifer*) and Coco Palm (*Cocos nucifera*). This same source (pp. 419-24) has a brief description of the tapping and processing of palm sugar.

[33] On the early sugar trade between Formosa/Taiwan and mainland China, see Mazumdar, *Sugar and Society in China*, pp. 41, 206-7, 264.

[34] Glamann, pp. 157-66. From the mid-seventeenth century, Java sugar displaced Chinese sugar in the VOC's shipments to Europe, but the demand there for South-East Asian sugar was erratic in the extreme. It competed with Brazilian and Caribbean sugar only in fairly exceptional circumstances: at the end of the 1640s, for example, when the Portugese-Dutch conflict in Brazil reduced the latter's supplies to the Amsterdam market, and for a short period in the 1720s when nearly 70 per cent of the sugar exported from Batavia was sent to Holland. For much of the early modern period, however, South-East Asian sugar was regarded as ballast in the VOC's shipments to Amsterdam (i.e. it was not the prime commercial purpose of the voyage). Glamann notes that 'sugar, during the rest of the Company's lifetime, remained a commodity the main sales of which took place in Asia'. Nonetheless, at various times in the 1780s and again in the 1790s, the VOC strongly encouraged the production of sugar in Java, largely with a view to meeting demand in Europe.

not altogether consistent — to have peaked quite early in the eighteenth century and to have remained in the doldrums thereafter.[35]

As far as sugar production is concerned, the situation further east in the *Pasisir* is only really documented — and then only imperfectly — from quite late in the century, and output appears subsequently to have fluctuated fairly dramatically between 1800 and 1830. A rough estimate would be that by the end of the 1820s, the *Pasisir* was annually producing/exporting around 55 000 piculs, or approximately 3300 metric tons [MT], a figure which (if reliable) came near to matching the 60 000 piculs said to have been manufactured (and presumably exported) contemporaneously in the *Ommelanden* and other parts of West Java.[36] Even so, by international standards — and by those of contemporary Asia — this was a commercially insignificant amount.

---

[35] Around 1710, there were some 131 mills operating in the *Ommelanden*, with a claimed potential productive capacity totalling approximately 6500 tons of sugar a year and an actual production of some 4000 tons (Glamann, p. 164). Subsequent output cannot be confidently quantified: it must be assumed to have been very much lower after the massacre of many of Batavia's Chinese settlers (who virtually ran the sugar industry) in 1740. During the 1750s, sugar production can scarcely have exceeded an annual average of 3750 tons. (The trade in sugar produced in the Batavia hinterland was monopolised by the VOC.) In the period 1751-60, the company consigned a total of 32 250 tons of (apparently) Batavia sugar to its other Asiatic factories, and somewhere between 2500 and 5000 tons to *factorij* Nederland (Glamann, p. 166). These figures do not take into account what Glamann (p. 165) describes as 'a constant small sale in the Indonesian archipelago (including sales in Batavia)'. After the mid-century, production appears to have picked up somewhat, though the number of mills continued to fall; J Hooyman says there were only fifty-five in 1779 ('Verhandelingen over den Tegenwoordigen Staat van den Landbouw in de Ommelanden van Batavia', *Verhandelingen van het Bataviaasch Genootschap van Kunsten en Wetenschappen*, vol. 1, 1779, pp. 173-263, here p. 241), but the same author cites a production figure of nearly 7000 MT for 1767, which he evidently reckoned was a pretty good year (pp. 212-13). Peter Creutzberg (*Indonesia's Export Crops*, vol. 1 of Peter Boomgaard (ed.), *Changing Economy in Indonesia*, The Hague, Nijhoff, 1975, p. 63) has annual exports from the Batavia *Ommelanden* at around 5000-6000 MT toward the end of the eighteenth century.

[36] For an extended discussion, see Robert Van Niel, *Java's Northeast Coast 1740-1840*, Leiden, CNWS Publications, 2005, pp. 133-53; and de Haan, *Oud Batavia*, vol. 1, 1935, pp. 325-6. According to the data laboriously collected by Van Niel (*Northeast Coast*, appendix 13), sugar production in the *Pasisir* amounted to an all-time (and quite exceptional) recorded high of 51 000 piculs in 1803, falling steeply to a little over 23 000 piculs in 1804 and to 20 829 piculs in 1805. This would suggest that de Haan's figure of 20 000 piculs for 1815 is perfectly plausible. 55 000 piculs had been achieved in the *Pasisir* by the end of the 1820s as a whole, up from a purported 20 000 piculs in 1815. The West Java output circa 1829 appears to have fallen by 50 per cent over the previous decade and a half (de Haan, *Oud Batavia*, vol. 1, p. 324; Van Niel, *Northeast Coast*, p. 343).

From the 1830s onward, however, the situation changed radically. Around the beginning of the decade, Java was exporting scarcely 7000 MT of sugar annually. Twenty years later (in 1851), the quantity had risen to well over 100 000 MT; by the early 1870s exports stood at twice that amount. And output continued to mount, so that by 1885, the end of the period with which we are concerned, exports stood at a figure in excess of 400 000 MT.[37]

Global comparisons are important in establishing the full extent of Javanese sugar's remarkable trajectory in the mid-nineteenth century. Early data on this score are scarce and notably incomplete, but one estimate is that total world production of sugar amounted toward the close of the eighteenth century to no more 263 000 MT in total. (This was before the massive disruption to supply in the Atlantic Zone occasioned by the great slave revolt on St Domingue, though the estimate probably took no account, for example, of the massive amounts of sugar in the form of *gur* produced in India, or of China's unquantified output of the commodity).[38] Similarly qualified, 'world' production was calculated at around 644 000 MT circa 1840, and had risen to something in the region of 1 million MT a decade later, before approaching 4 million MT by the mid-1880s. In short — taking the figures for known sugar production at their face value and assuming the certain fact that almost all Java's recorded output at this time was exported — during the middle decades of the nineteenth century Java had risen from a position of almost total inconsequence in the international sugar economy to one in which it accounted for around 10 per cent of the world's recorded sugar output.

That figure would be much higher — approaching 20 per cent — if cane sugar production alone was taken into account, for by 1885 some 50 per cent or more of the world's recorded output of the commodity took the form of (northern European) beet sugar. As we have just seen, the manufacture of sugar from beet had begun in Europe during the Napoleonic Wars, but it was not until the 1840s and 1850s that it began to be produced in commercially appreciable quantities with a thoroughly viable

---

[37] See Appendix 2, 'Java Sugar Production and Exports 1830-1885', in Creutzberg, pp. 63-76.

[38] See Tomich, p. 15; PhG Chalmin, 'Important Trends in Sugar Diplomacy before 1914', in Albert & Graves, *Crisis and Change*, p. 12. As indicated above, the estimate must be regarded as no more than rough, and excludes much Asian sugar production that took place outside the European colonial sphere.

technology. After that, its output increased exponentially, potentially threatening to wipe cane sugar off the market. It was, therefore, one of the significant outcomes of the industrial project in Java that Asian cane sugar, by far the greater part of it from the Dutch colony, came to play such a major role in world trade. Without it, sugar manufactured from beet would have dominated the international sugar economy from about 1880 onward. Even so, the continued high profile of industrially manufactured cane sugar was predicated on far-reaching changes in the world market.

During the formative period of the industrial project in sugar, throughout the middle decades of the nineteenth century, Java's main markets were in the West, initially primarily in Amsterdam and subsequently in London. From the late nineteenth century onward, Java's industrial sugar factories started to find that the bulk of their sales were beginning to take place elsewhere in Asia itself, as industrially manufactured and refined white sugar began to be preferred by consumers who had previously been supplied by indigenous handicraft-producers of non-centrifugal sugar. Indeed, by the 1920s, all the major outlets for Java sugar were located in Asia. Though this development took some time to become fully apparent, as early as the 1880s the tipping point had already been reached in which less Java sugar went 'west of Suez' (the standard contemporary designation) than to markets elsewhere in the world. Until then, the island's output was firmly integrated into a global commodity chain that moved its raw sugar from colonial periphery to a (quasi-)metropolitan core in Holland and the United Kingdom, where it was subsequently processed (i.e. refined) for distribution to European consumers.

After that, however, this bilateral relationship broke down and was replaced by one in which (colonial) Dutch capital and Indonesian resources of land and labour were combined to produce a commodity marketed 'exogenously' elsewhere in the East. Java had begun the nineteenth century, as we have seen, as a minor sector in a vast Asian production area in which the commodity was manufactured by pre-industrial means in places as far-flung as Bengal in northern India and a group of islands immediately to the south of Japan. It ended the century, however, as the 'Oriental Cuba', the Asian powerhouse of industrial sugar manufacture on the very front rank of the international sugar economy. It is to the evolution of this powerhouse, in the form of the advent of steam and steel on a colonial frontier and the industrial factory to which it gave birth, that we now turn.

2   A Creole Prometheus: Steam, Paddle Boats and Sugar Factories

During the middle decades of the nineteenth century, Prometheus came to Java, and did so in the shape of the technologies of steam, iron and (eventually) steel. In so far, moreover, as it invoked colonial ingenuity and invention as well as metropolitan transfer, Prometheus took on a distinctively Creole, hybrid character.[39] As one recent writer has remarked of technology (and much else):

> the Netherlands East Indies is such an alluring place to study, because it appears to exist simultaneously at the further reaches of modernity and close to its most dynamic centre.[40]

His point provides an apt motif for what follows, specifically in its applicability to the men and machines not only of the colony's sugar industry in the mid-nineteenth century but also of the larger imperialism of which they formed an essential part. The history of the Dutch colonial presence in nineteenth-century Java has been occluded to a degree by notions of a *Tempo Doeloe* — literally a 'time past', but with similar connotations to the myth of the ante-bellum American South — which became the subject for a deal of post-colonial nostalgia in the Netherlands itself.[41] On this reading,

---

[39] For the Creole character of the 'Old Indies World' in general, see Ulbe Bosma and Remco Raben, *Being 'Dutch' in the Indies: A History of Creolisation and Empire, 1500-1920*, translated by Wendie Shaffer, Athens, Ohio/ Singapore, Ohio University Press/ Singapore University Press, 2008.

[40] Rudolph Mrazek, *Engineers of Happy Land: Technology and Nationalism in a Colony*, Princeton, NJ, Princeton University Press, 2002, p. xv.

[41] The *locus classicus*, with a very heavy emphasis on photographic evidence, is E Breton de Nijs [aka Rob Nieuwenhuijs], *Tempo Doeloe: Fotografische Documenten uit het Oude Indie, 1870-1914*, Amsterdam, Querido, 1961; but see also EM Beekman, 'Introduction', Rob

a largely 'pre-modern' order prevailed in the colony during the middle decades of the nineteenth century and was swept away only toward the century's end by economic crises and a sharp increase in the inflow of European capital and, subsequently, of self-consciously 'expatriate' personnel. The colony was not the sort of place, in short, where an industrial project was likely to thrive: on the contrary, in such a location sugar production was likely to be a thoroughly old-fashioned affair.

In fact, nothing could be further from the truth. Metropolitan Holland itself may have been slow to take up the advances of the industrial revolution.[42] In its Asian colony, however, Prometheus was clearly in evidence on the frontiers of Dutch power in the Indonesian archipelago by the middle decades of the century.[43]

Nieuwenhuijs, *Mirror of the Indies: A History of Dutch Colonial Literature*, translated by Frans van Roosevelt, Amherst, University of Massachusetts Press, 1982, pp. xiii-xxiii; Beekman, *Troubled Pleasures: Dutch Colonial Literature from the East Indies, 1600-1950*, New York, Clarendon Press, 1996. In the latter work Beekman built a fantastical picture of an Indies community 'that was anything but Dutch' (p. 328), characterised by 'constant conflict' between 'the vast network of officials of the colonial civil service' and the world of 'planters, merchants ... settlers' (p. 335). The upshot of such imaginings was a confusing mélange that derives both from bad history and a simplistic approach to the contribution of imaginative literature to an understanding of colonial society. For a sophisticated modern re-analysis, see Joost Cote, 'Romancing the Indies: The Literary Construction of *Tempo Doeloe*', in Joost Cote & Loes Westerbeek (eds), *Recalling the Indies: Colonial Culture & Postcolonial Identities*, Amsterdam, Aksant, 2005, pp. 133-72. See also G Roger Knight, 'A Case of Mistaken Identity? *Suikerlords* and Ladies, *Tempo Doeloe* and the Dutch Colonial Communities in Nineteenth Century Java', *Social Identities*, vol. 7, no. 3, 2001, pp. 379-91.

[42] This remains, nonetheless, an issue on which the jury is perhaps still out. As Keetie E Sluyterman remarks (in *Dutch Enterprise in the Twentieth Century*, London & New York, Routledge, 2005, pp. 23-6), '[t]he Netherlands were late in catching up with the opportunities shaped by the First Industrial Revolution: the use of steam power and mechanisation in the textile and machinery industry [and the] rise of modern manufacturing industry in Holland only began in the 1860s'. Other research, however, complicates the picture somewhat. For a succinct introduction, see Jan Luiten van Zanden & Arthur van Riel, *The Strictures of Inheritance: The Dutch Economy in the Nineteenth Century*, Princeton, NJ & Oxford, Princeton University Press, 2004, pp. 4-6.

[43] For the role of steam navigation in cementing Dutch power in the erstwhile Netherlands Indies, see JNFM à Campo, *Engines of Empire: Steam Shipping and State Formation in Colonial Indonesia*, Hilversum, Verloren, 2005 (though Campo is predominantly concerned with a later period than that covered here). On the links between technology and imperial expansion in general, see the classic accounts in Daniel R Headrick, *The Tools of Empire: Technology and European Imperialism in the Nineteenth Century*, New York, Oxford University Press, 1981; Headrick, *The Tentacles of Progress: Technology Transfer in the Age of Imperialism, 1850-1940*, New York, Oxford University Press, 1988.

Paddle Boats and Sugar Factories

In the West, the nineteenth-century advance of steam and steel came to be epitomised in the cotton mill, at least in so far as the sphere of large-scale commodity production was concerned. Worldwide, on the other hand, the major connotations of steam power in the mid-century decades arguably had more to do with transportation (including its military applications), in the form of railway engines and steam boats. Indeed, the heavily armed steamer became Imperialism's mobile 'weapon of mass destruction' par excellence. Steam-powered, ocean-going vessels began to ply international waters in the 1810s and became fully effective a decade later. Famously, the *Savannah*, using a (then commonplace) combination of steam and sail, crossed the Atlantic from New York to Liverpool in 1819. Prior to that, various pioneering steamers had begun to ply British coastal waters.[44]

Of course, in the global picture, railways as well as steamers mattered a great deal and, in some locations, did so in connection with the manufacture of sugar. In Cuba in particular — from the 1850s onward the greatest of all the world's cane sugar exporters — the railway grew along with sugar. Indeed, its precocious appearance there, as early as the 1830s, had everything to do with moving the commodity and virtually nothing to do with passenger transport.[45] In Java, on the other hand, the railway was a relatively late arrival in the 1870s (after which it expanded exponentially). There, in the predominantly maritime world of the Indies archipelago, the mid-century connection between sugar and steam — figurative and literal — took the form of the paddle steamer and its 'screw'-propelled successor.

Even so, too exclusive a concentration on steamers and railways can be misleading. Along with the nautical application of steam and its use as motive power on the 'iron road', the stationary steam engine had also become an established presence globally during the middle decades of the nineteenth century (and in some locations well before that). This held not only for textiles (as in the Indian subcontinent and Japan) but also — and crucially — for sugar. In places as far apart as Java and Cuba or the Indian subcontinent and Guyana, the steam-operated sugar factory came to define

---

[44] John Kennedy, *The History of Steam Navigation*, Liverpool, Charles Birchall, 1903, pp. 11-36.

[45] Gert J Oostindie, 'Cuban Railroads 1830-1868: Origins and Effects of Progressive Enterpreneurialism', *Caribbean Studies*, vol. 20, nos. 3-4, 1988, pp. 24-45; Curry-Machado, *Cuban Sugar*, p. 11.

the land frontier of colonialism imperialism just as surely as the steamer marked it out at sea. The innards of the sugar factory and the paddle steamer — and, of course, the railway engine — had many similarities as far as technology was concerned, and all three operated with a certain degree of synchronicity on the colonial frontier. It was only around the mid-century that steam machinery started to become industry-specific to such a degree that it began to create exclusive, specialist fields of experience and knowledge.[46]

In the Indies, the 'nautical' part of the story of steam, steel and sugar began in the mid-1820s. A pioneering steamer, built in Surabaya in East Java, was first put into commercial service to connect the main colonial cities along the island's north coast. This hybrid, Creole vessel, very much a local creation despite its metropolitan antecedents, was named *Van der Capellen* in honour of the colony's first Governor-General. Built in Java by local workmen, using locally hewn teak, it was fitted with twin engines of 25 horsepower from the ubiqitious Liverpool firm of Fawcett Preston, the same firm that supplied steam-powered sugar mills in appreciable numbers to the Caribbean. Initially used for civilian purposes, the *Van der Capellen* was subsequently employed to carry troops and supplies during the Java War of 1825-30.[47] Distracted by the war — a challenge to colonial hegemony in Central Java with potentially dire consequences for its power throughout the island — the Indies Government did not embark seriously and strenuously on fastening its grip on the Indonesian archipelago as a whole until the following decade. It was in this context that the Dutch quickly began to appreciate the utility of steam power — and of paddle steamers in particular.

The little steamers were valued for their manoeuvrability, their shallow draught and assured speed. Not the least of their attractions, moreover, was their capacity, particularly at night, for inspiring terror in those who had not hitherto encountered them. Names like *Merapi* (a very active volcano in Central Java), *Vesuvius* and *Etna* were richly evocative of the effect they were presumed to have. Writing in 1834, Johannes van den Bosch, by then installed in The Hague as Minister of Colonies after a stint as Governor-General in the Indies, took a firm grasp of the imperial advantages. To his successor, JC Baud, he commended a steam vessel he was about

---

[46] See e.g. Curry-Machado, *Cuban Sugar*, p. 55.

[47] CA Gibson-Hill, 'The Steamers Employed in Asian Water, 1819-39', *Journal of the Malayan Branch of the Royal Asiatic Society*, vol. 27, 1954, pp. 131-4, 158. On Fawcett, see Tann, 'Steam and Sugar', pp. 71-5.

to dispatch to the Indies in terms of its ability to carry a large body of troops 'in the face of the monsoon': in other words, he commended it for its ability to circumvent the limitations traditionally imposed on navigation 'above and below the winds'. In this particular instance, the Minister was over-sanguine in his expectations: the boat in question sank in deep water during its early trials near Rotterdam.[48]

The Minister's point, however, was a valid one and paddle steamers — at least those that managed to stay afloat — quickly proved their worth. Under the aegis of the van den Bosch-Baud regime at the Colonial Office, and no doubt with the encouragement of the technologically-minded Dutch monarch himself, the assembly of steamers in the Indies Government's own Surabaya dockyard, using mechanical parts sent out from Holland, soon began in earnest — though it was perhaps another decade before they began to prove their worth. After that, however, their story takes on a dynamic of its own. In 1846, and again two years after that, paddle steamers participated successfully in military expeditions against some of the petty states of the as-yet unconquered island of Bali. In 1849, they also made possible the rapid deployment of troops to suppress a major uprising in Java itself.[49]

Men and Machines in Sugar: Transnational Networks and Global 'Diaspora'

Nonetheless, Prometheus's significance in the Indies was far from being confined to military conquest. It also extended into the field of economic conquest in the shape of sugar factories, whose own smoke-stacks, paralleling those of the paddle boats, became a ubiquitous feature of the lowlands of Java's eastern and central districts during the middle decades of the century. Beginning rather slowly a few years on either side of 1830, the majority of Java's one hundred or so colonial sugar factories could, within less than thirty years, boast the use of steam in at least part of their operations. These developments had far-reaching consequences for Java's position in what was increasingly becoming an international sugar economy.

---

[48] See van den Bosch to Baud, 15.9.1834 & 15.12.1834, in JJ Westendorp Boerma (ed.), *Briefwisseling tussen J van den Bosch en JC Baud*, vol. 1, Utrecht, Kemink en Zoon, 1956, pp. 182-3, 189. For the ignominious end of this particular paddle steamer, see MG de Boer, *Leven en Bedrijf van Gerhard Moritz Roentgen, Grondvester van de Nederlandsche Stoomboot-Maatschappij, Thans Maatschappij voor Scheeps- en Werktuigbouw 'Fijenoord', 1823-1923*, Groningen, Noordhoff, 1923, pp. 105-6.

[49] *KV*, 1849, p. 25.

Most immediately, they drew to Java several individuals with a degree of expertise in handling steam-operated machinery — and in the making of sugar with such machinery — that was not yet available locally. Whether they were indeed 'mechanics' [*mechanist*] or 'engineers' [*ingenieur*] — the distinction seems to have been a fairly fluid one — was at this date largely a matter of semantics.[50] The Dutch have a nicely-honed word for them: they were *werktuigkundig*, or 'knowledgeable with machines'. In other words, these were people who, by virtue of their experiential training in the foundries and shipyards of north-western Europe, were qualified to participate in the overseas, international transmission — and local adaptation — of the technology of industrialism. In the memorable phrase of a remarkable recent study of their presence in the Spanish Caribbean, they were people of 'versatile skills', recruited through agents, advertisements and, of course, the solicitation of relatives and friends who had gone before.[51] Their presence in the Indies in dockyards, sugar factories and the like hence reflected a global 'diaspora'. It was one in which experientially qualified people — variously, engineers or mechanics, sugar makers, iron masters and skilled artisans — re-located to 'the colonies' in the hope of making their fortune or at least of enjoying a better, more adventurous life than was possible in the metropolis.

Those who worked in the sugar factories, in particular, gained something of a reputation for being 'difficult'. They were a 'problem' from the moment they landed, one high-placed colonial official contended in the mid-1840s: they made 'absurd' demands and then lapsed into 'idleness' when they failed to obtain what they wanted.[52] Indisputably, their rarity-value allowed them a charmed existence. For example, the Netherlands-born sugar boiler at one north Java sugar factory in the mid-1850s, a certain Andries Renninghof from Amsterdam, was dismissed for having taken to

---

[50] It was not long to remain so, however. See e.g. Conrad Dixon, 'The Rise of the Engineer in the Nineteenth Century', in Gordon Jackson & David M Williams (eds), *Shipping, Technology, and Imperialism: Papers Presented to the Third British-Dutch Maritime History Conference*, Farnham, Ashgate, 1996, pp. 231-41.

[51] See the chapter entitled 'Engineering Migration' in Curry-Machado, *Cuban Sugar*, pp. 49-71. Although Curry-Machado's prime focus is Cuba and the Caribbean, what he says has major resonances for the contemporary situation in the industrialising sugar regions of Asia — and for Java in particular.

[52] Marginal comments of the Director of Cultivations in E & L Saportas, 'Rapport over den toestand van het suiker fabriekwezen op Java', in Exh. 24.4.1847/28.

the bottle and having trashed the house of a fellow employee on a drunken spree. Nonetheless, he was able to find immediate re-employment in another factory further along the coast — an opportunity which would surely not have presented itself in his native Holland (and he was still there a decade later). Indeed, it was apparent at this juncture that such people — at least when sober — were as much sought after as they were indispensable. In seeking a replacement, Renninghof's employers found that they were negotiating with a man who was '*meer mechanist dan suikerkooker*' ['more a mechanic than a sugar boiler'], but took him on for want of anyone better qualified.[53]

Ambitious and foot-loose, they were prepared to follow overseas the crates of industrial machinery that were beginning to make their way to what once might have been considered the 'ends of the earth'. At times — in the 1830s and early 1840s, at least — the 'ends of the earth' looked all the more attractive because of the downturn in the engineering sector of the economies of Western Europe. In the United Kingdom alone, in 1837-38, around one-third of the members of the Society of Journeymen Steam-Engine Makers were in receipt of relief from the Society, and in 1841-42 the figure was a little under one-quarter.[54]

Cuba — by the mid-nineteenth century the country with the biggest and most advanced cane sugar industry in the world — became the prime focus for such migrants, brought there (recruitment itself being very various) under the auspices of the Cuban elite who owned the island's sugar factories. The members of this Cuban elite had a far-reaching belief in the value and feasibility of technological innovation (made possible, in turn by the cheap labour of an enslaved African workforce), and were the world's biggest importers of steam-operated sugar machinery, the bulk of it initially of British origin but subsequently (from the 1840s onward) predominantly of North American manufacture.

Accordingly, Cuba's sugar owners had an internationally disproportionate need for skilled individuals to install, maintain and operate this machinery. Such people were mostly foreigners, brought there by transnational networks from a variety of engineering backgrounds. As has recently been remarked,

> the more influential of the Cuban elite ... displayed an active personal interest in international developments and took advantage of their periodic trips

---

[53] NFB, 10.7.1852/67; JVFB, 1852-3, pp. 23-5; NFB, 1.2.1854/109; Factorij to A'dam, 26.4.1854/284.

[54] Curry-Machado, *Cuban Sugar*, pp. 54-5.

to Europe or North America in order to check up on the latest models and innovations.[55]

In short, their continuous search for improvements in sugar production took them beyond the confines of their own empire and brought them into contact with globally developing industrial centres.[56] They were likewise important agents in the development of global migratory networks that extended beyond the shipment of involuntary workers to the provisioning of their factories with people well-versed in the ways of steam and steel.

Java, of course, was a good deal more distant from the industrial regions on either side of the north Atlantic than was its Caribbean antipode. Whereas it took only a matter of weeks to sail from the United Kingdom to Cuba (and less than that from New York or one of the other industrial centres of the United States), and many *maquinistas* took the opportunity of spending the industry's off-season in the States or in Europe[57], it frequently took the better part of four months to travel from Western Europe to Java. Although this journey-time was more than halved late in the 1840s for those with the financial means to undertake the so-called Overland Route (see below), a combination of cost and voyage-duration made employment in 'the Indies' much more of a year-round occupation than was the case in the Caribbean. Even so, the colonial communities of mid-century Java were far from being as 'isolated' or 'remote' as has sometimes been posited. As we shall see, there were many important parallels with Cuba in the way things played out in Java with respect both to the technology of sugar manufacture and to the provenance of the skilled individuals on whom its successful transfer — and adaptation — was predicated.

In the case of the Netherlands and its great Asian colony, moreover, there is a more specific, albeit (presently) largely submerged narrative here. It concerns the extent to which, as the nineteenth century progressed, a country like the post-1830 Netherlands, which was by then devoid of its more industrialised 'Belgian' south and was significantly less developed in terms of steam and steel than the United Kingdom or the east coast of the United States, nonetheless began to 'graduate' technologically skilled [*werktuigkundig*] artisans through the agency, in both their metropolitan and

---

[55] Curry-Machado, *Cuban Sugar*, p. 40.
[56] Curry-Machado, 'Cuban Phoenix', p. 35.
[57] Curry-Machado, *Cuban Sugar*, pp. 75-6.

colonial manifestations, of its military institutions and naval dockyards.[58] In the context of the present discussion, it was the latter that were very much to the fore.

From Dockyard to Sugar Factory: Mr Lawson and Colonel Lucassen

A man like Alexander Lawson, a young man whose career progressed from paddle boats to sugar factories, was somebody who might hence have been encountered in Cuba or Mauritius or India — or virtually anywhere in the world where steam-operated machinery had been, or was being, installed in the mid-century decades. As it was, he found himself in Java. Born in the Scottish coastal town of Dundee in 1819, he was the youngest surviving child of some ten siblings.[59] His father was in business there, latterly as a manufacturer of jute sacking and the employer of some fifty or so workmen — the steam-driven mills that turned jute into fabric being famously the main industry of nineteenth-century Dundee. Clearly a person of some substance, he was nonetheless a relatively small entrepreneur rather than one of the town's 'jute barons'.

His business was not big enough, perhaps, to attract or hold a younger son. For whatever reason, Alexander Lawson turned away from jute, and looked instead for an opening in the industries that this world commodity had attracted to the town. Foundries and shipyards were established in Dundee from the early nineteenth century onward to service its jute manufacturing enterprises. Given what we know of his subsequent career, it seems quite possible — though we do not know for certain — that Lawson served an apprenticeship in one of them. He may well have been trained, for example, by the Dundee Foundry Company or its successor Gourlay & Co, a mechanical engineering firm that traced its origins back to the 1790s.[60]

---

[58] On the metropolitan aspect of this subject, see in particular Geert Verbong, 'Opleiding en Beroep', in HW Lintsen (ed.), *Geschiedenis van de Techniek in Nederland: De Wording van een Moderne Samenleving 1800-1890*, Part 5: *Techniek, Beroep en Praktijk*, Zutphen, Walburg Pers, 1994, pp. 21-83.

[59] Alexander Lawson was born in Dundee (Scotland) on 1 July 1819 and died in Tegal (Java) on 18 July 1877. His parents were William Lawson (of Dundee) and Mary Hill. He married twice. His first wife was Harriet Aitkins (born in Dundee 1824, died in Tegal 1859), and his second wife was the Java-born Anna Maria Leroy (dates unknown). I am grateful for details of Lawson's background in Dundee, and for his family history prior to his arrival in Rotterdam, to Catherine McKay (personal communication, 2010), who has conducted extensive genealogical research on the family.

[60] SGE Lythe, 'Shipbuilding at Dundee Down to 1914', *Scottish Journal of Political*

What is certain, however, is that Alexander Lawson did not stay long in his home-town. By 1846, at the latest, the twenty-seven-year-old had left Dundee and re-located to the Netherlands, to the Dutch port of Rotterdam. He was employed there by the Nederlandsche Stoomboot Maatschappij [Netherlands Steamboat Company] or NSBM, an engineering and shipbuilding firm with a yard at Feijenoord on the southern outskirts of the city. (The yard has long since gone, but its location is preserved in the name of one of Holland's most famous soccer teams.)[61] By 1846, moreover, he was also a married man, the husband of Harriet Aitkins who appears, like Lawson himself, to have come from Dundee. Nonetheless, during that same year there was a major interruption to the young couple's married life — and when it was resumed, it was on the other side of the world. For in the middle of 1846, Alexander Lawson left Rotterdam and sailed to Java.

For some years, the NSBM had been in the business of building or supplying equipment for paddle steamers.[62] However, it was still a fledgling operation, kept going perhaps because Anthony van Hoboken, the great Rotterdam merchant and ship-owner, had a stake in it[63], but also because the Dutch kingdom was very short of such enterprises, especially after the secession of its 'Belgian' provinces in 1830. The NSBM under the direction of Gerhard Moritz Roentgen was hence something of a pioneering enterprise, heavily dependent on state patronage. In 1845-46, the company had been commissioned to construct two steam-operated paddle boats, the *Onrust* and the *Borneo*, for service in the Indies, and by the middle of 1846, the frames, engines and mechanical parts for the *Onrust* were ready for dispatch to

---

Economy, vol. 11, no. 3, 1964, pp. 219-32. For a richly informative survey of engine-building in nineteenth-century Dundee, see http://www.steamindex.com/manlocos/manulist.htm (accessed 12 January 2009). I would like to thank Mr Bruce Dorward for kindly providing information on the engineering workshops and shipyards of nineteenth-century Dundee.

[61] The information in this and the following two paragraphs (unless otherwise indicated) comes from VMK, 30.5.1846/21-305 & VMK, 2.11.1846/411 and the enclosures therein. On the origins of the NSBM, see Jan M Dirkzwager, 'A Case of Transfer of Technology: Ship Design and Construction in Nineteenth-Century Netherlands', in Gordon Jackson & David M Williams (eds), *Shipping, Technology, and Imperialism: Papers Presented to the Third British-Dutch Maritime History Conference*, Farnham, Ashgate, 1996, pp. 189-210, here p. 190.

[62] Their first such contract appears to have dated from 1834, and related to the paddle steamers *Hecla* and *Eterna*. See Bram Oosterwijk, *Koning van de Koopvaart: Anthony van Hoboken (1756-1850)*, Rotterdam, Stichting Historische Publicaties Roterodamum, 1983, p. 198.

[63] Oosterwijk, p. 271.

Surabaya. Loaded on board the Dutch merchant ship Bato, the mechanical innards of the paddle boat left Rotterdam on 25 June, together with a group of eight *machinisten en werklieden* [mechanics and skilled operatives] who were to be in charge of completing the *Onrust* when it arrived at its destination, which would have been around mid-November 1846.

Lawson was the only non-Dutchman among them, and — as the team's leader — was also the most highly paid. He got a salary of 300 guilders a month, as opposed to his assistant's 200 guilders and the 4-6 guilders a day paid as wages to the others. Prior to departure, he arranged for more than a third of his salary to be paid to his wife, whom he left behind in Europe — temporarily, as it turned out. On board the *Bato*, he and his deputy, the twenty-two year old JF Mossel — who came from the town of Hellevoetsluis, down-river from Rotterdam itself — travelled first-class, whereas the remainder of the group were second-class passengers. All in all, his salary — two-thirds of that accorded a relatively high-ranking official such as an Assistant *Resident* in Government service in the colony to which he was sailing — and the style of his shipboard accommodation suggest that Lawson was a highly valued and skilled *werktuigkundige*. It also points to the way in which a young and ambitious 'engineer' could greatly improve his chances of advancing and making good money by opting to 'go out to the colonies'.

Back in Europe, for instance, it seems unlikely that a man in his late twenties — however able — would have been put in charge of a major project such as that which Lawson undertook in Surabaya, where his job was to supervise the assembly of the *Onrust* (and the later arriving *Borneo*) in the Indies Government's dockyard. To give it its full and proper title, the dockyard was called *De Fabriek voor de Marine, het Stoomwezen en de Nijverheid* [or the Factory for the Navy, Steam Power and Industry]. Located in Java's second and already most 'industrial' city, it was a sizeable establishment, whose 'new iron and copper foundries left little to be desired'. A very few years after Lawson's arrival there, the dockyard was reckoned to have a workforce more than 800-strong, and its proud boast was to have assembled the Dutch warship *Admiraal van Kingsbergen* in the course of three-and-a-half-months from parts sent out from Holland.[64]

Work on the *Onrust* and *Borneo* took somewhat longer — indicative perhaps of the amount of manufacturing which actually had to take place in Surabaya despite

---

[64] *KV*, 1853, pp. 209-10.

the notionally prefabricated nature of the steamers — and it was only around the middle of 1848 that they were nearing completion. The *Onrust* became part of what was, in effect, a colonial war-fleet. Around 1850, there were eleven such steamers.[65] The *Borneo* was put into service of a different yet equally imperial kind, carrying letters and passengers from Batavia to Singapore, there to connect with the newly developed Overland Mail route to Europe (see below).[66]

Lawson's work in Surabaya must have finished late in 1848. He did not, however, return to Rotterdam or Scotland. Instead — and having already arranged for Harriet Aitkins to come out to join him — he moved from dockyard to sugar industry. His skills were evidently sought after. Taking up what proved to be permanent residence in the Indies, Alexander Lawson became engineer in charge at two adjoining steam-operated sugar factories in Tegal Residency on the north coast of Central Java. Built only a few years earlier, in 1841-42, the Kemanglen and Doekoewringin sugar factories could lay claim to being among the technologically most sophisticated and up-to-date factories in the entire colony. Both were equipped with machinery from the celebrated French-Belgian manufacturers Derosne et Cail, a firm that also supplied equipment to the French beet sugar industry and to colonial sugar producers in the Caribbean.

The two factories in Tegal were owned by a retired Indies military man, Colonel Theodore Lucassen, who may well have got to hear of Lawson while the latter was still in Surabaya, where Lucassen's recently deceased father-in-law, the senior Indies official, DFW Pietermaat, had held the position of *Resident*.[67] In any event, it was Lucassen personally who arranged for Lawson to be allowed to stay in Java and who arranged for his transfer to the north coast. Lawson, at this stage, was still a British subject, and leave to remain in the Dutch colony was not something that would have happened automatically. A deal of string-pulling would have been involved, something that should not have been too difficult for Lucassen, whose career and

---

[65] *KV*, 1853, pp. 36-8.

[66] By 1849 the 'Nederlandsche Eskader' in the Indies had thirteen steamers, including the *Onrust* and *Borneo*; it used steamers for the speedy movement of troops to Banten 1849, and it used the steamers *Batavia*, *Phoenix* and *Borneo* to carry the mail between Batavia and Singapore (for the newly opened steamer route to Suez via Ceylon). For all this see *KV*, 1850 pp. 15-26.

[67] Susanna Pietermaat, Lucassen's second wife, was a daughter of DFW Pietermaat (1790-1848), who was Resident of Batavia from 1834-37, and Resident of Surabaya from 1839-48. See *NP*, vol. 21, 1933-34, pp. 252-4.

contacts in Java, extending back over a period of more than three decades, presumably still carried a certain weight in Batavia.

Indeed, string-pulling was Lucassen's forte. His ancestors were country gentry from the borderlands of the Netherlands and Germany, and he himself had been born in a castle [*ridderslot*].[68] He subsequently entered the army early enough to be captured in Napoleon's campaign in Russia but was repatriated quickly enough to join the first Dutch military contingents dispatched to Java in 1816, when the colony was restored by the British. Once there, he evidently settled into the milieu of the 'Old Indies World' without too much difficulty, and in 1821 (at the age of twenty-nine) he married a sixteen-year-old, colonial-born woman of a 'good' family. Lucassen pursued a military path — smoothed no doubt by the connections established during the Napoleonic era — which culminated in his appointment as *Inspecteur en Chef Militaire Administratie* [Inspector and Head of the Military Administration] in the Indies.

Figure 4: An industrial pioneer in Java sugar: Colonel Theodore Lucassen.
Source: Koninklijk Instituut voor Taal-, Land- en Volkenkunde, Leiden, no. 47A24

A keen breeder, Lucassen had five children by his first wife and a further seven by his second, Susanna ('Suzette') Pietermaat. Indeed, he claimed it was the plethora of offspring who were the driving force behind his need to obtain a sugar contract. A military pension alone was totally insufficient to maintain his brood in the bourgeois style to which his clan was becoming accustomed. At the beginning of the 1840s, knowing the right people and having an ambitious plan for constructing a sugar factory of advanced design in the colony that he had just left, he was able to obtain access to the Dutch king. Willem the First, even though on the verge of precipitately

---

[68] For the Lucassen family, see *NP*, vol. 5, 1914, pp. 269-77; & *NP*, vol. 53, 1967, pp. 168-78.

abandoning his throne, was still very much the CEO of the Netherlands-Inc, and his patronage made all the difference. Schemes of that kind were dear to the headstrong monarch's heart, and he put pressure on the Colonial Office to secure a sugar contract for Lucassen — in the face of opposition from officials in Batavia, and despite Colonial Minister JC Baud's patent dislike of the man.[69]

Influence and Expertise: Theodore Lucassen and Hubertus Hoevenaar

Lucassen, contract in hand, arrived back in Java (not without mishap, including a shipwreck) in 1841. He was not alone, however, for he had brought with him to the colony a small contingent of mechanics and the like from northern France and the Low Countries. Two of them, indeed, were engineers or mechanics supplied by the same French firm, Derosne et Cail, which had also supplied the machinery.[70] Crucially, moreover, Lucassen had sailed to Java in the company of Hubertus Hoevenaar, the stepson of an old Netherlands associate and distant relative of Lucassen's, and members of Hoevenaar's immediate family, including his mother, Arnoudina Ringeling and his stepfather, Paulus Hoevenaar.[71]

---

[69] C Fasseur, *The Politics of Colonial Exploitation*, translated and edited by RE Elson & Ary Kraal, Southeast Asia Program, Cornell University, Ithaca, NY, 1992, pp. 186-7; Leidelmeijer, *Grootbedrijf*, pp. 155-62; Baud to van den Bosch, 29.7.1835, in Westendorp Boerma, *Briefwisseling*, vol. 2, p. 180; Th. Lucassen to Baud, 27.3.1845, NA, Collectie Baud, 723.

[70] The team of artisans and skilled operatives which Lucassen and his then associate, Otto Carel Holmberg de Beckfelt (who also built two sugar factories operating on Government Contract in the vicinity), brought with them to Tegal in 1841 consisted of Daniel Gilquin (born in Utrecht, 24 years old); Maurice Cellier (born in Astoune — as it appears to have been spelt — in France, 31 years old); Jules Daniel Boudaro (born in Paris, 28 years old); Louis Zoude (born in Doornik, Belgium, 22 years old); Michel Roux (born in Lyon, 25 years old); Hypolite Lachaume (born in St. Mequalt, as it appears to have been spelt, France, 27 years old); Louis Feray (date of birth unknown, France, 27 years old). See IB, 9.2.1842/20, MK, 2630. It was Roux and Feray who were (or had been) employees of Derosne et Cail.

[71] On the Ringeling and Hoevenaar families, see *DNL*, vol. 32, 1914, pp. 230-6 ; *DNL*, vol. 41, 1923, pp. 300, 360-1; *NP*, vol. 53, 1967, p. 169; ARM Mommers, 'Brabant van Generaliteitsland tot Gewest', Proefschrift, Rijksuniversiteit Leiden, 1953, p. 419; the Marriage Certificate of Hubertus Paulus Hoevenaar, 2 June 1813; the Death Certificate of Hubertus Paulus Hoevenaar, 3 January 1814; and the Marriage Certificate of Paulus Hubertus Hoevenaar, 3 April 1817, Gemeente Archief, Amsterdam. Hubertus Paulus Hoevenaar had lived (and died) on the Prinsengracht 'bij de Beerenstraat [*sic*] No. 271'. [Present-day street numbers around the intersection Prinsengracht/Berenstraat are in the high 400s. No. 271 would have been the *wijknommer* or ward-number.] Melanie Hoevenaar (born in Sablonville, Paris, 1831; died in Paris, 1881) was the daughter of Paulus Hubertus

The point about the younger Hoevenaar, however, was not his distant consanguinity with Lucassen (whose second wife, Susanna Antoinette Pietermaat [1814-84] was Arnoudina Ringeling's niece), but his direct experience in the industrial manufacture of sugar. Evidently intended as the corner-stone of the edifice that Lucassen was set on erecting in the colony, Hubertus Hoevenaar appears to have been brought out to Java because of *what* he knew rather than *who* he knew. His father, also called Hubertus Hoevenaar, had been a medical doctor with a practice on the Prinsengracht (one of Amsterdam's three 'grand canals' lined with the mansions of the rich — or, in the case of the Prinsengracht — with those of the merely well-to-do). It may have been a disease from the adjacent Jordaan slums that killed the young man — he was scarcely twenty-eight — a few months prior to the birth of his only child in 1814. His mother, Arnoudina Ringeling (1792-1854), came from an Amsterdam family with Caribbean connections, and subsequently married her late husband's brother.

The Hoevenaars were not in origin, however, an urban family. Rather, they were country gentry from deeply rural Brabant, in the south-east of the Netherlands. Even so, Paulus Hoevenaar (Hubertus's stepfather) was said to have had some money invested in the great engineering firm Cockerill et Cie at Seraing in Belgium (money which he reportedly lost in the firm's temporary collapse in 1840). If this is correct, it may well explain why his stepson had been placed with the Belgian firm — at that time one of the largest engineering and iron-working firms in Western Europe — a few years earlier, presumably as a 'gentleman apprentice' of some kind.[72]

Hoevenaar (born in Geldermalsen, 1784), whom Arnoudina had married in 1817. Paulus Hoevenaar died in Tegal in 1844 (PC Bloys van Treslong Prins, *Genealogische en Heraldische Gedenkwaardigheden Betreffende Europeanen op Java*, vol. 1, Batavia, Albrecht, 1934, p. 1), and his widow subsequently returned to Europe, where she died (in Paris) in 1854. Melanie, however, continued living *en famille* in Tegal. See *DNL*, vol. 32, 1914, pp. 231-3. The father of Hubertus (senior) and Paulus Hoevenaar, Cornelis Theodorus Hoevenaar, was clearly a country gentleman and was variously described as 'without occupation' (on his younger son's death certificate) and subsequently as '*Vrederegter*' ['Justice of the Peace'] at Boxtel, in the south-eastern part of the Netherlands (in his elder son's marriage certificate, 3 April 1817; likewise in the Amsterdam Stadsarchief). Before that he had held office as a Sheriff [variously *Schout* or *Schepen*] at other towns in Brabant.

[72] See the entry on Cockerill in the *Oxford Dictionary of National Biography*, edited by HCG Matthew and Brian Harrison, vol. 11, Oxford, Oxford University Press, 2004; Suzy Pasleau, *John Cockerill: Itineraire d'Un Geant Industriel*, Alleur-Liege, Belgium, Editions Du Perron, 1992; Robert Halleux, *Cockerill: Deux Siecles de Technologie*, Alleur-Liege, Belgium, Editions Du Perron, 1992.

The enterprise that the younger Hoevenaar joined in Java involved not only Lucassen, moreover, but also his erstwhile brother-in-law, *Jonkheer* Otto Carel Holmberg de Beckfelt, a newly ennobled ex-Indies official whose dealings in Court circles in The Hague bordered on the nefarious. We shall meet him again in a subsequent chapter. Like Lucassen he, too, manipulated his connections in Holland to obtain a concession to manufacture sugar on contract to the Indies Government. Neither Lucassen nor Holmberg, however, would have had either any real experience of making sugar or knowledge about the steam equipment used in its industrial manufacture, despite some airy assurances that they had 'inspected' sugar factories and machine ateliers in the beet sugar districts of northern France. Holmberg had led a charmed existence as a high-ranking Government official in Java for more than two decades (his chicanery having largely been rewarded by promotion), and Lucassen was an ex-military man whose position (*Inspecteur en Chef Militaire Administratie*) was essentially an administrative one, concerned with budgeting and supplies. He may indeed have had an excellent head for figures (he was later to be in dispute with Hoevenaar about account-keeping at the Tegal factories), but there is no evidence that he had any head for machines or any practical experience with steam engineering or the making of sugar.

Hubertus Hoevenaar, on the other hand, possessed these qualities in full. Not only had he worked for some years in Cockerill's factory at Seraing, but subsequently, in the autumn of 1839, he had found employment in the Campaign (the sugar-manufacturing season) at the Arras sugar factories owned by Louis Francois-Xavier Crespel-Delisse, the key pioneering figure in the French beet sugar industry.[73] In short, he had everything that his patrons so obviously lacked (barring money — Lucassen was later to claim that he had to pay off the young man's debts in Belgium before he could take him literally and metaphorically on board).

What Hubertus Hoevenaar did lack, however, on arriving in Java in 1842 at the age of twenty-seven or twenty-eight, was a wife. Given the connection with Lucassen, the logical thing would have been for him to wed one of the Colonel's daughters, who had accompanied their father on the family's return voyage to Java.

---

[73] Lucassen to van den Bosch, 30 November 1839, as quoted in Leidelmeijer, *Grootbedrijf*, p. 158. Louis Francois-Xavier Crespel-Delisse (1789-1864) had first set up in business in Arras in 1814, and at the height of his career owned and operated six beet sugar factories in Picardie. See the entry under his name in http://www.encyclopedie.picardie.fr (accessed 15 August 2014).

Nonetheless, for whatever reason — and it may even have been affection rather than calculation — he married instead one of Holmberg's daughters. Anna Marciana Catherina Holmberg de Beckfelt had likewise accompanied her father, who was by then a widower of almost ten years' standing, when he, too, sailed back to the island in 1841. Holmberg's eldest child, she had been born in the 'remote' town of Rembang on the island's Northeast Coast, where her father had currently been posted, in 1823.

We shall return to the Hoevenaar-Holmberg couple's story in a later chapter. The immediate impact of their marriage, however, was that Hubertus Hoevenaar was 'lost' to Lucassen, something for which it looks as if Lucassen attempted to compensate by marrying one of his daughters to another Dutchman with claims to experience with steam-driven machinery. The individual concerned was one Gerardus Johannes Netscher (1822-1877), who had arrived in Surabaya in 1845 or thereabouts as an assistant to the Indies' Government's 'Chief Engineer for Steam-power'. He married into the Lucassen family two years later, and, as the husband of Mathilde Theodora Charlotte Lucassen (1828-1906), was for some years the de facto *administrateur* [general manager] of the Colonel's sugar factories. Subsequently, however, he fell foul of colonial officialdom in Tegal — and perhaps of his irascible father-in-law as well. For whatever reason, the arrangement at the Tegal factories did not work out, and the young man returned (presumably together with his wife) to a position with the Indies Government in their Surabaya dockyard.[74] This was the point at which Alexander Lawson came on the scene. Moving in the opposite direction to Netscher, from dockyard to sugar factory, he became the Colonel's key technical man.

We do not know much about Lawson's years with the elder Lucassen and subsequently with Theodore RN and Donald Lucassen, the two sons who took over management of the business after their father's death in 1854. It was presumably on Lawson's advice that they bought the big new steam mill that was installed in 1859 to compliment the Derosne machinery set up in the boiling house some seventeen years earlier.[75] Meanwhile, Theodore RN Lucassen had bought the Kemanglen factory from his father's joint heirs and, parting company with his stepbrother (who remained based in Java), had become an absentee owner. This opened the way for Lawson. In

---

[74] See *NP*, vol. 53, 1967, pp. 169-70; 'Stamboek NI Ambtenaren', NA, MK; B Gunawan & D Valenbreder, 'De Kwestie Netscher: De Verhouding Ambtenaar-Particulier op Java in de Periode 1845-1855', Working paper no. 2, Vakgroep Zuid en Zuidoost Azie, Anthropologisch-Sociologische Centrum, University of Amsterdam, 1978.

[75] NHMR, 4978.

1874, after the Scot had been there for a quarter of a century, he was appointed as the *administrateur* of the Kemanglen factory. Hence Lawson reached the pinnacle of any sugar man's career. It looks as if at the same time he also put his savings into the enterprise: as well as being the *administrateur*, he had a 25 per cent interest in Kemanglen as a part-lessee.[76]

By then, Lawson had established a family locally and may well have abandoned any plan — if he had ever had one — of returning to Scotland. Harriet Aitkins had born him six children at Kemanglen, and died shortly after the birth of the last. Two years later, in 1861, Lawson remarried a Java-born woman, Anna Maria Leroy, and had four more children with her. Little or nothing appears to have survived relating to their lives together. Presumably, as Kemanglen's *administrateur* and his wife, they had spent their final years together in the lordly mansion that the owners had built adjacent to the factory. One admiring contemporary who had enjoyed the Lucassens' hospitality there in the 1850s described it as an 'Indo-European palace'.[77] There would have been servants aplenty, horses and carriage on call, and lavish hospitality — signifying, in short, a style of life, with its huge high-ceilinged rooms and vast verandah, that was at some considerable remove from anything that Lawson would have known back in Dundee half a century earlier.

There remained one thing from the Scottish connection, however, that Lawson would not have escaped. This was the commodity that had been the staple of his father's business in Dundee. Initially, the Java industry, in which Lawson spent the greater part of his life, packed most of its sugar into *keranjang* [baskets] made locally from the woven leaves of palms and other trees and plants. From around the mid-century onward, however, the predominant mode of packing sugar began to change. Increasingly, it was packed in sacks manufactured from jute. Known universally as 'gunny bags' — the term had a Sanskrit origin — they were at a later phase in the industry's history generally supplied from Bengal. Before that, however, there is a strong likelihood that they came from Dundee, prior to the supplanting of production there by the development of a huge jute industry in Calcutta and elsewhere in the subcontinent. In short, the very packaging of sugar — along with steam and steel — was part of the same global trajectory that had taken Lawson himself from one side of the world to the other.

---

[76] NHMR, 4978.
[77] SA Budding, *Neêrlands-Oost-Indië: Reizen over Java, Madura, Makassar […]: Gedaan Gedurende het Tijdvak van 1852-1857*, vol. 1, Rotterdam, Wijt, 1859, p. 148.

In July 1877, midway through the sugar Campaign and perhaps exhausted by its demands on the factory's *administrateur*, Alexander Lawson died, at the age of fifty-eight, and was buried next to Harriet Aitkins in the little European cemetery at the nearby Adiwerna sugar factory.[78] The history of his and Harriet's surviving offspring — and of his subsequent Java family — is yet to be uncovered. It is a reasonable assumption, however, that most of them married locally — as had Lawson himself in the case of his second wife — and became part of the Creole colonial society that typified 'Dutch' Java during the nineteenth and early twentieth century. That Creole character, moreover, extended into the industry in which he had spent the greater part of his life: global in one respect, it was Creole in another.

A Creole Prometheus

Prometheus's appearance on the Indies' frontier, as has already been suggested, had a distinctively Creole or hybrid dimension. The point is crucial to an understanding of the story of technology and technicians on the so-called colonial periphery of Java in the mid-nineteenth century. It is a mistake to conceive of that story exclusively in terms of unproblematic diffusion of technology from the West. As has been argued apropos of some older accounts of the subject, a common feature of many of these histories is that they present science and technology as a 'black box' — in effect, a hermetically sealed system of knowledge and its application which was simply transferred, holus-bolus, from one location to another. Recently, historians have begun to open that box and have demonstrated, for example, ways in which engineers, technicians and users negotiate technological change: groups or individuals adapt technologies to their own needs, and use technologies in ways not originally intended, or choose not to use them at all.[79]

Indeed, one leading student of the subject has remarked, in relation to the global 'dissemination' and 'transfer' of technology, that it is 'the complexity of the processes by which the ideas or inventions exchanged are introduced into the receiving society'

---

[78] 'Alexander Lawson / echtgenoot van Anna Maria Le Roy / geb. te Dundee 1819 / overt 18 Juli 1877. Sacred to the memory of / Harriet Aitkins / spouse of Alexander Lawson / who died September 1859 / aged 35 years.' See Bloys van Treslong Prins, *Europeanen op Java*, vol. 1, p. 1.

[79] I am drawing gratefully here on the ongoing work of the University of Wageningen scholar, Harro Maat. See, for example, 'Agricultural Sciences in Colonial Indonesia', *Historia Scientiarum*, vol. 16, no. 3, 2007, pp. 244-63.

which stands out; and that we need to pay close attention to 'the ways in which scientific knowledge and imported technologies are altered and innovated upon while being worked into new social and cultural contexts'.[80] Likewise, it can be argued that 'a theory of Eurocentric diffusion ... tends to reduce a rich historical record into simplistic binary oppositions: cores and peripheries, metropoles and colonies; oppressors and oppressed'.[81]

Accordingly, we need to think of the industrial project evolving around sugar production in nineteenth-century Java in terms of Creole technology and science — of a technology and science, that is to say, which was both metropolitan and colonial in its inspiration. Within this framework of understanding, technology — and its accompanying science in the sugar industry of Java in the mid-nineteenth century — has to be related not simply to the diffusion from the metropolis of technology and its attendant science but also to their evolution on the colonial frontier itself.

People as well as machines are central to an understanding of what took place, and the history of FJH Baijer, the 'Iron King' of Surabaya in the mid-nineteenth century, is a prime case in point.[82] Nowhere else in mid-nineteenth-century Java was the connection between sugar, steam and iron quite so palpable as in the East Java metropolis. As one noted historian of the city has remarked, 'spearheading the industrial revolution in the Netherlands Indies was the sugar industry ... [and] by the mid-1850s, two thirds of the mills in the districts around Surabaya operated with steam ...'[83] Baijer was the proprietor of a series of iron foundries and machine workshops in and around the city from the early 1840s through to his death there in 1879. Born in the Low Countries around 1807, Baijer spent the whole of his adult life in the Indies, apart from a return visit to Holland in 1863-64. He had begun as an employee in the Indies Government's Surabaya dockyard and *Constructie-Winkel* [engineering workshop] and was described when he left it in 1841 as *werktuigkundig*

---

[80] Michael Adas, 'The Problem of Paradigms: Patterns of Scientific and Technological Transfer from 1880 to 1950', *Journal of the Japan-Netherlands Institute*, vol. 4, 1996, pp. 277-85.

[81] Storey, p. 2.

[82] For Baijer, See GH von Faber, *Oud Soerabaia*, Soerabaia, Gemeente Soerabaia, 1931, pp. 170-7.

[83] See Howard W Dick, *Surabaya: City of Work*, Athens, Ohio, Ohio University Press, 2002, pp. 253-9; Dick, 'Nineteenth Century Industrialisation: A Missed Opportunity?', in J Thomas Lindblad (ed.), *New Challenges in the Modern Economic History of Indonesia*, Leiden, Programme of Indonesian Studies, Leiden University, 1993, pp. 123-49.

— the term which, as we have already seen, neatly embraced the possibility of 'engineer', 'mechanic' and anybody else who had a recognised claim to skill and experiences in the manufacture and manipulation of machinery.

Baijer's best-known enterprises were De Phoenix and the appropriately much longer enduring De Volharding [The Perseverance], which continued as a major engineering works in Surabaya into the twentieth century. Baijer was not a solitary figure, however. Indeed, even by the date of Edwards's arrival there in 1846, Surabaya was already on the way to becoming, with its iron masters, foundries and engineering workshops, the key centre for servicing the emergent industrial project in Java sugar. There was, for example, the ex-London ironmaster, Charles Gill, who brought his family to Java in the 1840s and set up in the foundry business in Surabaya at about the same time as Baijer. His descendants were still to be found in the colony three-quarters of a century later.[84]

Nonetheless, it was Baijer's enterprise that most neatly encapsulates key themes of the present argument. During the 1860s, his engineering yards, foundries and workshops attained a considerable reputation in the Indies — and beyond. In 1866, for example, they were sought out by a visiting group of Japanese officials and businesspeople. Baijer probably thought more highly of an official inspection by Governor-General Pieter Mijer two years later.[85] Nonetheless, Japanese interest was undoubtedly indicative of the extent to which Surabaya was — apparently — on the way to becoming a South-East Asian counterpart, in terms of industrial plants, of Calcutta, Shanghai and Hong Kong.

Without being isolated from the Netherlands, Baijer's several enterprises were nonetheless emphatically 'of the Indies' rather than mere transplants of metropolitan models. It was not simply the case, as the leading modern historian of the city has expressed it, that 'Surabaya had become an outpost of industrial Europe'.[86] Rather, Surabaya had become the centre in the Indies of a Creole technology and science that drew its inspiration both from the metropolis and the colony itself: it was part-European and part-Indies.

---

[84] Information on the Gill family kindly supplied by Peter Christiaans from the files of the Centraal Bureau voor Genealogie, Den Haag.
[85] Faber, *Oud Soerabaia*, p. 173.
[86] Dick, *Surabaya*, p. 261.

To be sure, the overwhelming bulk of the industrial equipment installed in Java's colonial sugar factories in the mid-century decades was imported from Western Europe, from manufacturers in the United Kingdom, France and the Netherlands. Toward the end of the period, some of it also began to be sourced in Germany. By the mid-nineteenth century, such manufacturers found a large market in 'the colonies'; and by its closing decades, one large enterprise in Scotland even had as its telegraphic address 'Colonial, Glasgow'.[87] As we saw in an earlier chapter, steam-operated mills for grinding sugar cane were exported from the United Kingdom to the Caribbean from the late eighteenth century onward, and by the 1820s, developments in the boiling house had started to follow suit. In both the United Kingdom and continental Europe, factories and workshops began to specialise in fabricating virtually the entire 'package' of boiling house equipment, which was then broken down into its component parts and transported for re-erection in colonial locations.

Nonetheless, the development was altogether more ambiguous in character than it might initially appear. For example, although in the 1840s the London engineering firm of Robinson boasted that their new milling machinery was so configured as to need a minimum of on-site expertise to install or re-locate it, too much should not be read into statements of this kind. In fact, as the history of individuals such as Lawson makes clear, Java's mid-century sugar industry had a nucleus of technically highly skilled people, brought there to look after their considerable investments in machinery by an Indies bourgeoisie of sugar manufacturers, financiers and merchants (to whom we shall return subsequently). Indeed, Robinson's simultaneous assurance to their potential customers that their new mill 'may be erected and set to work *by a local engineer, colonial mechanic, or intelligent manager*' points in precisely that direction [emphasis added].[88] In short, their machinery was not only adapted to the colonial frontier but also then adaptable on that frontier itself.

---

[87] John McNiell & Co's advertisement promised '[s]ugar machinery including all requisites for sugar plantations and refineries'. See HC Prinsen Geerligs, *Cane Sugar and its Manufacture*, Altrincham (Manchester), Norman Rodger, 1909 [endpapers].

[88] [HO & A Robinson], *Description of Robinson's Steam Cane Mill*, London, [no publisher stated], 1845, pp. 1-8. As the firm was at pains to make clear, their new steam mill was 'the production of engineers of practical experience in the sugar colonies and India ... whereas the usual machinery, to do it justice, requires a first-rate British mechanical engineer to erect it properly, provided with erecting drawings, and in some machinery with special instructions from the maker'. The pamphlet carries the notice: 'Further particulars ... on application to Messers H.O. and A. Robinson, Engineers, Mill Wall Iron Works and Engine Factory, Poplar, near London (where specimens may be seen), or at 12 Old Jewry-chambers, Cheapside, London'.

A facility for adaptation was quickly developed there. Indeed, given the poor quality of the equipment emanating from Dutch yards around the mid-century (equipment from Belgium, the United Kingdom and France was a different matter), Creole technology and science had, of necessity, to evolve in order to deal with it. The machinery that was sent out from Holland at the end of the 1840s for the reconstruction of the Wonopringgo sugar factory on the north coast of Central Java, for example, was so bad that the factory's owners came to suspect the dealings of the brothers JE & LA Saportas, shady colonial adventurers and *soi-disant* 'experts', whom they had contracted to arrange its supply.[89] To start with, there was no packing list with the crates of equipment, which made for endless difficulties when metres of otherwise anonymous-looking pipes and valves were concerned. Worse still, some of the apparatus, as supplied, was so bad that it had to be sent immediately to the Atelier Baijer at Surabaya to be reconstructed.[90]

Moreover, Baijer's enterprise was not the only one thus engaged. In 1853, for example, an entire sugar mill had been manufactured at the Government dockyard, and during the sugar Campaign, generally lasting from May through September, the yard was kept busy repairing machinery from the many sugar factories in the nearby Brantas delta and eastward along the coast in Pasuruan and adjacent Probolingo.[91] What is also obvious, however, is that sugar factories remote from the facilities of Surabaya and the *Oosthoek* (Java's Eastern Salient) quickly developed their own repair shops, with skilled personnel in attendance. When, in 1850, some of the newly installed equipment at Wonopringgo was damaged in operation, it could be sent for repair to the Djatibarang factory, westward along the coast in Tegal Residency, where a skilled European operative was employed. A Rotterdam newspaper clipping from the end of the decade records his widowed mother's grief at receiving news of his recent death in Java of 'my beloved eldest son ... Franciscus Adrianus Bergmans ... in life, Engineer [*Ingenieur*] at the sugar factories in Tegal'.[92]

---

[89] For some of the difficulty attendant on the renovation, see e.g. Factorij to A'dam, 26.8.1848/325 & 28.11.1848/338.

[90] Factorij to A'dam, 28.11.1848/338.

[91] *KV*, 1853, pp. 209-10. By 1857 (KV, 1858, p. 130), this connection with the sugar industry had been severed. The *fabriek* could only be used for 'private' work in exceptional circumstances.

[92] Factorij to A'dam, 24.6.1850/24 & 27.7.1850/27. On Bergmans, see newspaper clipping in the files of the *Centraal Bureau voor Genealogie*, Den Haag.

In terms of the size of their operations, the pace being set on the colonial 'periphery' by the larger, more centralised 'ateliers' and dockyards in Java was largely in step with — or, perhaps, even in advance of — what was going on at the metropolitan 'centre'. Leastways, in respect to the number of workers on their books, mid-century engineering works in both Holland and Java appear to have been roughly comparable. The biggest of the Dutch shipbuilding and engineering works around the mid-century was Paul van Vlissingen's and Abraham Dudok van Heel's Koninklijke Fabriek voor Stoom-en-Andere Werktuigen [Royal Factory for Steam-and-Other Machinery] on the Oostenburg in Amsterdam. The firm was said to have had around 1600 workers in its employ circa 1857, but five years later the workforce had dropped back to between 850 and 900.[93] The NSM's Feijenoord dockyard in Rotterdam — where Lawson had been working prior to his departure for Java in 1847 — appears to have been a significantly smaller enterprise: it was said that when its orders ran out in the following year, some 700 men were laid off.[94]

Meanwhile, across the world, in distant Surabaya, Baijer's workforce was (circa 1860) reportedly around 750-strong, while the Government dockyard and foundry (circa 1853) employed 800 or more workers. Some of Surabaya's predominantly Javanese workers were designated as 'Coolies', but most were described as *werklieden*, implying that they were by no means in the category of unskilled labour.[95] In the 1860s, for example, in the case of Baijer's establishment, Jhr [*Jonkheer*] Mr WT Gevers Deynoot, a visiting dignitary from the Netherlands, made special mention of its Javanese workers as being both *handig en gevat* [adroit and clever].[96] We do not know how Lawson experienced the great workshop and dockyard in Surabaya where he was in charge of assembling the *Onrust* and the *Borneo*. Nonetheless, it is reasonable to assume that he would rapidly have found himself being initiated into the ways of Creole technology. They were ways that were, no doubt, different from those of the NSM dockyard at Feijenoord which he had left four months earlier, but they were geared very effectively to local circumstances.

---

[93] MG de Boer, *Geschiedenis der Amsterdamsche Stoomvaart*, Amsterdam, Scheltema & Holkema's Boekhandel, 1921, vol. 1, pp. 78-9.

[94] De Boer, *Roengen*, p. 151.

[95] Faber, *Oud Soerabaia*, p. 172; *KV*, 1853, pp. 209-10.

[96] Jhr Mr WT Gevers Deynoot, *Herinneringen eener Reis naar Nederlandsch Indië in 1862*, The Hague, Nijhoff, 1864, p. 95.

Sugar, Steam and Steel

The skilled character of much of the workforce, one that included people designated as 'Chinese-Indonesians' as well as 'native' Javanese (allowance needs to be made for the problematic nature of ethnic identification of this kind), is easily lost from sight.[97] Given the essentially colonial nature of the archive on which we have to rely, the Europeans, with their prior training in the industrial centres of North-West Europe, stand out. Even so, they were obviously not alone. The case of the manufacture of sugar is better documented than that of the industrial establishments in Surabaya itself. Highly skilled Chinese-Indonesian sugar makers were a ubiquitous feature of the mid-century industry (and for long afterwards). Wearing an apparently characteristic kind of bowler hat, they are to be seen in one antique photograph of a major mid-century factory, taken around 1870. It shows a hierarchy of management — with the European *administrateur* and his colleagues at its apex — arranged on the steps at the front of the *fabriek*.[98] Some twenty or more years earlier, in the mid-1840s, it had been reported that most sugar factories were actually 'run' by Chinese-Indonesians.[99] A decade later, at the Wonopringgo factory, the newly installed *administrateur*, Thomas Edwards, employed skilled Chinese-Indonesians to oversee work in the boiling house (because he felt that Javanese workers were 'not reliable'). Indeed, it was an important part of his plan to bring the factory up to scratch.[100]

Nor was it only skilled Chinese who were involved. Visiting the steam-operated Boedoeran sugar factory in East Java in the early 1860s, the Singapore-born William Barrington d'Almeida (he was later to become a barrister in the United Kingdom) observed that 'the men employed to boil the juice are Chinese but the most important branches of the machinery are managed by Javanese'.[101] WT Gevers Deynoot made similar observations about the sugar factories that he visited at around the same time.[102] Likewise, it was reported in the mid-1840s that it was Javanese workmen

---

[97] A report on the Java industry in 1846 recorded that in the specific case of the Lucassen factories in Tegal (see above), the Derosne apparatus was operated by Javanese workers. See E & L Saportas, in Exh 24.4.1847/28.

[98] See the photograph of the Tjipiring sugar factory in Semarang Residency, reproduced in Breton de Nijs, p. 61.

[99] E & L Saportas, in Exh. 24.4.1847/28.

[100] Factorij to A'dam, 26.4.1854/284.

[101] WB d'Almeida, *Life in Java: With Sketches of the Javanese*, vol. 2, London, Hurst & Blackett, 1864, pp. 268-9.

[102] Gevers Deynoot, *Herinneringen*, p. 128.

Figure 5: A sugar factory's hierarchy of management: Tjepiring, North-Central Java in the 1860s.
Source: Koninklijk Instituut voor Taal-, Land- en Volkenkunde, Leiden, no. 503826

who operated the French-made, Derosne apparatus installed at Theodore Lucassen's factories in Tegal Residency.[103] Perhaps most interesting of all, the Koning Willem II factory near Surabaya, one of the biggest and most technologically advanced in the colony, employed during the 1860s a small number of Javanese workers designated as *inlandsche assisten machinists* [assistant-mechanics], who evidently worked alongside — at a quarter of the pay or less — the factory's sole European *mechanist*.[104]

In short, the inventory of steam-operated machinery in Java in the mid-nineteenth century has to be understood in a dual context: not simply one of diffusion

---

[103] E & L Saportas, in Exh 24.4.1847/28.
[104] Leidelmeijer, *Grootbedrijf*, p. 348: 'Bijlage E-II. Uitgaven aan personeel kosten bij suikerfabieken Sentanen Lor en Koning Willem II te Soerabaija'.

from the metropolis but also of the evolution of Creole technology and science in the colony itself. For example, the story that in Java (as in other 'sugar colonies') it was commonplace around the mid-century for Vacuum Pans to be used for the final 'boiling' of sugar into a near-solid state — they were said to be fitted with bolt-down hatches so that the sugar could then be dug out — is suggestive of a potent capacity for adaptation.[105]

The evolution, in this respect among others, of a distinctively hybrid, Creole form that was part-colonial, part-metropolitan in its inspiration, did not go unchallenged. Indeed, it was the subject of a hostile dialogue, running over several decades in the middle of the nineteenth century. As late as 1878, for example, a Netherlands-based writer was still able to deplore the 'backwardness' of the Java sugar industry. In this article (signed Delft, September 1878), the writer is quite explicit in his attack on Creole technology in sugar manufacturing in the colony: he recommended '*verbetering der fabricage door de toepassing der in Europa algemeen als goed erkende methoden van werken*' ['improvement in manufacture *through the application of well-recognised European modes of manufacture*'; emphasis added].[106]

Polemic of this kind had a long pre-history in the strained relations between soi-disant metropolitan experts and the Creole manufacturers in the colony. In the 1850s, for example, we find Thomas Edwards, the formidable *administrateur* of the Wonopringgo sugar factory (to whom we shall return in the following chapter), engaged in a defense of Creole science and practice — and taking up the cudgels

---

[105] See John Scoffern, *The Manufacture of Sugar in the Colonies and at Home*, London, Longman, Brown, Green and Longmans, 1849, p. 91. Scoffern himself, however, was highly critical of the use of new technology by colonial planters, particularly with regard to the way in which some of them operated their Vacuum Pans, citing stiff or overboiled sugar as a common occurrence. The practice of overboiling led to the complete separation of molasses and sugar. A direct result of this practice was the need for liquoring to improve its colour, which led to additional loss of product. Scoffern quotes a letter from a Dr Evans, (possibly EW Evans, the author of *The Sugar-Planter's Manual: Being a Treatise on the Art of Obtaining Sugar from the Sugar-Cane*, London, Longman, Brown, Green and Longmans, 1847), who wrote of Vacuum Pans in Java being fitted with large apertures through which the stiff boiled sugar was shoveled out, an occurrence that slowed production and added to the original cost of the Pan. The sugar at that stage should have been crystalline, still coated with molasses, damp and readily pumped out without manual assistance. I am indebted to Dr Andrew Ratledge for kindly communicating this information.

[106] F van Heumen, 'Over de Fabricage van Suiker uit Suikerriet', *Tijdschrijft voor Nederlandsch Indie* (Nieuwe Reeks), vol. 7, no. 2, 1878, pp. 216-18.

against one such expert from the University of Utrecht, who had been hired by the Dutch Colonial Office to investigate the Java industry. Edwards was evidently not somebody who tolerated fools lightly. Presented with a copy of Professor GJ Mulder's recommendations for improvements in sugar-manufacturing techniques in Java, he did not mince his words. 'I beg to say', he wrote to his employer's local representatives (who were clearly only too happy to pass on his comments to Amsterdam), 'with all deference to the great name and worldwide reputation of that gentleman … [his proposal was quite] the worst that has ever come under my notice'. He went on to suggest that, although its author 'may be the first chemist in the world … I take leave to say that he knows nothing whatever about Sugar mills'. The problem, from the colonial manufacturers' point of view, was that 'improvements' advocated by Mulder would undermine an economy of production predicated on the extensive use of cane-trash in the boiler house. More intensive crushing left it virtually useless as fuel, and double crushing, as advocated by Mulder, notoriously fouled the mills with broken cane. If there was an economically feasible alternative to existing practices, Edwards had no doubt whatsoever that 'no recommendation will be needed to induce [the manufacturers] to obtain the best presses that can be had for money'.[107]

Edwards could be so scathing, moreover, because he was fully conversant with global developments in sugar manufacturing. His was emphatically not the reaction of the scientifically ill-informed and technologically retrograde. 'Of late years', he was able to inform his employers in 1861, 'many scientific and practical men have written on the manufacture of sugar from cane juice, [and] … I have a long list of extracts from different writers … now before me'.[108] It comes as no surprise, therefore, to find that in the 1850s he was an early member, along with (locally) a couple of members of the Lucassen clan and the *Resident* of Pekalongan, of the newly formed Nederlandsch-Indische Maatschappij van Nijverheid [Netherlands-Indies Industrial Society].[109]

---

[107] Edwards to Factorij, 2.8.1856/1036, in Factorij to A'dam, 9.8.1856/480. The episode is discussed, in its broader context, in Leidelmeijer, *Grootbedrijf*, pp. 195-224.

[108] Edwards to Factorij, 24.12.1860, in Factorij to A'dam, 2.1.1861/ 915.

[109] For a list of the members, see 'Lijst van Leden', *Tijdschrift voor Nijverheid*, in *NI*, vol. 3, 1856, Batavia, Lange en Co, pp. 105-12. President of the Society was SD Schiff, the Director of Cultivations — effectively the CEO of the *Cultuurstelsel*; and in line with the aspirations of Creole science and technology, the Society produced its own Batavia-printed journal. Similar aspirations had been evinced in Surabaya in 1851 in the formation of the 'East Java Division' of the metropolitan-based Koninglijk Instituut voor Ingeniers. See *Almanak en Naamregister van Nederlandsch-Indië*, Batavia, 1827-64, here 1857, p. 303.

As these examples indicate, there was nothing remotely isolated about the evolution of technology and science in Java during the mid-century decades. Not only intellectually but physically, contact between Europe and the colonial frontier was central to it — and by the late 1840s this latter was a great deal easier and quicker than it had been previously. For those who could afford it, the distance in time between the colonial Indies and metropolitan Holland was significantly less, in the mid-century decades preceding the opening of the Suez Canal and direct steamer connections between Europe and Asia, than has often been supposed. Indeed, the single most important development (before the arrival of the aeroplane) in closing the time-gap between Europe and 'the East' had taken place some decades earlier, with the establishment during the 1840s of a regular Overland Mail passenger steamer route from Singapore to Marseilles or Southampton via the Red Sea and the Egyptian land-bridge. A journey that had previously taken three-and-a-half or four months via sail and the Cape was reduced to a little over five weeks.[110]

It was hence possible for Edwards — paid to do so by his employers — to make a swift trip to Europe in 1857-58 to order new equipment for Wonopringgo and to specify his requirements in person at the 'Millwall Iron Works & Engine Factory' of the well-known manufacturing firm of Robinson, on the eastern, Thames-side outskirts of London. This ensured that the new machinery would be ready in time for installation at Wonopringgo in the 'dead' period at the end of the 1858 Campaign. Departing for Europe in October 1857, thanks to the Overland Mail, Edwards could be securely back at Wonopringgo by early May 1858, in good time for the beginning of the manufacturing season for which his presence was indispensable.[111] Baijer, the 'Iron King' of Surabaya and Edwards's erstwhile employer (see above) was to make a similar journey with a similar purpose in 1864-65.[112]

The full significance of that ongoing interconnectedness, however, is only something that can be appreciated in the context of the way in which the industrial

---

[110] Femme Gastra, 'The Experience of Travelling to the Dutch East Indies by the Overland Route, 1844-1869', in Gordon Jackson & David M Williams (eds), pp. 120-37.

[111] 'Edwards leaves for Europe with this Mail', the NHM Batavia *factorij* informed Head Office early in October 1857, and asked them to put 5000 guilders at his disposal (Factory to A'dam, 10.10.1857/2105, NHMA). He began his return voyage at the end of February 1858, in company with some of the machinery from Robinsons, and resumed management at Wonopringgo on 14 May 1858. See Factorij to A'dam, 25.3.1858/63; Factorij to A'dam, 7.6.1858/650.

[112] Faber, *Oud Soerabaia*, p. 173.

project in sugar evolved in Java during the middle decades of the nineteenth century. It is to this that we can now turn.

3 The Industrial Sugar Factory: Wonopringgo, Thomas Edwards and the Nederlandsche Handel-Maatschappij (NHM)

As late as the 1870s, a painter's representation of a sugar factory on the north coast of Central Java made conspicuous reference to its purportedly picturesque aspects.[113] The place appears to be located in wilderness; a few 'blacks', as they would have been referred to then (it might be a particularly remote part of the Caribbean), are scattered in desultory fashion in the foreground; and a 'pioneering' European cabin bravely flies the Dutch flag. Although a belching chimney forms part of the picture, it is possible to feel that it is only there out of a need somehow to add variety to a scene otherwise totally lacking in animation or purpose. In fact, however, it is the vital clue to what was actually being depicted: an industrial site in constant day-and-night operation for a substantial part of the year, operating with a disciplined workforce of several hundred labourers, its grinding mills fed with rail-hauled cane and, within its walls and in day-and-night operation, an array of apparatus that was fully the match (by the time the painting was made) for most other leading sectors of the contemporary international sugar economy.

The rise of the industrial factory was central to all this. As has been widely observed, the arrival of steam operation and more specifically, though not exclusively, the steam engine, entailed the need for economies of scale to justify its use wherever it was installed. Technological advance necessitated larger units of production and the concentration of production in one place. It also raised issues of how to concentrate labour in a single location and how to subject labour to the degree of discipline which large units of production require if they are to operate smoothly — or indeed, operate

---

[113] See Figure 6 overleaf.

Figure 6: A deceptively tranquil scene: the Kemanglen sugar factory, North-Central Java in the 1860s.
Source: Courtesy of the author

at all.[114] Unsurprisingly, these were all issues played out within the context of the industrial project in sugar which got underway in Java during the 1830s and 1840s and developed exponentially thereafter.

There is, of course, no single pace-setting model of what constitutes 'industrialisation', and the immediate focus here is on technological innovation. This, far from constituting a clean and decisive break with the past, took place (at least until late in the nineteenth century) on a largely incremental basis that mixed the new with the old in a myriad of possible permutations. The revolution in the technology of sugar manufacture — and the word 'revolution' does seem appropriate, given the

---

[114] In the context of a wide literature on 'the factory', I have relied primarily here on the discussion relating to its development in metropolitan Holland in van Zanden & van Riel, pp. 227-35.

almost total transformation of the production process that it eventually involved — was paradoxically at once rapid and delayed in the middle decades of the nineteenth century: brand new, state-of-the-art apparatus rubbed shoulders with much older and 'obsolete' equipment, as was typical throughout the major sectors of the international sugar economy of the day. Something similar, as we shall see, might be said about the organisation of industrial labour in factory (and field): older forms of subordination existed alongside, and in tandem with, ways of recruitment and discipline which had a much more 'modern' appearance.

The Mid-century Progression of the Industrial Project

Just how far the industrial project in Java sugar had progressed in the decades between Alexander Lawson's arrival in the colony at the end of the 1840s and his death at the Kemanglen sugar factory in 1874 is evidenced by both the machines and the men who often came out with them. On present evidence, at least, we cannot be sure that Thomas Edwards, an Englishman who arrived in the colony early in the 1840s, came together with a consignment of sugar-making equipment. What is certain, however, is that he spent the rest of his life in its company. Indeed, his career in the colony spanned the third quarter of the nineteenth century, which saw sugar production in Java shift firmly and decisively into an industrial phase that crucially underpinned the colony's rise to international eminence as an exporter of cane sugar outclassed only by Cuba.

Artisan Sugar Manufacture in Java and Early Attempts to Industrialise Production

Before the 1820s, the manufacture of sugar in the Dutch colony largely approximated the 'Chinese' style found elsewhere in South-East Asia.[115] The mills employed were simple constructions, generally made up of two upright wooden rollers that were set in motion by water-buffalo yoked to an overhead beam. The juice thus obtained was then boiled down into sugar in open pans, often little more than cauldrons set over direct heat.

On a technological level, in the Batavia *Ommelanden* as elsewhere in the colony, with very few exceptions, the industry's manufacturing sector remained rudimentary, to an extent that led contemporary commentators to compare it unfavourably with the

---

[115] Leidelmeijer, *Grootbedrijf*, pp. 69-82.

Figure 7: Artisan sugar production: a 'pre-industrial' mill operated by water-buffalo.
Source: Courtesy of the author

great sugar industries of the Caribbean. It suffered likewise from its location, which, although near to the terminus of the Chinese junk trade and VOC headquarters, made it heavily dependent on a supply of workers from elsewhere. A further factor of considerable importance was the policy of the VOC toward the sugar industry, which was both restrictionist and erratic.[116] Moreover, it seems perfectly possible that by the late eighteenth century, the sugar industry in the *Ommelanden* was suffering from a severe ecological crisis.[117] Unsurprisingly, perhaps, by the opening decades of the nineteenth century, the industry there had come to be widely regarded as moribund. Recent research, however, has suggested that this picture is somewhat overdrawn and that moves were indeed afoot late in the eighteenth century and early in the nineteenth to update the industry's production methods.[118]

---

[116] Peter Boomgaard, *Children of the Colonial State*, Amsterdam, Free University Press, 1989, p. 30.

[117] See Leonard Blusse, *Strange Company: Chinese Settlers, Mestizo Women, and the Dutch in VOC Batavia*, Dordrecht, Foris Publications, 1986, pp. 15-34.

[118] Leidelmeijer, *Grootbedrijf*, pp. 95-112.

Nonetheless, attempts to modernise the industry, in the sense of catching up with Caribbean best practice, met with only limited success prior to 1830. The two largest such operations were both located in West Java, where proximity to the port of Batavia perhaps conferred some advantage, but where — as in the *Ommelanden* — a scarcity of locally available labour was a possibly fatal drawback. One of these pioneering ventures was on the Pamanoekan and Tjiassem estate (aka 'P&T') — a vast tract of land alienated by Lieutenant Governor Thomas Stamford Raffles during the British occupation of the island between 1811 and 1816, and still in the hands of some of his cronies and their associates during the decade that followed.

It was they who established an elaborate sugar manufactury on the estate, located at the 'up-country' settlement of Subang, on the edge of West Java's mountainous interior.[119] From a colonial standpoint at least, Subang was a remote and somewhat isolated spot. Nonetheless, it was there, at the beginning of the 1830s, that the Vacuum Pan — the sine qua non, as we have seen, of the mid-century industrial project in sugar worldwide — may have made its first appearance in Java.[120] Despite or perhaps because of all this, however, the P&T estate was by then virtually bankrupt, and developments there stalled for a decade or more. Elsewhere in West Java, during the course of the 1820s, the Batavia-based firm of Trail & Co bought a steam engine, almost certainly the first in Java to be used for that purpose, to run a large sugar-making operation that they owned in the coastal lowlands near Bekasi, to the east of Batavia, where it complimented other up-to-date machinery similarly imported from manufacturers in the United Kingdom.[121] Despite these early harbingers, however, it

---

[119] On Subang in the 1820s, see G Roger Knight, 'From Plantation to Padi Field: The Origins of the Nineteenth Century Transformation of Java's Sugar Industry', *Modern Asian Studies*, vol. 14, no. 2, 1980, pp. 177-204.

[120] John Pitcairn (*administrateur*, P&T) to van den Bosch, 14.8.1830, NA, Collectie van den Bosch, 426: 'I am anxious to inform your excellency that a machine lately invented in England for boiling sugar by steam has been sent out to me, which will likely arrive in the course of this year. It possesses many advantages over the present mode of boiling sugar …' See also JE de Sturler [Secretaris Pekalongan] to van den Bosch, 2 September 1830, in regard to what he (mistakenly) designates as a '*Trek Fournius*' ['Draft Furnace'] on the P&T estate. He says it ought to be copied by the Government's sugar contractors and that Mr Loudon, formerly Administrator of P&T, by then living in Pekalongan, '*verhaalde mij dat het van de nieuwste ondervinding is, en er een ingenier uit Engeland is gezonden geweest om het interigten*' ['told me that it was of the very latest invention and that an engineer had been sent out from England to install it']. See NA, Collectie van den Bosch, 216.

[121] 'AV Batavia', 1824, vol. 3, p. 23, NA, Collectie Schneither, 84. For Trail & Co's importation of Machinery (from the United Kingdom), see IB, 13.8.1827/8, MK, 2507; IB,

was only in the following decade, with the inauguration in 1830 of the *Cultuurstelsel*, that significant progress began to be made on the industrial project in sugar.

The *Cultuurstelsel* and the Industrial Project in Sugar

The *Cultuurstelsel*, or System of [State] Cultivations, represented an attempt by the Dutch colonial state to commandeer peasant land and labour for the purposes of export commodity production. The principal crops were envisaged as coffee, sugar and indigo-producing crops, though this list was not exhaustive. Discussion of the agrarian aspects of the *Stelsel* can wait until later in the book. From the immediate standpoint of the manufacture of sugar, however, the essential fact was that the *Stelsel* inaugurated a period of far-reaching technological modernisation in the Java industry.

The factories initially established under its aegis represented a marked advance on what had gone before, at least in those parts of Central and East Java where the *Stelsel*'s remodelling of the sugar industry was largely concentrated. Primarily, this meant that the new (or in some few cases, revamped) factories were equipped (for the most part) with iron, horizontally-set, triple-roller mills for the grinding of cane. Indeed, their installation became one of the key stipulations in the agreements entered into with the Indies Government by the 'Contractor' entrepreneurs — mostly Europeans with an admixture of Chinese-Indonesians (the latter were formally excluded from contracts late in the 1830s) — who were the industry's mainstay during the mid-century decades. As well as 'modern' mills, the Contractors' factories were likewise usually possessed of sets of equipment in the boiling house, a modified version of the 'Jamaica train', which marked an improvement in terms of efficiency on earlier 'Chinese' arrangements.

Nonetheless, all this was still at some remove from what was technically possible by the 1830s and 1840s. Indeed, with a few notable exceptions, developments in Java during this period were scarcely on par with the contemporary industries of the Indian subcontinent or Mauritius. Thereafter, however, in terms of the technology and science of sugar production, Java drew away decisively from its erstwhile counterparts.

The central developments of the sugar revolution of the nineteenth century, as has been argued, took place in the boiling house, as well as in the milling of cane itself. Initially, the Java industry was rather slow to take up the Vacuum Pan and

---

24.5.1824/2, MK, 2476 & IB, 29.3.1823/4, MK, 2468.

associated steam-operation in this key sector of production. When it finally did so, however, progress was substantial and rapid. Indeed, by the late 1850s steam-operated equipment of one kind or another was to be found in the boiling houses of more than half of the nearly 100 factories working on contract to the Indies Government, and in virtually all of them by 1870.[122] In the case of the heavily 'sugared' adjoining Residencies of Pekalongan and Tegal on the north coast of Central Java, for example, the earliest Vacuum Pans were installed at the beginning of the 1840s, where they worked in conjunction with some of the most advanced (Derosne et Cail) equipment to be found anywhere in the world at that date. Even so, at that date these were pioneering ventures and, Java-wide, factories similarly equipped were in a tiny minority. Within the next decade and a half, however, Vacuum Pans became very much the norm. Indeed, by the late 1860s, only one of the factories in Pekalongan-Tegal still operated solely with open pans in the old style.[123]

By then, Java had largely caught up with developments elsewhere in the international sugar economy, particularly those taking place in the New World. In this respect, the comparison between Java and Cuba is a particularly potent one. Destined to be Java's occidental counterpart for the remainder of the colonial era, the Caribbean island overtook Brazil in the mid-nineteenth century as the world's single largest producer-exporter of cane sugar. In part, at least, it did so because of innovation in the field of manufacturing technology which transformed Cuba into the most technologically advanced sugar industry in the New World. In addition to the

---

[122] Leidelmeijer (*Grootbedrijf*, p. 138) has established that nearly 60 per cent of the colony's ninety-six contract sugar factories (fifty-six in all) were equipped with Vacuum Pans circa 1857. A degree of possible ambiguity exists as to the nature of the *stoomtoestellen* [steam equipment] installed at some few factories, in so far as the reference (in documentation relating to the industry collected by the well-known Umbgrove *Commissie* in the mid-1850s) may be to steam-heated, but 'open', clarifying and evaporating pans (i.e. 'Wetzels', 'Gadsdens' and the like) rather than to Vacuum Pans per se. See *SU*, Bijl D. Nonetheless, in the greater majority of cases referred to by Leidelmeijer (at least fifty of Java's total of ninety-six 'Contract' sugar factories), the reference is clearly to Vacuum Pans, unambiguously defined by their *luchtledige* [reduced-pressure], 'closed' character. Moreover, in some cases where the Umbgrove documentation (itself using very varied terminology supplied by the officials of the sugar-producing Residencies) is apparently ambiguous re *stoomtoestellen* — as in the four Lucassen and Holmberg factories in Tegal — we know from other sources that these factories were indeed fitted with Vacuum Pans.

[123] JVFB, vol. 24, 1848-49, pp. 76-7; 'Overzigt Tegal', NA, Collectie Umbgrove, pp. 1-5; JVFB, vol. 37, 1861-62, appendix; *KV*, 1867-68, p. 124.

installation of steam-driven mills at the beginning of the 1860s, the Caribbean island was said to have perhaps as many as seventy-seven factories equipped with Vacuum Pans — and associated steam equipment in the boiling house. If this calculation is roughly correct, Java — with its fifty-six or so Vacuum Pans — was not so very far behind.

To be sure, the comparison can be overstated. It seems doubtful, for example, whether either of Java's most advanced sugar factories at the time — Wonopringgo on the north coast of Central Java and Koning Willem II in East Java — matched in technological finesse such mid-century Cuba factories as Acana, in Matanzas province.[124] Even so, the Java sugar industry of the mid-nineteenth century evidently possessed factories which — by the very mixed standards of the day in respect to the machinery of manufacture — were broadly comparable with those of other similarly advanced sectors of the international sugar economy.

The Evolution of the Wonopringgo Sugar Factory

The Wonopringgo sugar factory was located in Pekalongan Residency, near the foot of the mountains that form the southern fringe of the coastal plain of Central Java. To its north, the level country of intensively cultivated, irrigated rice fields extends through the district of Pekajangan down to the outskirts of the town of Pekalongan itself, while almost immediately to the factory's south, in the district of Sawangan (Karanganyar), the land becomes undulating, leading to the foothills of the massif that separates the *Pasisir* from the interior of Central Java. Streams coming down from the mountains made Wonopringgo a particularly good location for a factory that, until quite late in the nineteenth century, depended heavily on water power for grinding its cane, while its proximity to the densely populated coastal plain ensured a ready supply of labour.

To designate the original installation there, built at the beginning of the 1830s, as a 'factory' would be to use something of a misnomer. Its early history, however, exerts a fascination not only because of what it was not, but because of the extent to which it complicates any narrative of the *Cultuurstelsel* predicated on notions of a 'command economy' that was imposed in a thoroughly businesslike and coherent

---

[124] I am grateful to Dr Curry-Machado for drawing my attention to the Acana mill, which was among the most advanced of its day.

Figure 8: Mid-nineteenth-century industrialisation: there is no extant painting or photograph of the Wonopringgo sugar factory in the mid-century decades. This contemporary view of the Pangka factory further along the north coast of Central Java provides some indication of what Wonopringo must have been like.
Source: Koninklijk Instituut voor Taal-, Land- en Volkenkunde, Leiden, no. 47D4

fashion. In this part of the colony, at least, nothing could be further from the truth. The story begins in 1830, at the very onset of the *Cultuurstelsel* and of the state's drive to expand sugar production, when the Dutch authorities in Pekalongan, no doubt panicked by the sheer force of the edicts coming from the gubernatorial palace at Buitenzorg, decided to order the planting of sugar cane in the Pekajangan district, to the south of Pekalongan town. (They probably hoped that the location was sufficiently removed from the indigo fields not to do any damage to what they reasonably suspected was the Residency's most promising commodity.) The area of land involved amounted to no more than 80 *bau* (about 55 hectares) — around a tenth of the amount of land being planted for the developed Wonopringgo factory some quarter of a century later — but the project caused endless trouble.

In order to get the ripening cane processed into sugar, and in the absence of other takers, the Residency authorities contracted a local Chinese-Indonesian, identified as one Gou Kang Tjou in Dutch accounts, to buy the cane and build a mill. Since Gou appeared to have no money of his own, Pekalongan's leading Chinese merchant, *Nonya* [Mrs] Oei Taylo — in a deal she was later to regret — advanced the cash. Meanwhile, the *Bupati* of Pekalongan, together with an allegedly penniless Arab trader — who was probably called Sarif Schan, and who was an Islamic functionary attached to the Regent's Court — were likewise prevailed upon to stand surety for Gou, as was one of the Residency's Dutch *controleurs* or district officers.[125]

What Gou did with his money was to build a primitive processing plant in the long-established 'Chinese' manner. Officially inspected by the Dutch authorities in 1834, it was said to be already ruinous: a bamboo shed housed half a dozen small wooden roller-mills (in the local, 'Japara' style) for grinding the cane, and a building that served simultaneously as a boiling house and living quarters was equipped with a set of six iron cauldrons. The resultant sugar, so badly made that most of it had liquified, was stored in a tumbledown warehouse on the site, and the entire enterprise was valued at the derisory sum of between 800 and 1000 guilders. Recriminations over Gou's venture helped foul relations between the *Bupati*, Oei Taylo and the Residency for at least the next decade: the venture exposed the *Bupati* to the claims against Gou, and he found himself being sued for 15 000 guilders by *Nonya* Taylo. Since his salary from the Dutch amounted to no more than 12 000 guilders a year, this was obviously a very serious matter for the already heavily indebted *Bupati*. Indeed, it was serious enough for him to bring it up with Governor-General *ad interim* JC Baud when the latter visited the Residency in 1834.

As if this was not enough, a plan was also hatched, further bedeviling Gou's venture. The plan was to transfer the whole operation southwards to a new site, in Karanganyer, where a well-connected European Contractor was installing himself.[126]

---

[125] For the information in this and the following paragraphs, see L Vitalis, 'Rapport Pekalongan 1834', pp. 35-6, NA, Collectie Baud, 460; 'Rapport omtrent de suikermolen te Wonopringgo', in L Vitalis to Directeur Cultuurs, 10.3.1834/25, ANRI, Archief Cultuurs, no. 333, Exh. 13.3.1834/761; 'Brieven aankomende van de Directeur van Cultuurs 1832', AD, Pekalongan, no. 80; Cultuurverslag Pekalongan, 1834, pp. 1-14, ANRI, Arsip Cultuurs, 1624; IB, 25.5.1833/3, MK, 2847; IB, 5.7.1834/3, MK, 2852; IB, 3.10.1834/7, MK, 2853; IB 24.12.1834/10, MK, 2853.

[126] See AV, Pekalongan, 1831 & 1832 [unpaginated] & Directeur Cultuurs to Resident Pekalongan, 13.3.1832/390 together with enclosed letter De Sturler to Governor-General,

This individual, the Scots-born Alexander Loudon, was a favorite of the all-powerful Governor-General, Johannes van den Bosch — and had as his business partner a retired army officer, JG de Sturler, whose niece was the Governor-General's wife.[127]

Loudon himself subsequently moved to richer pastures in neighbouring Semarang Residency. The Karanganyer speculation, succinctly described by one Dutch official as being located on a site anything but suitable for a sugar factory, was abandoned, and the centre of operations moved back to Wonopringgo, where European Contractors were installed to manage things. The new *concessionaires* were the offspring of an earlier Governor-General, the formidable HW Daendals, but they appeared to have inherited little of their father's drive or acumen.[128] Around 1839, they erected a new factory on the Wonopringgo site, but the operation quickly changed hands, and by 1841 it was owned by the Semarang-based commodity trading firm of Tissot & Co[129], in conjunction with their Batavia associates, Lagnier & Co. The several successive Contractors who now ran the operation proved scarcely more adept than Gou, except in so far as they had managed to get some money from the Indies

---

7.3.1832 (extract) and AD, Pekalongan, nos. 1-3 & 80. Loudon had petitioned the Batavia Government against the granting of a contract to Gou, arguing that it would jeopardise his supplies of cane and be the 'ruin' of his own Karanganyar venture, for which he had already bought 'expensive English iron machinery'. Accordingly, the Director of Cultivations (the 'CEO' of the *Stelsel*) refused to ratify Gou's contract and journeyed to Pekalongan to decide if cane should go to Gou or Loudon. The *Resident* remarked that 'from the above, it can be sufficiently seen, how unfair it would be, to ruin the Chinese contractor in order to accommodate someone [i.e. Loudon] who is already well-provided for'. He observed that 'Wonopringgo' Cane would have to be carted 4-5 *palen* (7.5 kilometres) to Loudon's mill at Karanganyar. As of 1832, ratification of Gou's contract remained postponed: 'Messers Loudon and De Sturler, so I understand, have prevented ratification so far by their repeated petitions, since these gentlemen are convinced that they have a claim to the cane which was originally planted for the Wonopringgo mill'.

[127] Westendorp Boerma, *Briefwisseling*, vol. 2, p. 260.

[128] The brothers CJ and AD Daendals took over Loudon's contract at Karanganyar (IB, 12.12.1838/10, MK, 2589). They already held a concession to manufacture sugar in neighbouring Semarang Residency. As former Contractors, they were being sued by the Indies Government in 1843 for non-delivery of sugar. See Extract IB, 13.2.1843/11 in AD, Pekalongan, no. 100.

[129] The head of the firm, the Marseilles-born Jean Marie Tissot, had arrived in Java in 1810. He was for some time active as a coffee planter in the Principalities. By the late 1820s, however, he had gravitated to Semarang, where he set up in business in some form of association with a member of the local Chinese-Indonesian business community, known, it is thought, as Tan Oeko.

Government[130] to finance the building of an 'industrial' factory on the site, with two triple iron-roller mills for grinding the cane and something rather more elaborate than Gou's cauldrons for boiling the juice down into sugar. Even so, the operation was badly undercapitalised and lacked some vital equipment. Most importantly, it was dependent on a single water-wheel, which had insufficient power to run both mills simultaneously, with the result that the grinding season was unduly prolonged and much of the cane had dried out before it could be crushed. In any event, the mills were in very poor condition. Nor were matters helped, it was reported, by the fact that the Contractors had insufficient funds to buy the firewood needed for boiling the sugar, and hence had to rely entirely on burning cane-trash.[131]

The situation changed decisively in the mid-1840s. Both Tissot and Lagnier were heavily involved in the sale of Dutch cotton goods on consignment from the Nederlandsche Handel-Maatschappij (Netherlands Trading Society) or NHM[132]; and with the collapse of their business ventures in 1843, their assets, such as they were, including the Wonopringgo factory, passed into the hands of the Batavia branch-office or *factorij* of the NHM.[133] Unable to find a buyer at what they regarded as a realistic price, they then set about converting the run-down sugar works into a modern factory.

The new Netherlands-based owners were the biggest Western business-house operating in the colony in the mid-nineteenth century and both the commercial agent of the Indies Government and (until 1850) its bankers. As such, the NHM enjoyed what seemed, at times, the status of a quasi-governmental enterprise. By virtue of their political connections, as well as the large amount of capital at their disposal — nominally 34.5 million guilders, subscribed by mostly Dutch stockholders[134] — and

---

[130] At the close of 1844, the outstanding loan from the Indies treasury amounted to 30 000 guilders. See 'Lijst ... Kultuurondernemingen ... Ultimo December 1844', in Exh. 1.2.1847/22.

[131] For the state of Wonopringgo at the time that it came into the NHM's hands in 1844, see 'Nota betreffende de Fabriek Wono Pringo door den Heer CA Granpré Molière', NFB, 31.12.1844/669.

[132] WFM Mansvelt, *Geschiedenis van de Nederlandsche Handel-Maatschappij*, vol. 2, Haarlem, [1924-1926], pp. 19, 39.

[133] NFB, 4.6.1843/614 & 29.8.1844/655; Mansvelt, vol. 2, pp. 18-19 & 39-40.

[134] When the NHM was established in 1824, the Dutch King, Willem I, was the largest single shareholder (Mansvelt, vol. 2, p. 226). For an authoritative recent overview of the company's history, see Ton de Graaf, *Voor Handel en Maatschappij: Geschiedenis van de Nederlandsche Handel-Maatschappij, 1824-1964*, Amsterdam, Boom, 2012.

by virtue, also, of the wide scope of their business, they played a dominant role in the commercial life of the Indies (and a major role in the Netherlands itself). During the mid-century decades, they developed extensive interests in the Java sugar industry. Indeed, around 1860 nearly one-fifth of the colony's major sugar factories, most of them in the north coast Residencies of Central Java, had contracts of some sort with the NHM for the sale of that part of their output which they were not committed to deliver to the Government — which also sold its sugar through the agency of the NHM.[135] Wonopringgo itself, however, was the first, and for almost a quarter of a century, the sole directly-owned speculation in sugar manufacture in which the NHM were involved. Accordingly, the firm's Batavia *factorij* lavished a good deal of attention on it (not least in the form of monthly letters to Amsterdam cataloguing developments there, something for which the historian can be duly grateful!). The firm ended up converting it into a 'model' factory on parallel lines to the cotton mills that the NHM had already established in the Netherlands.

They began on the right footing in 1847 by re-negotiating the contract for Wonopringgo (for a further twenty years) on a basis that obliged the firm to deliver to the Government only as much sugar as was needed to cover the state's expenses incurred in organising the cultivation of the cane (primarily so-called crop payments to peasant cane growers). This was provided under the standard arrangement prevailing under the *Cultuurstelsel*. The remainder of the factory's output remained at the 'free disposal' of the manufacturer.[136] This was a favourable (though not unique) arrangement, which meant that as sugar prices experienced renewed buoyancy toward the end of the 1840s, the NHM could hope to profit from increased production at Wonopringgo to a greater degree than the majority of factories in Java circa, whose contracts stipulated that the greater part or the whole of their output had to be consigned to the Government at a preordained price. Having thus settled the matter of 'free disposal' and gone on to order several ship-loads of new equipment, the *factorij* then set about finding somebody to manage the enterprise efficiently. In 1852, they found him.

---

[135] See Chapter 5 below.

[136] See Contract 6.4.1848/1, enclosed in Factorij to A'dam, 25.4.1848/318; JVFB, vol. 23, 1847-8, p. 60.

'Even Though an Englishman ...': Thomas Edwards (1814-1864)

Since the NHM had been founded in the mid-1820s with a view to wresting the commerce of Java from the (potential) control of the British, the appointment by its Batavia branch of an individual by the name of Thomas Edwards as Wonopringgo's *administrateur* [general manager] may have been seen as a provocation by Head Office, and clearly needed to be justified. 'Even though an Englishman', as the *factorij* readily conceded in reporting on matters to Amsterdam, Edwards stood head and shoulders above the many other applicants for the position, which had been advertised in June 1852 in the colony's sole — and Government-run — newspaper, the *Javasche Courant*.[137]

He was one of the industry's first 'professionals', in so far as his job was a salaried one (and the NHM rejected subsequent attempts on his part to lease the factory from them). As such, he received 500 guilders a month (the same base salary as an Assistant *Resident* in Government service) together with an annual bonus linked to the factory's output, free accommodation at Wonopringgo and 'all that which is normally provided free of charge to the Administrator of a sugar factory'.[138] The essential point about Edwards, however, was not only that he was already an experienced sugar factory manager, who had been *administrateur* of two other such enterprises in Java during the preceding half-decade, but also that he had considerable experience with steam-operated machinery. This was crucial, since by this date Wonopringgo had become a large and well-equipped enterprise, in whose manufacturing process steam played a crucial role.

The extent of this advance is partly obscured by the relatively late arrival in the industry, at least in appreciable numbers, of steam-driven mills for grinding cane. Indeed, shortly after the mid-century there were said to be only ten steam engines operating sugar mills in the whole of Java, with four more in the offing.[139] This meant that only around 10 per cent of the big Java factories operating around 1860 had steam mills: in Cuba, almost exactly contemporaneously, the figure was around

---

[137] NFB, 10.7.1852/67.
[138] NFB, 10.7.1852/67.
[139] *KV, 1863*, Bijl W, *Nota betrekkelijk de werking van stoommachinerien op de suikerfabrieken voor het in beweging brengen van de molen* [Note concerning the operation of steam machinery in sugar factories with reference to how the mills are powered].

70 per cent.[140] At Wonopringgo itself during the mid-century decades, motive power for grinding of the factory's cane continued to come from two big water-wheels (a second water-wheel was brought to Wonopringgo from Loudon's now abandoned and part-demolished factory at Karanganyer) rather than a steam engine.[141] Even so (and as will be argued subsequently), there was nothing necessarily retrograde about the continued adherence to water power in the Java sugar industry in the mid-nineteenth century: for the factories, water was a 'free' and plentiful resource, at least in the case of those situated, as was Wonopringgo, near abundant supplies from the nearby mountains. The essential point, moreover, was that throughout mid-century Java, water-power was harnessed in association with a great deal of technologically advanced machinery.

Wonopringgo was a prime case in point. Following their assumption of ownership at the factory in 1844, the NHM came up with substantial amounts of money to re-equip it in a manner befitting what was by far and away the colony's richest and most powerful business enterprise.[142] First, two new mills for grinding the cane were installed in 1845: exploiting its commercial contacts in the Indies, the firm was able to have one of them (made by the Dutch firm of Van Vlissingen) shipped from the Surabaya warehouse of their agency there. These in turn were replaced at the end of the following decade by up-to-the-minute milling equipment, imported from the London engineering firm of Robinson, whose yard Edwards had visited in person to order machinery to his precise specifications during a six-month visit to the United Kingdom in 1857-58. (The equipment was still there — and still operational — early in the twentieth century.) This was similar machinery to that which Robinson was exporting contemporaneously to Cuba.[143] Though still predominantly water-

---

[140] Tann, 'Steam and Sugar', p. 72.

[141] Edwards's description is summarised as follows: the north mill wheel was 30 foot across (diameter) and 7 foot 10 inches wide, and the south wheel was 20 foot by 3 foot 7 inches. See enclosure in Factorij to A'dam, 25.2.1853/192.

[142] For the information in this and the following paragraphs, see 'Nota betreffende de Fabriek Wono Pringo door den Heer CA Granpré Molière', in NFB, 31.12.1844/669; Factorij to A'dam, 1.8.1845/233; Factorij to A'dam, 17.9.1845/236; Factorij to A'dam, 29.11.1847/305; JC Teengs [Report on Wonopringgo], Batavia, 27.6.1850, in Factorij to A'dam, 24.7.1850/29; Factorij to A'dam, 25.9.1854/316; Edwards to Factorij, 9.9.1854/826, in Factorij to A'dam, 11.10.1854/320; JVFB, vol. 35, 1859-1860, p. 255; Heijning to De Directie der Vereeniging van Suikerfabrieken te Passoeroean, 20.12.1863, in Factorij to A'dam, 25.1.1864/1225; Mansvelt, vol. 2, pp. 363-6.

[143] Curry-Machado, *Cuban Sugar*, p. 47.

powered, Wonopringgo was also possessed by this date of an auxiliary steam engine, for those occasions during the 'dry season' when there was insufficient water to fully operate the mill. The heart of the 'new' Wonopringgo, however, was located in the boiling house where the cane-juice was cleansed, concentrated into *tjing* [thick juice] and subsequently transformed into sugar. When the firm had taken over the factory in 1844, the 'boiling house' was just that: an array of some fifty-two iron cauldrons (in Dutch, *ketels*) and a *magazijn* or warehouse with room for 7000 pots. The semi-liquid sugar was left to set in these pots and (sometimes) 'clayed', meaning that the pots were sealed with wet clay, the water from which percolated through the setting mass, taking impurities with it and leaving several layers of fine white sugar in its wake.

Here, the changes wrought by the NHM were nothing short of revolutionary: a set of four Vacuum Pans — the NHM evidently did nothing by halves — was installed there circa 1850, after a massive and prolonged effort. It took a month to drag them (presumably using labour commandeered from the local population) the sixteen kilometres from the wharf at Pekalongan to the factory site at Wonopringgo. It took considerably longer than that to get them operating properly, something which caused both considerable dissent among the factory's European personnel and the premature departure of the 'engineer' in charge of the assembly of the new apparatus. Even so, it was all worth it, since (as explained earlier) the Vacuum Pans made it possible to complete the penultimate stages of manufacture in a way that ensured both more and better sugar and a far greater efficiency of operation. Wonopringgo was thereby launched on a trajectory that made it one of the most productive and profitable sugar factories in Java in the mid-nineteenth century. Given the ample provision of Vacuum Pans, moreover, it also seems to have proved possible — on one occasion at least — to use them for reducing the cane-juice to a *tjing* as well as for boiling that syrup to near-setting point. As Thomas Edwards was to remark subsequently to his employers: '[T]he system of evaporation *in vacuo* is much superior. The work is brought together, the superintendence is much easier … [emphasis in original]'.[144]

The trouble was, however, that this made very heavy demands on the boilers, meaning that fuel was required at a prohibitive cost. Hence, the reduction to *tjing*

---

[144] For this and the material in the following paragraph, see Factorij to A'dam, 11.10.1854/320, appendix; Edwards to Factorij, 9.9.1854/826.

appears to have continued to take place (for the most part) at Wonopringgo in the mid-nineteenth century in similar open *platte batterijen* [steam-heated batteries] to those found in most contemporary factories in Java. What singled out Wonopringgo was the extensive use of bone charcoal in the manufacturing process. Prior to being pumped into the Vacuum Pans, the cane-juice was twice treated with bone charcoal during the cleansing (using Taylor filters) and concentration process.

Meanwhile, the new apparatus in the boiling house was complemented by the installation of a Centrifuge that spun the nearly 'finished' sugar into crystalline form. Initially installed (in 1854) so that some of Wonopringgo's output could be marketed direct and without the need for further refining (Australia was the intended destination)[145], a whole bank of Centrifuges would subsequently become a ubiquitous feature of the production line. In the 1860s, however, the sole Centrifuge operated alongside older systems for draining the sugar of molasses in *gemetselde steenen bakken* [specially constructed brick troughs], which supplanted or supplemented the more conventional clay pots. A small pottery, a plant for manufacturing bone charcoal, a saw-mill, an iron foundry and a rudimentary fitters' workshop completed the mid-century inventory of Wonopringgo: an industrial complex located, somewhat incongruously — as pioneering factories worldwide tended to be — in the midst of farm-land and forest. With no more than a touch of hyperbole, Edwards remarked to his employers after almost a decade in their service that Wonopringgo was

> [o]ne of the most complete [factories] in Java — nothing has ever been refused by you which I have thought might conduce to an improved manufacture, and although other administrators may have shown more ability, not one, I dare to affirm, has been more animated by a more constant and earnest desire for improvement than myself.[146]

From Whitchurch to Java: A Transnational Trajectory

Edwards's predecessor at Wonopringgo had been somebody with minimal experience of steam and steel. He was a former warehouse keeper and prior to that captain of a sailing ship.[147] The new appointee was a man of a very different stamp. His career was

---

[145] Factorij to A'dam, 25.9.1854/316.

[146] Edwards to Factorij, 24.12.1860, in Factorij to A'dam, 2.1.1861/ 915.

[147] J Stokhekker, *administrateur* of Wonopringgo, 1844-51. Before becoming a *pakhuismeester* [warehouse-keeper] for the NHM in 1840-41, he was *gezagvoeder* [commander] of the Schooner *Calypso*. See JVFB, vol. 16, 1840/41, p. 3.

akin to that of Alexander Lawson, Hubertus Hoevenaar and the other *werktuigkundig* individuals whose vital connection to the sugar industry is discussed at various points in the present account. That is to say, he was part of that transnational 'diaspora' of skilled individuals, initially at least with qualifications that were experiental rather than formal, who roamed the booming sectors of the global industrialising economy during the middle decades of the nineteenth century and who formed part of a 'network of knowledge' that was international in character.

Thomas Edwards himself had been born in the Shropshire town of Whitchurch, in the Welsh borders of England, in fairly good agricultural country which produced many cattle — and much leather. His father was by trade a leather worker — a currier who treated and softened the hides after they left the tannery — as his own father had been before him. Curriers were in decline, however, and as a youth Edwards gravitated (along with many of those working in the leather industry) toward the rapidly industrialising areas of south Lancashire, some eighty or so kilometres to the north. By the 1830s, the districts lying between Manchester and Liverpool — where his uncle, Robert Broadhurst Hill, was a substantial man of business — had become the cradle of industrial development in the United Kingdom. It was no accident that the world's first passenger railway had opened there in 1831, and the area was home to a number of major foundries and engineering works, and to the collieries that supplied them with fuel. Edwards had experience in both.

He was first employed at the Haydock colliery, south-east of Liverpool, at that time the largest coal mine in south Lancashire. At Haydock, as we know from a few surviving fragments of letters and diaries kept by his younger brother Robert, Thomas Edwards learned technical drawing, and experienced going down the pit itself. Down there, he was teased by the women workers — 'the queerest concerns you ever saw', Tom told his brother — who laboured along with men on the coalface or in the tunnels. Moving on from the colliery, he worked for a time, presumably again as a 'gentleman apprentice', at the nearby Vulcan Foundry.[148] Vulcan, then at the beginning of an illustrious history of mechanical engineering which lasted until

---

[148] 'June 19th, 1833 — Tom left W'Church for Haydock and then went to Vulcan Town by the following month.' Extract from Robert Hill Edwards's First Journal (in possession of Elaine Nobbs, Charlottetown, PEI, and kindly transcribed for me by Mr Don Jardine, a direct descendant of Robert Hill Edwards, Tom Edwards's younger brother). Shortly after his arrival in Java, in the late months of 1842, Tom was already being spoken of as a *werktuigkundige* — a person expert with machines. See IB, 13.9.1842/1, MK, 2637.

late in the twentieth century, was owned and run by a son of George Stephenson (of 'Rocket' fame) and by Charles Tayleur, the Liverpool-based scion of a wealthy Shropshire family.[149] Tayleur's links to the Unitarian Dissenter congregations of his home county, to which the young Thomas Edwards also belonged (his late father had been a respected Unitarian preacher as well as being a leather worker)[150], may well explain his apprenticeship at the foundry.[151]

By the mid-1830s Vulcan was manufacturing steam locomotives and engines on an increasingly significant scale. It was a sizeable and important establishment, and obviously attracted some clever and ambitious young men. One of Thomas Edwards's contemporaries among the apprentices there, Daniel Gooch, was to become a famous engineer with the Great Western Railway in the United Kingdom, and subsequently its company chairman. Edwards left no account of his experience at Vulcan, but Gooch did. His diary enables us to reconstruct a picture of young Edwards trudging from his lodging at a farm in a nearby village, down a rough, unmade lane to where the not quite complete factory lay — still a green field-site but with the new Newton-le-Willows railway station, midway between Liverpool and Manchester, only a short distance away.[152]

---

[149] For information on the Vulcan Foundry in the 1830s and 1840s, see 'The Story of Vulcan Works from 1830 to 2002', prepared by Malcolm Siberry for MAN B & W Diesel Ltd, Ruston, UK, posted at http://www.enginemuseum.org/bbv.html (accessed 15 August 2014).

[150] See the obituary notice (by the town's Unitarian Minister, the Rev. John Philp) in the Unitarian publication, *The Monthly Repository of Theology and General Literature*, vol. 20, 1825, p. 181.

[151] The family of Charles Tayleur (1775-1854) owned an estate near Market Drayton in the north of the county and possibly a town house in Shrewsbury [information from http://www.enginemuseum.org/sor.html (accessed 15 August 2014)]. Their number may have included some very prominent Unitarian Dissenters. In the late eighteenth century, William Tayleur of Shrewsbury (where Unitarianism was very strong among the 'better sort', who had two chapels in the town), an Oxford Fellow and London Barrister, was a noted Unitarian. See John Seed, 'Gentlemen Dissenters: The Social and Political Meanings of Rational Dissent in the 1770s and 1780s', *The Historical Journal*, vol. 28, no. 2, June, 1985, pp. 299-325.

[152] Gooch began his distinguished career at the Vulcan Foundry as an apprentice in January 1834. He recorded in his diaries: 'On the 28th January 1834, I left home to go and work at the Vulcan Foundry, near Warrington in Lancashire, under Mr. Robert Stephenson. He and Mr. Tayleur of Liverpool had just built their works – indeed they were not quite finished – when I went there. The works were constructed chiefly for building locomotives. When I arrived at the Newton Junction late in the evening, I found Mr. Charles Tayleur, the Manager of the Vulcan Works, in the waiting room. I had a letter from Mr. Stephenson for him, and presented it with my great awe to him, as the arbitrator of my future. He, however, spoke

There is no surviving record of any of Vulcan's machinery having being sent to Java at this time, but Edwards, at least, made the journey. Why there and not to Cuba, where so many young engineering 'exiles' found their way around that time? Possibly the issue of slavery ruled this choice out. Brought up — as we have just seen — in the Dissenter communities of north-west England, and hence into an abolitionist tradition, Edwards may possibly have ruled out Cuba — with its thousands upon thousands of black African slaves incarcerated in factory barracks — on those grounds if no other. However that may be, Edwards arrived at the age of twenty-seven in Batavia in August 1842 on board a ship, the *Warlock*, which had left Liverpool in April of that year.[153] Most probably, he did so at the behest of his first employer in Java, Thomas Benjamin Hofland, though again we cannot be quite sure of exactly what happened and what the connection was.

Leastways, Hofland was the person who supported Edwards's application to the colonial authorities, a few weeks after his landing there, for permission to remain in Java.[154] One of the colony's richest men, together with his brother Peter, TB Hofland had recently bought the P&T estate in West Java from the British interests who had owned it for the previous twenty years, and he was also the proprietor of several sugar factories in East Java's *Oosthoek* districts. The Hoflands were both Asian-born and had arrived in Java from the Indian subcontinent during the course of the 1820s.[155] Together with their Amsterdam-born partner Johann Erich Banck, and in cahoots with Chinese-Indonesian business interests in Surabaya, they made a great deal of money in the *Oosthoek* in the following decade supplying sugar on contract to the Indies Government.[156]

---

in a kind, friendly way to me, and this did much to reassure me … The works were situated about a mile from the Moss; down a wretched dirty lane with ruts a foot deep. I had to be in the works not later than ten minutes past six in the morning, and a dreadful walk it was in the dark when I first went there' [from www.enginemuseum.org/sor.html (accessed 15 August 2014)].

[153] *Javasche Courant*, 13 August 1842.
[154] IB, 13.9.1842/1, MK, 2637.
[155] On the Hoflands, see Bosma and Raben, pp. 126-8.
[156] The NHM's Batavia *factorij* advanced the Hoflands more than 1 million guilders to buy Pamanoekan and Tjiassem, on the security of its output of sugar and coffee. See Factorij to A'dam, 5.9.1840/1527 & 29.11.1841/1819. As to the brothers' financial relation to the East Java Chinese, it was reported by the *factorij* in the early 1850s 'that the Chinaman Kwee Yang

It was not there, however, but at P&T that Edwards found his first job in Java. In taking over the estate, the Hoflands, it has to be assumed, aimed to follow up their success in the sugar industry of East Java with something similar at P&T. Within a few years they had built a second factory elsewhere on the property, in addition to the Subang operation that they had inherited from their British predecessors.[157] TB Hofland's application to the Indies Government for permission to prolong Edwards's stay on the estate made explicit reference to the fact that the sugar works were of 'such a character that a capable machinist needed to be continually employed there'.[158]

Indeed, to Edwards's expert eye the problems were evidently more far-reaching than that. Within a very few months, he was accompanying some of the equipment from Subang for repair at a machine workshop in Pasuruan in East Java, operated by a pair of British 'migrants', WJF Dudman and Thomas Reed Stavers.[159] Newly established in the booming sugar districts of Java's *Oosthoek*, such a workshop's existence was a further indication of the advancing frontier of the industrial manufacture of sugar in the colony in the middle decades of the nineteenth century — and of the transnational character of the technicians who supported it. Dudman and Stavers's venture was described by the Dutch *Resident* as being of 'great utility' to the area's sugar factories, and in 1842 its owners were lent the considerable sum of 12 000 guilders by the Indies Government to buy and ship from Europe 'a large iron smelting furnace and the equipment belonging to it'. Like Edwards himself, its proprietors were highly mobile and possessed of the kind of skills that gave them a chance of a better life in the colony than would have been the case 'at home'. Early in the century, Dudman & Co had been shipbuilders at Deptford in the lower reaches

---

Ho, died on July 7 (possibly in 1851) and that the Hoflands had considerable sums [*groote sommen*] on loan from him'. See 'Aantekeningen uit de Correspondentie Factorij', NHMA, 7999, file 588.

[157] In 1842, the *factorij* remarked on the 'substantial improvements recently effected' at Pamanoekan & Tjiassem, without, however, going into any detail. See Factorij to A'dam, 8.1.1842/1858. For a description of the sugar-making equipment at P&T in the 1840s, see Assistant Res. Krawang, 'Verslag omtrent den Toestand der Verkoopte en den Verhuurde Landen in der Afd. Krawang', 16 March 1850, AD, Krawang, no. 9.

[158] IB, 11.2.1843/4, MK, 2642.

[159] For the information in this and the following paragraphs, see IB, 1.7.1843/23, MK, 2647; IB, 15.8.1840/20, MK, 2609; IB, 29.6.1841/5, MK, 2619; and the files on the Dudman brothers in the *Centraal Bureau voor Genealogie*, Den Haag (kindly supplied by Peter Christiaans). On Stavers, see Chapter 5, below.

of the Thames to the east of London, and it is fairly certain that the 'Java' Dudmans came from the same family.[160]

Stavers had been born in Deptford on the Thames Estuary in 1798 and died in the United Kingdom in 1867. Much of the later part of his life, however, was spent in Java, where he was described as a 'master shipwright and seaman' at the time of being given permission to settle in the colony in 1840.[161] He was not, however, the only member of his family to have settled on Java as the place to make his fortune. A brother, William 'Jack' Stavers — whom we shall meet again later — had found his way to the island some two decades earlier. Around the mid-century, William Stavers was the Government Contractor for the Koning Willem II sugar factory — one of the best equipped of its day — in East Java's Surabaya Residency. A nephew, Francis Dawson Stavers (1823-1864), also appears to have had a stake in the same operation.

Like Thomas Reed Stavers, WJF Dudman (1816-1868) likewise had kin living in Java. Following the termination of his connection with the workshop in East Java, he became partner in the Government sugar contract in the Rembang Residency on the north coast of Central Java. His brother, Robert Dudman, meanwhile, had enjoyed a career that had striking parallels with that of Thomas Edwards. In the early 1840s, he, too, was engaged in repairing sugar-making machinery in Java, in this instance on estates belonging to to the Dezentje family in the *Vorstenlanden* [Principalities] of Central Java. It was there that several score of European planters, with the recently deceased patriarch of the Dezentje family very prominent among them, had established themselves on 'estates' leased from the nobility of the princely Courts during the 1810s and 1820s. Like Edwards, Robert Dudman went on to become *administrateur* of a sugar factory — before dying in Surabaya in 1855.

On his journey to the sugar belt of the *Oosthoek*, Thomas Edwards may well have seen enough to convince him that his future lay there rather than in West Java, where there were few factories and where it appears that the Hoflands had drawn back from any plans to install up-to-date steam equipment.[162] For whatever reason, by 1846,

---

[160] See C Northcote Parkinson, *Trade in the Eastern Seas, 1793-1813*, London, Cass & Co, 1966 [1937], pp. 121, 128.

[161] See IB, 15.8.1840/20, NA, MK, 2609.

[162] For a description of the sugar-making equipment at P&T in the 1840s, see Assistant Res. Krawang, 'Verslag omtrent den Toestand der Verkoopte en den Verhuurde Landen in ... Krawang', 16 March 1850, AD, Krawang, no. 9. It would appear from these reports that there were no Vacuum Pans operating on the estate in around 1850.

within three years after his arriving there, Edwards and the Hoflands parted company. Meanwhile, he had found the domestic partner who remained with him for the rest of his life. Ann Baird had been born at Subang in 1826. She was almost certainly the daughter of Robert Webster Baird, the superintendent of the 'sugar works' there, and a local woman whose identity is presently unknown. In the normal way of things in the Indies colonial communities of Java in the nineteenth (and twentieth) century, Baird might well have 'recognised' his daughter, thereby conferring European status on her. However, Robert Baird died in the same year as she was born, and quite possibly before she was born.[163] As a result, Ann Baird remained 'un-recognised' and hence an *inlander* or native. (This was a 'mistake' that Edwards took pains to avoid with respect to his own children with Ann Baird.) Brought up, as we must presume, among her dead father's British colleagues — one or two of whom were still there in the early 1840s — she most likely met Edwards at Subang. What is certain is that she subsequently lived with him in East Java and later still at Wonopringgo.

Departing from P&T, Edwards first took himself to Surabaya, where Frans Jacob Hubert Baijer first employed him.[164] Later to be hailed as the city's 'Iron King', Baijer was at that time the proprietor of a recently established iron works and repair shop, the 'Phoenix' Fabriek voor Stoomwerktuigen [the Factory for Steam Machinery].[165] From there Edwards moved directly into the sugar industry of East Java which Baijer's enterprise had been created to service. It was presumably no coincidence that both the sugar factories at which Edwards subsequently worked (Padjarakan and Tjipiring) were in the process of installing — or had just installed — steam-operated machinery.[166] Accordingly, when the NHM *factorij* decided to employ him as their *administrateur* at Wonopringgo in 1852 they had obtained the services of one of the most experienced steam engineers in the colony.

Unsurprisingly, the NHM thought very highly of Edwards, whom they correctly saw as the cap-stone of their venture at Wonopringgo. Indeed, they thought well enough of him, and of his capacities as a man well-versed in the ways of steam

---

[163] See the notice of his death in *Bataviasche Courant*, 23 February 1826.

[164] IB, 2.11.1846/22, MK, 2688.

[165] IB, 2.11.1846/22, MK, 2688.

[166] See 'Opgave wegens de op Java werkende suikerfabrieken, Juni 1848', in NHMA, 9207. These brief details of Edwards's career in the Indies prior to this appointment at Wonopringgo come from his application (in 1857) for naturalisation as a Dutch citizen in NA, Archief Ministerie van Justitie, 2.09.01, dossier 4862.

and steel, to pay for a return voyage to Europe in 1857-58 on the expensive Overland Mail route so that he might order more machinery for Wonopringgo — and visit his family. It also appears that he took this opportunity of taking his and Ann Baird's two young daughters to join his mother, sister and brother-in-law in Edinburgh. He did so in the knowledge that they would receive the kind of education there that they could never hope to experience in remote Wonopringgo. The two young 'scholars ... born in Java' are recorded in the Edinburgh Census early in the following decade.[167]

Presumably, their father anticipated that the family would soon be reunited. Leastways, in 1862, despite considerable inducements to remain, he left the employment of the NHM, apparently with a view to returning to the United Kingdom. Instead, he lingered in Java and in 1864 took up employment with the Batavia firm of Maclaine Watson. Together with their close affiliates in Semarang and Surabaya, Maclaine Watson were at this time second only to the NHM's *factorij* in terms of the extent of their sugar interests. Edwards became the *administrateur* at their Gempol sugar factory, some 150 kilometres to the west of Wonopringgo, in Cirebon Residency.

What had happened to make him abandon his apparent plan to repatriate? Had he lost the money he would have saved from his salary and bonuses during his ten years at Wonopringgo? The year 1862, in which he took his long-projected departure from Wonopringgo, was a bad one for agricultural speculations in Java, and many firms and individuals had their fingers badly burnt. It seems possible that Edwards, having invested his money locally, might have been among them.[168] The most likely candidate for identification as the agent of Edwards's ruin was the entrepreneur and sugar-factory owner, Johannes Herderschee. His death in May 1862 (discussed in a subsequent chapter) exposed huge debts to 'private individuals' and brought about the collapse of the substantial Batavia firm of Van Ommeren, Reub & Co (see Chapter 5, below). Herderschee's Simbang sugar factory in Pekalongan was quite near to Wonopringgo, and it is highly likely that he and Edwards would have known each other well.

---

[167] I am grateful for this information to the research of Mrs Jill Hawkins, who has established that the two girls ('scholars' and 'born in Java') were living in the early 1860s in Edinburgh's 'New Town' with the Torrop family. (Edwards's widowed mother also lived with them.)

[168] On the crisis of 1862, see L de Bree, *Gedenkboek van de Javasche Bank*, vol. 2, Wetevreden, Kolff, 1928, pp. 47-62.

In any event, Edwards's tenure at the Gempol factory was a short one. It seems likely that he had used his trip to Europe in 1857-58 not only to lodge his children with his relatives but also to get advice about his health. His father had died at the age of thirty-five and his brother, Robert Hill Edwards, was grievously sick in Canada, where he had taken himself and his family to farm early in the 1840s. It is hard not to suspect that the chemical processes used in treating leather in the Edwards's family workshop back in Whitchurch all those years earlier had taken a terrible toll. Be that as it may, Thomas Edwards died near his new workplace, in the hillside village of Agalinga, a few kilometres from the Cirebon town of Madjalengka, on 13 November 1865. The sugar Campaign at Gempol would have ended for the year, and it was where he and Ann Baird had presumably gone to escape the heat of the plains. He was scarcely fifty years old. In what was, in effect, a posthumous tribute to what he had achieved at Wonopringgo in the decade he was there, the *Resident* of Pekalongan eulogised Wonopringgo two years after his death as

> without doubt one of the best looking [*schoonste*] and fit-for-purpose factories built on Java. No expense has been spared to apply everything that science found worthy to increase and improve the quality of output.[169]

Industrial Production and Productivity at Mid-century Wonopringgo

Edwards had remained at Wonopringgo for a full ten years. Under his management, the factory had flourished and become a profitable enterprise for both the owners and for Edwards himself. It had been transformed from a run-down, poorly performing factory into a large and well-equipped enterprise, with a commensurately extensive area of plantation. Back at the very beginning of sugar making there, early in the 1830s, Gou's pair of simple 'Chinese'-style wooden mills had had supplies of cane from some 80 *bau* (55 hectares) of 'plantation'. The industrial set-up for grinding cane and boiling down the juice at Wonopringgo created by the NHM was matched with an area under cane 10 times greater than that: something in excess of 800 *bau* (550 hectares) was planted in the vicinity every year.

In terms of output, moreover, Wonopinggo under NHM control was — or became — a convincing demonstration of the economies of scale associated with the rise of the industrial factory and of the productive potentials of steam and steel in one

---

[169] Resident Pekalongan to Director Binnenlands Bestur, 20.2.1867/674. Exh. 11.4.1868/91.

combination or another. One estimate was that 'Chinese'-style mills of the kind used by Gou produced at best around 2 piculs (around 125 kilograms) of sugar per day[170], whereas in the 1820s, Trail & Co's pioneering steam-driven mill in West Java (see above) was reckoned to be capable of a daily output of 30 piculs per day.[171] Used in combination with the steam-grinding of cane, or independently of it (as was widely the case in Java in the mid-nineteenth century, for reasons already explained), the steam-operated Vacuum Pan offered further improvements in the quality as well as the quantity of the product.

The NHM's Wonopringgo was not only a much larger enterprise than its predecessors, but also a much more productive one in terms of the quantities of sugar manufactured from a given area of cane. It is impossible (given the fragmentary sources available) to know how much sugar Gou Kang Tjou had actually produced at his (abortive) sugar works from his 80 *bau* of cane in the early 1830s: it may have been as little as 100 piculs or around 6300 kilograms, but the figure seems improbably low.[172] Altogether more satisfactory data relate to the state of affairs at Wonopringgo in the mid-1840s. In 1844, immediately prior to the NHM take-over, the output of the semi-industrialised factory was in the region of 14 000 piculs or 880 MT, obtained from some 700 *bau* (490 hectares) of cane. The visiting NHM executive who reported on this considered that the resultant sugar yield of 20 piculs per *bau* was a fairly respectable one, given the state of affairs there and the fact that only 600 *bau* of the planted cane had actually been harvested.[173]

Thereafter, however, things really took off. If the figure of 20 piculs per *bau* was thought quite reasonable in the 1840s, by the early 1860s something approaching or exceeding 50 piculs per *bau* was the norm at Wonopringgo. Indeed, in 1865 the figure reached an exceptional 58 piculs. Some of this increased productivity, of course, had to do with improved cultivation and the resultant higher yields of cane (though this improvement is unquantifiable on existing data). Even so, there can be little doubt

---

[170] Hooyman, 'Tegenwoordigen Staat', pp. 203-5.

[171] 'AV Batavia', 1824, vol. 3, p. 23, NA, Collectie Schneither, 84.

[172] Inspector of Cultivations Louis Vitalis found only about 70 piculs of 'good' sugar there in 1834, adding that a third of the stock had reverted to syrup. See 'Rapport omtrent de suikermolen te Wonopringgo', in Vitalis to Directeur Cultuurs, 10.3.1834/25, ANRI, Archief Cultuurs, no. 333, Exh. 13.3.1834/761.

[173] 'Nota betreffende de Fabriek Wono Pringo door den Heer C.A. Granpré Molière', 23.12.1844, in NFB, 31.12.1844.

that the evolution over time of the industrial project within the factory walls was primarily responsible. Far better equipped than the other two Government contract sugar factories operating in Pekalongan in the 1860s, Wonopringgo produced signicantly more sugar per hectare than other factories in the locality, such as nearby Sragie, and Kalimatie.[174]

The Factory and its Workforce

By the 1850s, Wonopringgo's many refinements included apparatus for producing gas so that the whole factory could be lit at night in relative safety, since continuous, twenty-four-hour operation was the sine qua non of an efficiently run Campaign. The military connotation of this term — used for the manufacturing season (which generally ran, as previously mentioned, from May to October, during the 'dry' monsoon when conditions underfoot allowed for the movement and ripening of cane) — was not inappropriate. There had to be a certain degree of precision and discipline if the schedule for harvesting and crushing was not to go badly awry, resulting in significant loss of sucrose content in the cane. As was the case globally, the rise of the industrial factory in Java was therefore intimately associated with the recruitment and disciplining of labour. Edwards spoke of Wonopringgo's need for 'three hundred men at 6 o'clock every morning' in and around the factory compound throughout the Campaign. In so doing, moreover, he laid specific emphasis on the particular needs of *industrial* production, for: 'I need scarcely say that in a sugar *fabriek* the work of the day cannot be put off till the morrow — everything must be done at the right time or the whole fabrication will soon come to a deadlock'. It was a situation in which, as he remarked, 'order and regularity' was of the essence.[175]

In the absence of the factory siren that was becoming common in the industrial enterprises with which Edwards himself would have been familiar in the United Kingdom, workers were perhaps summoned by gongs or drums (direct evidence is lacking) from surrounding villages specifically assigned to labour service at the factory. Unlike the turn-out in south Lancashire where Edwards had originally based himself,

---

[174] Between 1863 and 1869 Wonopringgo averaged some 53 piculs per *bau* (ppb), nearby Sragie averaged 35-62 ppb and the more distant Kalimatie about 43 ppb. See GG to MK, 8.2.1872/193/3, Exh. 20.11.1872/27.

[175] The information on labour at Wonopringgo in the mid-nineteenth century in this and the following two paragraphs is drawn from Edwards to Factorij NHM Batavia, 11.12.1858 & 15.12.1858, in NFB, 18.12.1858/430.

however, wages played only a minor part in labour recruitment for Wonopringgo in the mid-nineteenth century. Instead, the Government officials — both Dutch and Javanese — who were responsible for supplying workers to the factory relied on the corvée obligations imposed on the peasantry by the state.

As we shall see subsequently, the Dutch had inherited from the pre-colonial regime in Central Java a peasant labour service regime of formidable proportions. During the middle decades of the nineteenth century (albeit in circumstances that were to transform it), this regime was harnessed to the requirements of the commodity production of sugar, in the factory itself as well as in the field. Edwards's correspondence with his employers at Batavia (at a time when a local dispute appeared to imperil his supply of commandeered labour) makes it clear that 'Government Coolies', as they were called, were the mainstay of the factory's workforce. Whether he might have *preferred* 'free workers' to forced labour was immaterial for, as he informed the NHM,

> in the surrounding districts there is not a single peasant who is not subject to the orders of half a dozen different functionaries — that may not be written in the statute book — but is written in the book facts. Not one of the dwellers in the *desas* [villages] who has a household and a status, has the free disposal of his own time, and he cannot sell that to me which he himself is unable to dispose of.

To be sure, as elsewhere, Wonopringgo's commandeered workforce was accorded a daily dole by the factory, amounting to between fifteen and twenty *doits* [a copper coin notionally worth one-hundredth of a guilder] in the mid-century decades. As one leading Dutch economic historian has neatly observed, however, corvée under the *Cultuurstelsel* constituted a 'form of labour that was no less coerced for being remunerated by the payment of coins'.[176] Even so, although wages were hardly the key, the factory workforce that evolved over the mid-century decades was not a homogeneous one.

Along with the 'Government Coolies', who generally performed menial tasks, factories in the mid-nineteenth century like Wonopringgo also started to assemble a semi-permanent nucleus of *mandoors* [skilled operatives and foremen] who were employed to work with the machinery and to supervise the 'casual' workforce.

---

[176] Jan Luiten van Zanden, 'Linking Two Debates: Money Supply, Wage Labour and Economic Development in Java in the Nineteenth Century', p. 170, in Jan Lucassen (ed.), *Wages and Currency: Global Comparisons from Antiquity to the Twentieth Century*, Bern, Peter Lang, 2007, pp. 169-92.

Relatively few in numbers, these skilled workers were still a vital dimension to the industrial project.[177] Moreover, at some big factories — though not at Wonopringgo in the mid-century— manufacturers began to arrange to settle some part of the workforce in and around the factory compound, where they lived with their families.[178] These workers' quarters, housing a variety of skilled operatives as well as labourers, were to become a feature of the Java industry after the commandeered labour associated with the *Cultuurstelsel* began to be phased out during the third quarter of the nineteenth century. Their embryonic existence in some parts of the colony in around 1850, however, serves to underscore the distinctly heterogeneous nature of the industrial factory's workforce even when the *Stelsel* was at the peak of its operation.

It is to the way that land — as well as labour — was harnessed to the sugar industry in general throughout lowland Java during the middle decades of the nineteenth century, and to how this was articulated with the relations of production which had existed on the island before van den Bosch and his associates got to work there in the 1830s, that we can now turn.

---

[177] RE Elson, *Village Java under the Cultivation System*, Sydney, Allen & Unwin, 1994, pp. 209-10.

[178] Elson (*Village Java*, p. 212) cites the case of the very big and well-equipped Koning Willem II factory in East Java, 'where a large portion of the workers lived in three large factory compounds (named "London", "Paris" and "Singapore")'.

Part II

The 'Peasant' Economy, the Money Trail and the Bourgeoisie

4 Sugar without Slaves: The Agrarian Basis for the Industrial Project

Sugar is associated — perhaps indelibly — with plantations and slaves. Java, as things developed during the middle decades of the nineteenth century, had neither: or, at least, not in any way that related to the production of sugar. The 'sugar plantation' as conceived in the heavily Caribbean-centric literature did not exist there (or was found only on the margins of the industry). Neither did slavery, nor the indentured forms of labour that (in part) supplanted it in the New World and elsewhere. Ostensibly at least, commodity sugar production, as it developed on Java, belonged instead to a general, long-established, 'Asian' pattern, in which cane was raised by a 'peasant' workforce, utilising existing farm-land in conjunction with other crops.

As we shall see, a generalisation as broad as this runs the risk of seriously misrepresenting the agrarian basis of production that evolved in Java through the mid-century decades. Nonetheless, it does serve to highlight the major disparity between how the industry's raw material was produced and the classic situation of contemporaneous New World sugar manufacture. In the Dutch colony, the sugar industry expanded rapidly between the 1830s and 1880s, primarily but not exclusively under the aegis of the *Cultuurstelsel* or System of [State] Cultivations, which was inaugurated at the beginning of the period by Governor-General Johannes van den Bosch and his lieutenants. In contrast to the barrack slavery of transported Africans and the dominant monoculture of contemporary Cuba — Java's Caribbean antipode — Java sugar's expansion was predicated on raw material produced by local, peasant labour from cane fields that were created by the temporary amalgamation of scores of often minute irrigated rice fields or *sawah*. The *sawah* amalgamated in this way, however, remained within the domain of peasant agriculture and reverted

Figure 9: The founder of the *Cultuurstelsel*: **Governor-General Johannes van den Bosch.**
Source: Koninklijk Instituut voor Taal-, Land- en Volkenkunde, Leiden, no. 47A9

to 'peasant' cropping once the cane had been harvested — whereupon a fresh set of fields was prepared for the planting of the next season's sugar harvest. This was the famous system of *wisselbouw* or crop rotation which singled out Java's sugar industry from virtually all its major global counterparts.

Production of the industry's raw material did indeed take on some plantation-like characteristics, particularly after the *Cultuurstelsel* began to be phased out from about 1870 onwards. Over the course of time, cane ceased to be a 'peasant' crop in any meaningful sense of that word and came under the direct and close supervision of industry personnel. Even so, cane's continued location within the cycle of 'peasant' agriculture became and remained *the* defining characteristic of the Java industry. In this context, it is hardly possible to do more than skirt around (rather than address directly) the question of whether the 'peasantry' of mid-twentieth-century anthropology/sociology is a particularly useful concept to apply to the *bevolking* [i.e. the 'common people'] of the mid-nineteenth century. Colonial language-usage rarely if ever used the term *boer* or any other possible Dutch synonym for 'peasant', so, for better or for worse, we appear to be stuck with the term 'peasantry', however much the term might need to be qualified.

From Plantation to Padi-field

Well in advance of the inauguration of the *Stelsel* in 1830, the prime focus of commodity sugar production in Java had shifted from West Java, where it had been plantation-based, into the island's north-central and eastern districts, where sugar manufacture was based largely on the cultivation of cane in peasant rice fields. However tentatively, this shift was in evidence at various points along Java's Northeast Coast from at least the late eighteenth century onward, as was a context of state (i.e. VOC) intervention to promote it, something that likewise proved to be the way of the future.[179] From 1830 onward, however (as we shall see shortly), intervention of this kind took place in an unprecedented scale in the form of the *Cultuurstelsel* — as a result of which all vestiges of plantation-style production in the sense widely current in relation to sugar in the New World were swept away.

In consequence, and in further contrast to the situation in the Caribbean and elsewhere in the New World, sugar in Java was very far from being a monoculture, carried on (largely) in the absence of other significant cultivations. Indeed, the case was quite the contrary. Throughout the lowlands of the island's central and eastern districts, and in increasing quantities from 1830 onwards, cane was raised alongside other State Cultivations, notably crops for the dyestuff indigo, and — crucially — alongside main-crop 'peasant' rice and a variety of peasant-grown secondary crops or *palawija*, which ranged from sweet corn through to beans and onions. In short, the Java sugar complex was embedded within a very extensive multi-crop agrarian economy and located, however uneasily, within an elaborate annual cycle of peasant agriculture.

Eventually this degree of 'embedded-ness' became, or threatened to become, the industry's Achilles' heel. Predominantly, however, Java sugar's ability to exploit the land and labour of a densely settled peasantry was the key source of Java sugar's international comparative advantage. Even so, crucial questions remain about the dynamics of that exploitation: about how it was achieved and how it may have evolved over time. Categorically, in respect to agrarian matters, the *Stelsel* represented something altogether more far-reaching than 'business as usual'. As one leading modern scholar in the field has argued, 'the received view' that the *Cultuurstelsel* represented little more than 'the simple employment of existing methods of authority … is in need of some important clarification and qualification'.[180] As will be argued, the development of sugar as a State Cultivation in the middle decades of the nineteenth century, in tandem with the fiscal policies of the increasingly formidable colonial state, resulted in a situation in which the old ways of exploiting rural resources were melded with new ones.

---

[179] Knight, 'From Plantation to Padi-field', pp. 177-204.
[180] Elson, *Village Java*, pp. 183-4.

The key to this melding was the fact that rural Java on the eve of the *Cultuurstelsel* was far from being a simple, subsistence economy or one in which 'peasants' constituted a homogeneous social and economic formation. Indeed, rural resources of land and labour had long been organised for the commodity production of a variety of crops (sugar cane among them). In turn, this production was enmeshed in an elaborate regime of labour service which dated from the pre-colonial era but had in large measure survived subsequent Dutch colonial advance. One of its hallmarks was a rural working population organised quite specifically, it would seem, to provide both produce *and* labour to the state through the intermediary of the local elites of Javanese officials and headmen. Integral to this organisation, moreover, was a division of the rural workforce into categories of people who were differentiated (at least so it seemed to outsiders) in terms of the degree of their access to land, their 'preparedness' to offer themselves for labour service and other such considerations. It was on foundations such as these that the exploitation of land and labour evolved under the aegis of the *Cultuurstelsel* during the course of the mid-century decades.

Java Before the *Cultuurstelsel*: A 'Picnic' at Sea with Commissioner Nederburgh in 1798

A little scene enacted on the north coast of Central Java at the end of the eighteenth century, recorded in the published account of Commissioner SC Nederburgh's journey there in 1798[181], is highly instructive. Nederburgh's journey took place at a time when the Dutch Republic, temporary successor of the *ancien* regime in Holland and the Indies, was attempting to assert its control over the Indonesian possessions of the VOC, the monopoly trading company which had represented the power in 'the East' for the Netherlands for the previous two centuries, but which was now in bankruptcy. As the Republic's chief emissary, Mr Nederburgh — the title signified his status as a lawyer — was notionally the most powerful person in the colony: an individual who, in words of one recent authority, 'showed himself to be a man of a monstrous and delicate ego, whose desire for power knew no bounds'.[182] He would

---

[181] [Nederburgh, SC], *Journal der Reize van Mr SC Nederburgh, Gewezen Commissaris Generaal over Nederlands India, Langs Java's Noordoostkust, in 1798*, Amsterdam, W Holtrop, 1804, p. 3.

[182] Nederburgh had arrived in Java in 1793 as head of three Commissioners-General and 'became the supremo in Java until his return in 1799'. See Van Niel, *Java's Northeast Coast*, p. 53.

have travelled in some style, accompanied by a sizeable entourage, and he would have been received with high ceremony.

The journey would nonetheless have been a relatively slow one. The building of the great Post Road, a highway suited to European conveyances — with crucial assistance from teams of very Javanese water-buffalo on its more tortuous stretches — was still a decade away. Commissioner Nederburgh's progress through his realm took place, therefore, largely on-board ship. As such, it became the occasion for a repast at sea — a picnic on the water — which spoke eloquently of both colonial power and commodity production in Java in the late eighteenth century and of the legacy bequeathed by the colony's old order to the VOC's (eventual) successors in the mid-nineteenth century.

The Old Order: A Colonial Realm and Acquisition of Commodities

Sailing eastwards, the 500 kilometres from Batavia to Semarang — the main centre of Dutch power in Central Java and the seat of the powerful Governor of Java's Northeast Coast — Commissioner Nederburgh's vessel dropped anchor off the town of Pekalongan, a hundred kilometres or so west of his destination.[183] After heralding him with a nineteen-gun salute from the shore (at least, so they assured Nederburgh, who had been too far off to hear it), the chief local dignitaries hastened out to greet him in *praauws* laden with refreshments. Pekalongan was destined to become part of one of Java's key zones of industrialised sugar production during the course of the nineteenth century. In Nederburgh's day, however, sugar was still of minor importance there. Above all, rice — husked and unhusked *padi* grown by the area's peasantry — constituted the chief claim to the attention of the VOC and the people with whom the company dealt in its quest for commodities. Nevertheless, the relations of production that underpinned this quest, in Pekalongan itself and elsewhere in the Java lowlands by the end of the eighteenth century, remained a powerful influence on the progress of commodity production there in the century that followed — and on the production of sugar in particular.

The only individual specifically named in Nederburgh's account of the day he spent moored off the north coast of Central Java was the German-born 'Dutchman' Frederik Jacob Rothenbühler. Rothenbühler, who had arrived in Java three decades earlier when he was still in his teens, was about forty years old and the Dutch *Resident*

---

[183] See *Journal Nederburgh*, p. 3.

or — in his VOC guise — *Onderkoopman* (Subordinate Merchant) at Pekalongan. As such, he was the key figure in the colonial power structure in this part of provincial Java. By the time of Nederburgh's voyage, the *Resident* would have abandoned living in the increasingly dilapidated old Dutch fort, the *Beschermer* or Protector[184] with its stone walls and four bastions, built in the 1740s when the VOC had first made its appearance there. Like his counterparts elsewhere on Java's north coast (following local usage, the Dutch usually referred to these districts stretching eastwards from Cirebon as the *Pasisir*), he would have moved into altogether more congenial and airier accommodation in the nearby *Residentie*, the office-cum-residence of the chief official which lay at the physical centre of colonial power in the administrative divisions or Residencies of Java in the nineteenth century. What kind of man lived in the Pekalongan *Residentie* at the end of the eighteenth century is something that ultimately can only be guessed at. One later verdict on Rothenbühler — and one preserving a distinct flavour of a certain kind of late colonial sentiment — comes from F de Haan, the indefatigable Government archivist extra-ordinaire in Batavia from the early 1900s until the 1930s. De Haan, who was presumably fully familiar with the surviving written record, opined that the *Resident* was 'a very clever man but something of a bore with an exaggeratedly high opinion of the Native'.[185]

Rothenbühler was among that group of representatives of Dutch influence — VOC employees — who had begun to establish a presence on Java's north coast and in the island's Eastern Salient [the *Oosthoek*] from the middle of the eighteenth century onward. That presence was initially very much an armed one, but quickly settled down into something altogether more 'civil', dominated on the Dutch side by Company men who drew their incomes from commissions, trade on their own account and — in many cases — from whatever they could glean in the form of bribes and the like from the people with whom they dealt. In this latter respect, according to one modern authority, Rothenbühler 'was regarded as an honest and devoted servant of the company', which was a good deal more than could be said of many of his contemporaries.

In the decades that followed, institutionalisation proceeded inexorably, albeit at a slow and somewhat erratic pace, and the successors of Rothenbühler and his

---

[184] P Bleeker, 'Fragmenten eener Reis over Java', *Tijdschrift voor Nederlandsch-Indië*, vol. 2, 1849, pp. 262-70, here pp. 266-7.

[185] F de Haan, 'Personalia der Periode van het Engelsch Bestuur over Java', *Bijdragen tot de Taal-, Land-en Volkenkunde*, vol. 92, 1935, pp. 477-681, here p. 634.

ilk were gradually formed into a powerful bureaucracy of salaried officials, which became and remained one of the distinguishing hallmarks of the Dutch colonial state in the Indies.[186] Rothenbühler himself served under successive post-VOC regimes, including the regime established under the occupation of Java by the British between 1811 and 1816. Only with the colony's restoration to the Dutch did he finally retire, though not to the Europe that he had left in his youth. Instead, he settled himself near Surabaya, the 'capital' of East Java, as head of a household that boasted more than a hundred domestic slaves — among them, presumably, given the prevailing mores, a fair number of concubines and musicians as well as household servants.[187] Retirement evidently agreed with him: he lived there for another twenty years before dying, full of years, at the age of seventy-eight.

On that April day in 1798, however, Rothenbühler was not alone in sailing out to present his respects to Commissioner Nederburgh. With him on the flotilla of Indonesian craft were his three Javanese *Bupati* subordinates. Designated as Regenten or 'Regents' by the Dutch, they were there to represent the *Priyayi* elite at whose apex they stood. The most senior of them was Raden Adipati Jayaningrat, then thirty-two years of age. He had been the *Bupati* of Pekalongan since 1789, when he had been appointed by the Dutch to succeed his murdered father.[188]

Under the suzerainty of Mataram, the dominant Javanese state that the Dutch had encountered on their arrival on the island at the end of the sixteenth century, the *Priyayi* were both state functionaries ('courtiers') and local power-holders. They retained much of these complex loyalties well into the nineteenth century. In

---

[186] See HW van den Doel, *De Stille Macht: De Europese Binnenlands Bestuur op Java en Madoera, 1808-1942*, Amsterdam, Bert Bakker, 1994; and C Fasseur, *De Indologen: Ambtenaren voor de Oost, 1825-1950*, Amsterdam, Bert Bakker, 1993.

[187] Frederik Jacob Rothenbühler was born in Zweibrücken circa 1758, arrived in Java in 1771 and died in Surabaya on 21 April 1836. In 1809, he became *Gezaghebber* [Commander] of the *Oosthoek*, and by 1811 had become *Raad Extraord. van Indie Supernumerair*. In 1812, he was appointed, along with J Knops and PH van Lawick van Pabst, and under the direction of Colonel Colin Mackenzie, to what became known as the Mackenzie Land Tenure Commission, with a broad brief to inquire into reform of the existing Government system in Java. See Van Niel, *Northeast Coast*, pp. 26-7, 242; and Ketjen, E, 'Levensbericht van FJ Rothenbuhler', *Verhandelingen Bataviaasch Genootschap van Kunsten en Wetenschappen*, vol. 41, 1881, pp. 71-3. For the lifestyle of high officials of the era, *inter alia* their seraglios, and for developments in the administration in general, see Boomgaard, *Children of the Colonial State*, pp. 14-15.

[188] Van Niel, *Northeast Coast*, p. 83.

Pekalongan, for example, it was reported as late as the 1860s that the *Bupati* (as well as 'the common people') still perceived the Javanese Courts of Central Java as the centre of their world.[189] *Bupati* and lesser *Priyayi* officials constituted a 'native' administrative corps, known as the *Pangreh Praja*, which was a critical element in the reconstruction of the sugar industry in the mid-nineteenth century. As such, they were subject to Dutch pressure but also needed to be accommodated if colonial ends were indeed to be achieved.[190]

Along with the three *Bupati*, however, were two other individuals, neither Dutch nor Javanese, but of Chinese descent. Their presence on board the flotilla was a further indication, should one need it, of the complex nature of local power,

---

[189] 'Solo is immer de Negari van het land' ['Solo remains the centre of their realm'], PV, Pekalongan, 1857 [unpaginated], AD, Pekalongan, no. 5.

[190] The classic accounts are: Heather Sutherland, 'The Priyayi', *Indonesia*, vol. 19, 1975, pp. 57-79; Sutherland, *The Making of a Bureaucratic Elite*, Singapore, Heinemann, 1979; Onghokham, 'The Residency of Madiun: Priyayi and Peasant in the Nineteenth Century', PhD Diss, Yale, 1975; James Rush, *Opium to Java: Revenue Farming and Chinese Enterprise in Colonial Indonesia 1860-1910*, Ithaca, NY, Cornell University Press, 1990. The origins of the relationship between Dutch colonisers and Javanese and Chinese-Indonesian elites dated in this part of Java from the middle of the eighteenth century, when the whole of the island's northern *Pasisir* came under the suzerainty of the VOC. From the mid-eighteenth century onward, exploiting its new position of political power along the length of the *Pasisir* and utilising what were presumably existing Chinese commercial networks and connections with Javanese power-holders, the company began to demand rice and other commodities — including sugar — from the *Bupati* over whom it was now suzerain. For discussion of the dominant political economy of Java in the eighteenth and early nineteenth centuries with reference to specific regions, see e.g. Mason C Hoadley, *Towards a Feudal Mode of Production: West Java 1680-1800*, Singapore, Institute of Southeast Asian studies, 1994, pp. 3ff.; Luc Nagtegaal, *Riding the Dutch Tiger: The Dutch East India Company and the Northeast Coast of Java 1680-1743*, Leiden, KITLV Press, 1996; Gerrit Knaap, 'Maritime Trade in Small-Town Java around 1775', in Peter Boomgaard, Dick Kooiman & Henk Schulte Nordholt (eds), *Linking Destinies: Trade, Towns and Kin in Asian History*, Leiden, KITLV Press, 2008, pp. 81-98; Van Niel, *Northeast Coast*; Kwee Hui Kian, *The Political Economy of Java's Northeast Coast c. 1740-1800: Elite Synergy*, Leiden & Boston, Brill, 2006; PBR Carey, 'Waiting for the "Just King": The Agrarian World of South-Central Java from Giyanti (1755) to the Java war (1825)', *Modern Asian Studies*, vol. 20, no. 1, 1986, pp. 59-137; Boomgaard, *Children of the Colonial State*, pp. 11-31; Merle C Ricklefs, 'Some Statistical Evidence on Javanese Social, Economic and Demographic History in the Later Seventeenth and Eighteenth Centuries', *Modern Asian Studies*, vol. 20, no. 1, 1986, pp. 1-32; Ricklefs, *War, Culture and Economy in Java, 1677-1726*, Sydney, Allen & Unwin, 1993; Ricklefs, *Jogjakarta under Sultan Mangkubumi, 1749-1792: A History of the Division of Java*, London, Oxford University Press, 1974.

influence, wealth and ethnicity in the decades prior to the introduction of the *Cultuurstelsel*. In Pekalongan as in other parts of the *Pasisir*, the locally born Chinese-Indonesians were often termed *peranakan*, or 'sons of the soil'. Like many of their Dutch contemporaries, such people tended to be markedly acculturated to their Javanese milieu. In some cases, they had been settled on the island for generations, though — again like their Dutch counterparts — without necessarily losing ties to their homeland.[191]

Too much should not be made of the 'ethnic' distinctions implied in this terminology. The notionally tripartite division of colonial society into 'Europeans', 'Chinese' and 'Natives' was still some way off in the future. In the particular case of Pekalongan, for example, something of the awkwardness of trying to portray the situation within a latter-day ethnic terminology emerges from the fact that the area's 'Javanese' *Bupati* had Chinese forbears. Regent Jayaningrat of Pekalongan himself was quite unambiguously of part-Chinese descent, and early in the nineteenth century he was reckoned to derive two-thirds of his total income from the leasing of villages to Chinese-Indonesian interests, in an arrangement that had probably held good for some time prior to that. As one Dutch scholar has observed, 'these groups [Dutch, Javanese and Chinese] were not separate from one another, whether socially, politically or economically; in many respects they were indeed locked into mutual interdependency'.[192]

One of the two Chinese-Indonesian men accompanying Rothenbühler was the so-called Captain China of the town of Pekalongan itself. He was the person, that is to say, who was appointed by the Dutch to head the substantial community of Chinese-Indonesians who were settled there. Late in the eighteenth century, among the towns of the *Pasisir*, Pekalongan was reckoned to be second only to Semarang — the north-coast metropolis that gave access to the rich interior of Central Java

---

[191] See the succinct discussion in Rush, *Opium*, pp. 90-2. Several sources from the early nineteenth century reserve the term *peranakan* to describe locally settled Chinese who had converted to Islam. See e.g. Residency Report Semarang 1823 (Domis), pp. 288-9, NA, Collectie Schneither, 91, and 'Knops' Description 1814', Mackenzie Collection (Private), 79, p. 270, India Office Library, London. See also Mason C Hoadley, 'Javanese, Peranakan & Chinese Elites in Cirebon: Changing Ethnic Boundaries', *Journal of Asian Studies*, vol. 47, no. 3, 1988, pp. 503-17, here pp. 505-8; PBR Carey, 'Changing Javanese Perceptions of the Chinese Communities in Central Java', *Indonesia*, vol. 37, 1984, pp. 1-47, here pp. 3-16; Van Niel, *Northeast Coast*, pp. 101-20.

[192] Nagtegaal, *Dutch Tiger*, p. 5.

— in terms of the size of its Chinese community. By the 1820s, the town's Chinese quarter had a population of well over 1000 men, women and children. It was located across the river from the Javanese Regent's Court or *dalem*, the main mosque and the market, and comprised

> a row of dwelling houses, amounting to perhaps fifty to sixty. To the north and south it is defended by wooden palisades ... [T]he houses are joined one to another, with high stories; towards the west is the Kap-pit-tans residence, to the right of which is a garden, which may be about one acre in extent, beautifully shaded with trees ...[193]

The '*Kap-pit-an*' himself, however, was not the most important of the two Chinese-Indonesians aboard the boats that sailed out to greet Nederburgh. A person of altogether greater consequence was the leaseholder of the district of Ulujami, to the west of the town of Pekalongan itself. Leased from the VOC, Ulujami was at that time a rich, rice-producing area, described in the 1780s as 'the granary of Semarang'.[194] Run by Chinese-Indonesians, its workforce largely comprised Javanese peasants: around 1803, there were estimated to be about 8000 of them living there, not counting their children.[195]

---

[193] Ong Tae Hae, *The Chinaman Abroad: An Account of the Malayan Archipelago, Particularly Java*, translated by WH Medhurst, London, John Snow, 1850, pp. 11-12. According to 'Statistiek Pekalongan 1821', B/2, there were 668 men, 658 women and 928 children, approximately half of whom (664 adults, 406 children) lived in the Chinese *kampong* at Pekalongan itself (NA, Collectie Schneither, 90). Some twenty-five years later, the Chinese population there amounted to 1900 souls, out of a total urban population roughly estimated at 15 000: see Bleeker, 'Reis', pp. 266-7.

[194] On Ulujami, see Peter Boomgaard, 'A Bird's Eye View of the Economic and Social Development of the District of Comal, 1750-1940', in Hiroyoshi Kano, Frans Hüsken & Djoko Suryo (eds), *Beneath the Smoke of the Sugar Mill*, Yogyakarta, AKATIGA/Gadjah Mada University Press, 2001, pp. 9-37, here pp. 9-21; Ong, *Chinaman Abroad*, p. 13; Van Niel, *Northeast Coast*, pp. 108-9. The district of Ulujami (along with adjacent areas) was leased by the VOC to the Chinese Captain at Semarang, Tan Tok, and administered by his nephew Tan Tjienko ('... the same is no further subordinate to the Resident than only with respect to the shipping of produce, wherefore this post is one of the most agreeable that can be wished for ...'). See 'Rothenbuhler Report 1798', p. 64, Mackenzie Collection (Private), no. 7, India Office Library, London. The leasing of Ulujami to Chinese-Indonesian interests, which apparently dated from the outset of the VOC regime on the Northeast Coast in the 1740s, persisted until 1813 (John Bastin, *Raffles' Ideas on the Landrent System in Java*, The Hague, Nijhoff, 1954, pp. 164-6).

[195] 'Memorie van den Resident Willem Beekman ... 25 Augustus 1803' [unpaginated], in AD, Pekalongan, no. 48.

In European accounts, the leaseholder was called Tan Yok or Tan Tok.[196] He had presumably travelled from Semarang for the occasion, for he was the 'Captain China' there and member of one of the city's leading business families. His nephew, Tan Tjienko, actually managed the Ulujami estate. The 'Captain China's' descendants maintained links with Pekalongan and the neighbouring Residency of Tegal for much of the nineteenth century. The family's interests there (as we shall see) were accommodated in the colonial schemes for expanding the sugar industry in this part of the *Pasisir*, which began to come into play after 1830. Indeed, the Tan dynasty was one of Semarang's foremost mercantile clans in the nineteenth century: in common with the Han family of Surabaya the Tans were, as one recent researcher has observed,

> keen exploiters of the tax farming industry of the *Pasisir*. Assuredly, the Semarang and Surabaya Chinese captains were the foremost merchants of the key commodity of Central and East Java, rice, as well as sugar, salt and other products, shipping large quantities to Melaka, Johor, Siak and beyond ... The Towkays [i.e. big Chinese business men] collaborated closely with Company personnel in administrative, business and other matters ... [T]he Towkays certainly played their cards right. Company administrators on the *Pasisir* needed an economic partner who had local expertise, sufficient resources to cater for their needs, and was cooperative ... The keyword here is mutual benefit ...[197]

Commodity Production: Cotton, Indigo, Sugar and Rice

All those aboard the little flotilla, that is to say, were involved in the exploitation of commodity production in the region. By the late eighteenth century, production of this kind embraced the manufacture of the dyestuff indigo and of sugar as well as the production of cotton thread. Nonetheless, by far the greatest commodity produced

---

[196] Van Niel, *Northeast Coast*, p. 109.

[197] Kwee Hui Kian, 'Cultural Strategies, Economic Dominance: The Lineage of the Tan Bing in Nineteenth Century Semarang', in Boomgaard et al., *Linking Destinies*, pp. 197-218; Kwee, *The Political Economy of Java's Northeast Coast, c. 1740-1800*, pp. 164-71. Kwee notes, for example, that Tan Tiang Tjhing (1770-1833) had closer relations with the Dutch authorities in Semarang, and the VOC's Governor of the Northeast Coast, based at Semarang, defended the leasing of Ulujami to the Tans against queries from the Netherlands. (He was presumably in receipt of kick-backs for approving the deal.) The Tan family had various links to the sugar industry in this part of Java in the mid-nineteenth century. They extended into the Batang area to the east of Pekalongan town, and the Captain China of Semarang owned a sugar mill there as early as 1764. See Boomgaard, 'District of Comal', pp. 17-18.

and traded along the length and breadth of the *Pasisir* in the late eighteenth century and at the beginning of the nineteenth was rice.[198] Notionally at least, the bulk of production of all kinds reached the Dutch through the agency of the *Bupati*, in the form of contractually agreed 'Contingents' and 'Forced Deliveries'. In this respect, as in many others, conditions in the lowland localities of East and Central Java were so various as to make it sensible to speak not of one Java but of many. Nonetheless, we can make several broad generalisations. One is that the prevailing rural political economy fused elements of what is sometimes referred to as 'subsistence peasant cultivation' with wide-spread production of commodities for both local and distant markets. A second such generalisation is that the day-to-day business of accessing agricultural production was — and remained — heavily dependent on mutually advantageous understandings between the emergent colonial state and various powerful local interests.

These latter included, obviously enough, the *Bupati* and the Chinese-Indonesian traders and entrepreneurs with whom they were often closely associated. By the 1820s, however — a decade prior to the inauguration of the *Cultuurstelsel* and all that it implied for the evolution of commodities and the relations of production which underpinned their supply — they had been joined by others. Colonial resources had begun to remark upon the presence of Arabs — most likely locally acculturated or recently arrived members of the Hadhrami 'diaspora'[199] — as well as the even more recent arrival of a number of privately-operating European and Armenian traders dealing in commodities of one sort or another. In Semarang in 1825, for example, when the outbreak of the Dipanagara uprising ('the Java War') threatened the security of the town, the small contingent of merchant citizens who rode out against 'the rebels' (in many cases to their deaths) included individuals from both the latter ethnic groups.[200] In short, on the eve of the *Cultuurstelsel*, a diverse

---

[198] See e.g. Van Niel, *Northeast Coast*, pp. 121ff.

[199] William G Clarence-Smith, 'The Rise and Fall of Hadhrami Shipping in the Indian Ocean, c. 1750-c. 1940', in David Parkin & Ruth Barnes (eds), *Ships and the Development of Maritime Technology in the Indian Ocean*, London, Routledge Curzon, 2002, pp. 227-58; Frank Broeze, 'The Merchant Fleet of Java, 1820-1850', *Archipel*, vol. 18, 1979, pp. 251-69.

[200] PBR Carey, *The Power of Prophecy: Prince Dipanagara and the End of the Old Order in Java, 1785-1855*, Leiden, KITLV Press, 2008, pp. 613-14; Joseph Bremner to [?], Semarang, 4.9.1825, enclosure in J McLachlan [to Hugh MacMaster], London, 16.2.1826; Gillian Maclaine to Marjorie Maclaine, 8.10.1825 [copy], MacMaster MSS (in Private Possession, UK).

group of people controlled, or sought to control, commodity production through a variety of means.

Within this framework, a mass of fairly heterogeneous petty farming households carried on direct production, together with their attendant and (sometimes) dependent labourers — people whose significance will be discussed in some detail in the pages that follow. In standard terminology, they were 'peasants'. Some of their notionally surplus output may have been marketed directly. It is safe to assume, however, that the bulk of it was expropriated through imposts on crops authorised by the state and carried out through the agency of *Priyayi* power-holders.[201] At the same time, 'surplus' labour was likewise expropriated through the medium of corvée.

Indeed, labour service of one kind or another lay at the heart of all these arrangements. Just how central it was is indicated by the fact that the standard measurement of rural resources in lowland Java in the late eighteenth century was the *cacah*, a unit probably best described as combining land per se with the amount of labour service (and hence people) that it would provide.[202] In 1798, when Rothenbühler set about enumerating the resources of the Residency under his charge, he recorded the assets of Pekalongan's *Bupati* in terms of the number of *cacah* that they possessed.[203] In some of its dimensions at least, it may be argued that 'pre-colonial' Java (which the Dutch were increasingly infiltrating from the mid-eighteenth century onward) was possessed of a labour service regime whose only real parallel in the region was in distant Siam. Attempts by colonial regimes in the early nineteenth century to replace these arrangements with a direct tax on the cultivators

---

[201] Arrangements through which Chinese-Indonesians obtained control over the *Bupati*'s rights over the produce and manpower of the countryside, common enough everywhere on the north coast at the end of the eighteenth century, were particularly extensive in Pekalongan Residency. In 1808, for example, the Regent of Pekalongan was reckoned to derive two-thirds of his total income from the leasing of villages to Chinese interests. See 'Bijl. [no. 6] Behoorende tot de Memorie van den Paccalongangsche Resident JA Middelkoop', 1808, AD, Pekalongan, no. 48.

[202] Rothenbuhler, for instance, '… was aware that the word cacah means number, and that the complete expression would be *cacah karya*, or the amount of land necessary for the upkeep of one household capable of providing the ruler with one corvée labourer. The same *cacah karya* was also a unit of taxation, because, if no corvée was required, this unit should yield a specified amount of tax'. See Boomgaard, *Children of the Colonial State*, appendix 1: 'What is a cacah', p. 207.

[203] 'Rothenbuhler Report 1798', p. 64, Mackenzie Collection (Private), no. 7, India Office Library, London.

— the so-called *Landrente* — had only limited success in many areas[204], due in part at least to the resilience of an altogether older political economy. Indeed, in many areas of Java, members of *Priyayi* elite arranged to pay the *Landrente* (notionally) levied on 'their' villagers in return for harvest levies. In some districts, at least, they did so in association with local Chinese traders, who thereby gained access to commodities at favourable rates.

In short, on the eve of the introduction of the *Cultuurstelsel*, a long-standing system of imposts and levies — in kind and, above all, in labour — was still firmly in place in rural Java, and formed the basis for commodity production everywhere on the island with the exception of the *Ommelanden* around the colonial capital of Batavia. In one key dimension, the system was sanctioned by long usage and brute force, and 'legitimated' at a functional level by the cultivator's quest for security in a landscape in which settlement was still widely interspersed by forest and waste. The system was presumably also based on intricate, elaborate and time-honoured accommodations which permeated the entire rural political economy, and on the arrangements for general commodity production which were based on it.

Sugar as a 'State Cultivation' from 1830 till about 1880

Much has been written about the *Cultuurstelsel* and about the role sugar played in it. Perspectives have been rich and varied, many of them reflecting a fascination with its impact, both short- and long-term, on the socio-economy of rural Java.[205] From

---

[204] WR Hugenholtz, 'Landrentbelasting op Java, 1812-1920', Proefschrift, Universitiet Leiden, 2008; WR Hugenholtz, 'The Land Rent Question and its Solution, 1850-1920', in Robert Cribb (ed.), *The Late Colonial State in Indonesia: Political and Economic Foundations of the Netherlands Indies 1880-1842*, Leiden, KITLV Press, 1994, pp. 139-72.

[205] For a succinct introduction to the history of the era, see Vincent JH Houben, 'Java in the Nineteenth Century: Consolidation of a Territorial State', in Howard Dick et al., *The Emergence of a National Economy: An Economic History of Indonesia, 1800-2000*, Sydney, Asian Studies Association of Australia in association with Allen & Unwin, 2002, pp. 56-81. The account in the following pages draws extensively on, and is greatly indebted to, a number of accounts written over the last few decades, beginning with C Fasseur, *Kultuurstelsel en Koloniale Baten*, Leiden, Universitaire Pers, 1975 (translated and edited by RE Elson & Ary Kraal as *The Politics of Colonial Exploitation*, Ithaca NY, Southeast Asia Program, Cornell University, 1992); RE Elson, *Javanese Peasants and the Colonial Sugar Industry: Impact and Change in an East Java Residency, 1830-1940*, Singapore, Oxford University Press, 1984; Elson, *Village Java*; Lukman Soetrisno, 'The Sugar Industry and Rural Development: The Impact of Cane Cultivation for Export on Rural Java, 1830-1934', PhD Diss, Cornell University, 1980; MR Fernando, 'Peasants and Plantation: The Social Impact of the European Plantation Economy

the standpoint of the present argument, however, the crucial facts have to do with its role in making possible the industrial project. Developments post-1830 did not initiate the rise of sugar as a significant commodity in Java, but sugar did vastly expand its grip on the island. Indeed, during the decades that followed, sugar cane became the hegemonic — though, as we shall see, far from exclusive — crop in huge tracts of the lowlands of the island's eastern and central districts. It also became a major agricultural staple in those areas of the interior of Central Java — the so-called *Vorstenlanden* or Principalities of Yogyakarta and Surakarta — which existed outside the direct operation of the *Cultuurstelsel* itself.[206] Important as was the mid-century development of sugar production in the *Vorstenlanden*, however, it was in the so-called Government Lands (i.e. the directly ruled parts of the island) that the industrial project in sugar reached its highest stage of development. It did so under the aegis of that *Cultuurstelsel* that had been inaugurated in 1830 and was to last (as far as the raising of sugar cane itself was concerned) until its phased dismantlement during the 1870s and 1880s.

The way in which sugar production was organised within the framework of the *Cultuurstelsel* was essentially dualistic. The production of raw material took place on the basis of the commandeering by the state of Javanese peasant land and labour. At the same time, the state granted concessions to Government Contractors (all of whom were Dutch, Indies-Dutch or Chinese-Indonesians), whose business it was to ensure that peasant-raised cane was processed into commercial-grade sugar. In tandem, these two developments constituted the heart of the *Cultuurstelsel*. Compulsory peasant cultivation of cane took place under the supervision of Dutch and Javanese government officials and 'village' headmen. When ripe and ready for harvest, the

---

in Cirebon Residency from the Cultivation System to the End of the First Decade of the Twentieth Century', PhD diss, Monash University, Melbourne, 1982; Djoko Suryo, 'Social and Economic Life in Rural Semarang under Colonial Rule in the later Nineteenth Century', PhD Diss, Monash University, Melbourne, 1982; Robert Van Niel, *Java under the Cultivation System*, Leiden, KITLV Press, 1992; Frans van Baardewijk, *The Cultivation System: Java 1834-1880*, vol. 14 of Peter Boomgaard (ed.), *Changing Economy in Indonesia*, Amsterdam, Royal Tropical Institute (KIT), 1993.

[206] On the industry in the *Vorstenlanden*, see Bosma & Raben, pp. 121ff.; Bosma, 'Sugar and Dynasty in Yogyakarta', in Ulbe Bosma, Juan A Guisti-Cordero & G Roger Knight (eds), *Sugarlandia Revisited*, New York & Oxford, Berghahn Books, 2007, pp. 73-94 and — especially for its masterly account of the broader context of developments in the mid-nineteenth century in South-Central Java — see Vincent JH Houben, *Kraton and Kumpeni, Surakarta and Yogyakarta, 1830-1870*, Leiden, KITLV Press, 1994.

contracting manufacturers arranged for it to be cut and then carted to their mills, using a mixture of servile and notionally 'free' workers (see below).

In short, the *Cultuurstelsel* provided the Contractors with both an assured supply of raw material and much of the workforce necessary to process sugar in what remained, despite increasing amounts of new industrial-style equipment, a heavily labour-intensive industry. It did so, moreover, in a context in which each of the 100 or so 'contract' factories set up under the *Stelsel* was assigned a so-called *beschikkingskring* or, more simply put, a *kring* — a term that translates rather awkwardly as 'circle of disposal or exploitation'.[207] It was from fields within the *kring* that the factories contracted to the Indies Government obtained their raw material and drew much of their labour. Albeit in a thoroughly contingent fashion, this created a flexible basis for the production of its raw material, which set the Java industry apart from virtually all its major counterparts in the international sugar economy. As we shall see in a later chapter, it had profound consequences for the industry's continuity and ability to expand.

The Imperatives of Raising Cane

Famously, cane sugar worldwide required heavy inputs of labour into both plantation and manufacturing sectors if profitable levels of output were to be achieved and maintained. In nineteenth-century Java, these requirements were greater than almost anywhere else in the international economy of cane sugar. This was because its industry, virtually unique among major contemporary producers, eschewed the practice of ratooning, whereby cane was grown year after year from the stumps of the previous crop. Instead, in the case of Java, cane was generally planted anew each season, as was dictated by the system of crop rotation or *wisselbouw* which, as we have already seen, became the dominant mode of cane cultivation once the *Cultuurstelsel* had got underway.

Crop rotation, in turn, reflected both socio-economic and agricultural imperatives. It appears to have evolved in part as a way of minimising the disruption caused to 'village Java' by the rapid expansion post-1830 of sugar production, in so far as cane could be 'fitted in' to the existing agricultural cycle. Crop rotation also had other advantages. It allowed the rapid expansion of production through the planting

---

[207] See e.g. Elson, *Javanese Peasants*, pp. 35-46; and Fasseur, *Colonial Exploitation*, p. 34.

of cane on existing farm-land and — as contemporaries could not have failed to be aware — had the potential for producing the consistently high yields of cane for which Java became internationally renowned. Ratooning, while saving on labour, did so at a cost. In the agricultural conditions of the mid-nineteenth century, it invariably led to a steady and appreciable fall-off in yields after the first crop. Rotation and annual replanting suffered from no such disadvantage. Instead, they held out the promise of cane that was always 'first crop' and commensurately high-yielding.

Under the aegis of the *Stelsel*, the typical mid-nineteenth-century schedule of work in sugar began with the harvesting of *sawah* rice around April and May of each year. The land assigned to sugar was then repeatedly ploughed, using water-buffalo and wooden ploughs.[208] Contemporaneous with this process of opening up, drying out and 'sweetening' the soil [*uitzuuring*], there also took place the construction of access roads and — most important of all — an elaborate grid of ditches, designed as much to lead water off the standing cane as to irrigate it while in the early stages of growth. Cane was then planted in furrows using rooted cuttings taken from the tops of the previous year's planting of now ripened cane. Once planted — and planting was usually completed by September — the young cane needed to be kept free of weeds, banked-up, irrigated and sometimes fertilised, though this was rare in the mid-century. It was also necessary to construct, and keep in good order, stout bamboo fences around each plantation complex, which might otherwise suffer significant damage from the inroads of wild boar. After several months of growth, this demanding schedule of maintenance eased up considerably, since the semi-mature cane created sufficient shade to inhibit weed growth and, during the west-monsoon, was more likely to suffer from wet feet than from any shortage of water. Even so, adverse climatic conditions at any time during the twelve- to fifteen-month growing season could cause major upheavals in the 'normal' work process. Serious flooding, for example, could wash out the cane and necessitate replanting, while high winds might flatten large tracts of well-established plantation and require extensive work to stand the crop up again.

---

[208] See e.g. JJ Tichelaar, 'De Exploitatie eener Suikerfabriek, Zestig Jaar Geleden', *ASNI*, vol. 33, no. 2, 1925, pp. 248ff.; G Roger Knight, 'The Peasantry and the Cultivation of Cane in Nineteenth Century Java', in A Booth, WJ O'Malley & A Weidemann (eds), *Indonesian Economic History in the Dutch Colonial Era*, New Haven, Yale University Southeast Asian Series, 1990, pp. 49-66.

When a sufficient area of the plantation was ripe enough for harvest, the Campaign began, usually some time in May of the year subsequent to planting. By then, the onset of the east-monsoon would generally have begun to create sufficiently dry conditions underfoot. Workers could then go into the plantation to hack down the cane with knives, tie it up in bundles and stack the bundles on carts to be hauled to the factory by the ubiquitous water-buffalo. Only at a very few mid-century factories was haulage partially mechanised through the installation of an iron tramway along which wagons were pulled by draft-animals between plantation and mill. Arrangements like this began in the 1860s and became more common as the century progressed. Once the cane had arrived at the factory — speed was of the essence, since the sucrose content of the cane deteriorated rapidly once it was cut — it was offloaded by hand and passed into the mills.

Most of the work inside the mid-century factory, and the compound that surrounded it, was of an entirely unmechanised nature, and highly labour-intensive. The manufacturing process itself required a great deal of manual labour, as did the removal of the expressed cane [*ampas*] from the mills themselves and its drying for subsequent use as fuel in the boiler house. In fact, the factory's furnaces consumed fuel far in excess of their stock of *ampas*, and had to rely on a great deal of cutting and carting of timber, at (presumably) an ever-increasing distance from the factory itself. Once the sugar had been manufactured and dried, it had to be packed and transported — usually by cart, less commonly by water — to wharves and warehouses on the coast, from where it could be shipped to a major port for export overseas.

Sugar and Servility: Provisioning the Industry with Labour[209]

In an important sense, the mid-century Java industry was every bit as dependent on servile labour as were its contemporaries in Cuba and Brazil, where slavery remained the norm until the 1880s. Nonetheless, the differences between Java and the major New World producers again far outweighed the similarities. Labour in Cuba (in particular) in the mid-nineteenth century evolved strongly in the direction of the barrack slavery of black African workers, who were shipped across the Atlantic in

---

[209] For a general introduction, see G Roger Knight, 'Sugar and Servility: Themes of Forced Labor, Resistance and Accommodation in Mid-Nineteenth Century Java', in Edward Alpers, Gwyn Campbell & Michael Salman (eds), *Resisting Bondage in Indian Ocean, Africa and Asia*, London & New York, Routledge, 2006, pp. 69-81.

ever-growing numbers during the mid-century decades.[210] In Java, forced labour in sugar developed in quite different ways and from a profoundly different foundation.

The prime, initial reason for this difference was quite straightforward. Work in the island's mid-century sugar fields and factories represented in some key dimensions a servility imposed on a settled local population of farmers and labourers — peasants, in short — who had long been incorporated (as we have seen) into a highly developed regime of labour service to the state and its local intermediaries. Within this overall context, however, servility took complex forms. In terms of access to land, Java's peasantry was markedly differentiated internally. Some peasants held more land than others, while some peasants held no land at all and were dependent for access on a variety of forms of share-cropping, tenantry and the like. In turn, this historically skewed access to resources was a vital factor in the commandeering of labour. The hegemonic positioning of the sugar industry within the larger framework of the agrarian society was contingent, that is to say, not only on the determination of state power-holders to support it, but also on the particular social and economic formation of rural Java.

A Heterogeneous Workforce: Corvée Labour, 'Government Coolies' and 'Free' Workers

As was also the case in the mid-century New World, Cuba included, the extensive workforce harnessed to the many-faceted demands of the contemporary Java sugar industry took on a multiplicity of forms.[211] Indeed, the Java workforce was probably even more heterogeneous than its Caribbean counterpart. The architects of the *Cultuurstelsel* had decreed that compulsory labour service, performed as corvée in the guise of *Cultuurdienst*, or Cultivation Service (a rather nice feudal invention on the part of Dutch officials), constituted the invariable basis for the cultivation of cane itself. Nonetheless, the other sectors of sugar production were serviced in a thoroughly heterogeneous fashion. Cutting and carting of cane at most factories was done by workers recruited (notionally at least) by the Sugar Contractors themselves, without recourse to corvée; and (as we saw in an earlier chapter) different and differing

---

[210] See e.g. Laird W Bergad, *Cuban Rural Society in the Nineteenth Century: The Social and Economic History of Monoculture in Matanzas*, Princeton, NJ, Princeton University Press, 1990, pp. 190-203, 228-39.

[211] E.g. Bergad, *Cuban Rural Society*, pp. 245-62.

arrangements prevailed for the work performed in the factories in which the cane was processed into sugar.

To be sure, in this latter sector of production, some workers were indeed assigned to the industry on the putative basis of their labour obligations to the state (aka corvée) and its local *Priyayi* officials. Such workers were designated as 'Government Coolies'. To a degree that varied considerably over time and place, however, the contracting manufacturers who owned and ran the factories were also supposed to recruit people designated — this time in non-feudal Dutch — as *vrijwilligers*, literally 'volunteers' and hence 'free labourers'. Sometimes these workers were also referred to as 'Free Coolies'. The term 'Coolie' was already on its way to becoming a general designation for 'native' workers rather than a relatively specific term for those who manually shifted heavy things.

Moreover, virtually all categories of labour were in receipt of some form of monetary payment. In the case of cane growers, this took the form of so-called crop pay or *plantloon* (see below), while in the case of virtually all other industry workers it took the form of a wage or dole, at levels often determined by the state. Embedded within the factories, moreover, was a core of skilled or semi-skilled workers and artisans who were generally in receipt of cash advances for their work for the entire milling season, and hence subject to some form of indenture, albeit of an 'informal' kind. There was no state-enforced penal sanction applicable to them (as was subsequently the case, however, with indentured workers elsewhere in the Netherland Indies).

Skewed Access to Rural Resources and the Basis of the Industry's Labour Supply

In stark contrast to later stereotypes of an island singularly packed with people, the agricultural environment of Java in the early and mid-nineteenth century was one in which settlement was still rather widely scattered in a countryside relatively well covered in woodland that provided a home to 'bandits', wild boar — and tigers.[212] The demography of nineteenth-century Java is an art not a science.[213] Probably, then as now, most of Java's population was concentrated in the interior of Central and East

---

[212] The point is singularly well-made (and elaborated) in Elson, *Village Java*, pp. 1-13.

[213] For perhaps the sanest survey of the demography, see Boomgaard, *Children of the Colonial State*, pp. 139-98.

Java. Nonetheless, there is good reason to suppose that along both the north coast of Central Java and in the *Oosthoek* east of Surabaya, there existed in the 1830s and 1840s pockets of dense settlement in which intensive wet-rice [*sawah*] agriculture had long been practised. Post-1830, it was into these pockets that the revived sugar industry attempted to nestle. To this extent, it is indeed true that the *Cultuurstelsel* era was not established — as were many of its global counterparts — on an agrarian frontier in which cultivation was limited and population sparse. Even so, labour was far from super-abundant in Java in the mid-century decades, and only became so late in the century or in the early years of the twentieth.

Under these circumstances, the key to forced labour in Java in the mid-nineteenth century was *not* to be found primarily in the sheer weight of numbers in the countryside. Rather, it was located in the skewed access to resources that characterised peasant society. In turn, this skewed access facilitated the growth of a kind of rural proletariat, in however 'disguised' a form.[214] Contrary to a once fashionable scenario that posited the industry's exploitation of a substantially homogeneous peasantry, the subordination of labour to the requirements of the large-scale production of cane was predicated on an existing and growing differentiation among Java's rural population into complex varieties of 'haves' and 'have-nots'.

The crucial dimension of this skewed access was the presence in the countryside of locally highly variable numbers of landless (or functionally landless) and dependent households. Such households appear already to have existed in locally varying numbers in the 1830s and 1840s and were markedly on the increase thereafter.

---

[214] See the key observation of Brass and Bernstein (in a more general setting) concerning '... the extent to which smallholding linked to colonial plantations was internally differentiated in socio-economic terms: that is, on the one hand, the better-off peasants, composed of proprietors and/or tenants whose main income derived from the sale of the product of labour rather than labour power itself, and on the other those "peasants", the majority of whose incomes came from the sale of labour power and not its product, *and who were as a result never anything other than labourers with temporary/conditional access to land rather than peasants who sold their labour power*. In other words, the extent to which repeasantisation was not so much a unilinear, once-for-all transition as a multiple and continuous process of transformation, that itself *hid an accompanying and underlying trend toward proletarianisation/deproletarianisation* [emphasis added]'. See Tom Brass and Henry Bernstein, 'Introduction: Proletarianisation and Deproletarianisation on the Colonial Plantation', in E Valentine Daniel, Henry Bernstein & Tom Brass (eds), *Plantations, Peasants and Proletarians in Colonial Asia*, London, Frank Cass, 1992, pp.1-40, here p. 15.

Generally designated as *menumpang*, they were family units who lived in or adjacent to the compounds of landholders. As such, they were distinguishable from *budjang*, generally portrayed as male workers who were not yet married, and from itinerants.[215] From at least the 1850s onward, a propensity was commented upon in the colonial record for those landholders on whom corvée was imposed to send their dependent, client labourers as substitutes. By the 1850s and 1860s there were wide-spread reports that the landholding or (as they were referred to in some accounts) sikep strata of the peasantry avoided labour service, either in part or in its entirety, and dispatched their *menumpang* to the cane fields and factories in their stead.[216]

The implications of this for our understanding of forced labour in Java in the mid-nineteenth century are far-reaching. In the context of labour mobilisation in general, brutal disciplining of village heads charged with responsibility for the turn-out of labour was one recourse, and at certain times and places no doubt critical. All the same, this was only part of the story. Coercion of the workforce was only possible in a sustained and systematic way because of a political economy in the countryside which left increasing numbers of rural workers dependent for their survival on something other than their own means of subsistence. Cane's hegemony in the agricultural cycle played some part in underpinning this feature of peasant society, in so far as cane's claim to land and irrigation water may well have helped push some marginal elements among the landed peasantry into the (functionally) landless category.[217] So, too, did the growing pressure of population on land, as a result of what seems generally agreed to have been increasing numbers in the mid-century countryside. Equally important, however, and closely related to these two factors, was the historical existence in the countryside of groups of workers with (at best) only marginal access to land. In the case of at least some of the work required by the sugar industry, the state's ability

---

[215] For a brief guide to definitions (e.g. 'The entire group of landless families is normally indicated with the name (me)numpang'), see Boomgaard, *Children of the Colonial State*, pp. 59-67.

[216] For the situation as it had developed, e.g. in the Pekalongan area by the 1860s, see G Roger Knight, 'Peasant Labour and Capitalist Production in Late Colonial Indonesia: The Campaign at a North Java Sugar Factory 1840-1870', *Journal of Southeast Asian Studies*, vol. 19, no. 2, 1988, pp. 245-65, here p. 256; Knight, 'The Peasantry and the Cultivation of Cane', passim.

[217] See e.g. G Roger Knight, '"The People's Own Cultivations": Rice and Second Crops in Pekalongan Residency, North Java, 1800-1870', *Review of Malay and Indonesian Affairs*, vol. 19, no. 2, 1985, pp. 1-38.

effectively to enforce labour on its behalf was fairly clearly conditional on the degree of their presence.[218]

Indeed, it looks as if the locally varying ratio between landed and landless was indeed a key factor — possibly even *the* key factor — in the effective implementation of a system of servile labour in the sugar industry. Along the sugared north coast of Central Java, in particular, there were contrasts in the effectiveness of the *Cultuurstelsel* in promoting the expansion of the sugar industry which point to some such explanation. There was a revealing difference, for example, between the situation in the adjoining (and later amalgamated) Residencies of Tegal and Pekalongan. In this area of Central Java, sugar had been a very small-scale industry in the pre-1830 period, but a dozen or more sugar factories were subsequently established there under the aegis of the *Cultuurstelsel* — with very mixed results.

In Tegal Residency, and particularly in the districts immediately to the south of the city of Tegal itself, sugar had taken firm hold by the 1840s. For their owners, five of the six factories that operated there (Adiwerna, Djatibarang, Doekoewringin, Kemanglen and Pagongan) were profitable concerns. Further to the east, however, in Pekalongan Residency (and also in the eastern districts of Tegal itself), the situation of the three factories established there in the mid-nineteenth century (Wonopringgo, Sragie and Kalimatie) was rather different. Of these, Wonopringgo alone, in the quite exceptional circumstances outlined in the previous chapter, started to show a profit in the 1850s, whereas it was only in the following decade, that, taken as a whole, the sugar industry there began to flourish in terms of production and productivity.

Of course, there were many reasons for this. These reasons related to the over-exploitation of the area's agricultural resources and repeated clashes between the Residency, leading *Priyayi* and Chinese-Indonesian interests over a period of two decades or more. There may also have been significant ecological factors militating against the expansion of the industry. Nonetheless, one of the key differences between parts of Tegal and the Pekalongan Residency related to labour. In the former Residency,

---

[218] One highly respected authority apparently reads the prevalence of *menumpang* quite differently, viz. as a way of *escaping* the full burden of the demands for labour service (Elson, *Village Java*, p. 384, fn. 491). The point is well-taken, but little explanation is provided for *how* some sections of the rural working population were able to take this option, while the provenance of the information — an unnamed Dutch official's pronouncement on this score, circa 1852, in relation to one district (Ngawi) in Central Java — is suggestive rather than conclusive.

there appear to have been rather more working households available to the industry in the *beschikkingkringen* [formal zones of exploitation] which were assigned to each of the factories than in the latter. Altogether more striking, however, was the contrast between Tegal and Pekalongan in terms of the availability not simply of labour itself but of (functionally) landless labourers who were potentially 'available' to the industry. Data from the 1850s, collected in some detail by colonial officials, is crucial here. It suggests that *menumpang* and the like were present in much greater numbers in some locations along the sugared north coast than in others.[219] In particular, it appears that in the prime sugar areas of Tegal over 40 per cent of the peasant households were landless *menumpang*, as opposed to a figure of around 18 per cent in the sugar areas of Pekalongan.[220]

These figures are certainly not unproblematic. Nonetheless, they point (at the very least) to the importance of differential access to resources within the peasantry in explaining the varying rates at which the sugar industry managed to establish a hold on agrarian resources as a whole. Where the number of dependent households was insufficient to create an adequate pool of *menumpang* and other landless workers, the ability of the state and its local agents, both Dutch and Javanese, to foster the industry's growth through the sufficient allocation of labour was correspondingly impaired.

In short, what ultimately made forced labour feasible was the extent of well-established and expanding asymmetrical relations of production *within* the peasantry

---

[219] The point was noted by Dekker (W Dekker, 'Tussen Zelfvoorziening en Commerciele Landbouw', Docteraalscriptie, Vrije Universiteit, Amsterdam, 1978, pp. 56-7) more than a quarter of a century ago, but without any substantial discussion of its implications.

[220] *Landed and Landless Households in the Sugar Kring of Tegal and Pekalongan around 1856*:

Residency	Households in Kring			Total Kring area of factories	Households per ha of Kring		
	Total	Landed	Landless		Total	Landed	Landless
Tegal	38 528	22 469	16 059	2590/8	14.87	8.65	6.20
Pekalongan	12 347	10 109	2238	1050/3	11.75	9.62	2.13

Source: 'Cultuurverslag 1851', for the area of the factory *kring* (Exh. 15.4.1853/12) and for the landed/landless elements in the population, see the data from the 'Umbgrove Monographies' (cited extensively in Elson, *Village Java*, passim). For the Tegal and Pekalongan sugar factories see NA, Collectie Umbgrove. The relevant sections of each 'Monographie' are 'III Bevolking binnen den kring der Onderneming/Vervolg B/Inheemsche bevolking/3/Verdeeling'.

of the lowlands of Central and Eastern Java. Any other conclusion rests far too heavily on the supposed coercive abilities of a colonial state that was, in fact, far from enjoying untrammelled power over the disposal of rural resources. The mid-century Indies regime simply did not have the sinew to sustain the requirements of a modern 'command economy': it was as yet only a 'half-formed bureaucracy' (the phrase is Heather Sutherland's) that was obliged, *faute de mieux*, to mix coercion with accommodation of the Javanese elites, above and within the 'village', with whom it had perforce to deal. As one leading student of colonialism has remarked (in a non-specific context):

> the colonial state existed in relation to different modes of production, each animated by people distinct from each other, distinctions that were crucial if clear order were to be preserved and if capital were to exploit the labour power it found in the colonies. Such labour power was not simply there for the taking; rather, the state had to hitch itself to the interests of indigenous elites in order to gain access to the labour power that imperial capital needed. Each colonial state had to manage a particularly complex set of contradictions, if that state were to promote the interests of 'its' economic actors in a competitive world economy …[221]

Coercion and Accommodation

In this context, the apparently persuasive argument of one highly respected Java specialist that 'terror and brute force were the cement of the nineteenth century colonial order' needs to be treated with some caution.[222] In fact, the state had, of necessity, to tread a fine line in terms of authority between the strong arm and the blind eye as far as the exercise of power was concerned.[223] A great deal also depended on the experience and character of the state's officials. In Pekalongan Residency in the early 1860s, for example, the *Resident* noted wryly that the handful of European *Controleurs* [District Officers] were too young and green 'to penetrate the cunning

---

[221] Frederick Cooper, *Colonialism in Question: Theory, Knowledge, History*, Berkeley, University of California Press, 2005, p. 51.

[222] PBR Carey, 'Review of J van Goor, *Kooplieden, Predikanten en Bestuurders Overzee: Beeldvorming en Plaatsbepaling in een Andere Wereld*', *Itinerario*, vol. 8, no. 1, 1984, p. 162.

[223] See e.g. G Roger Knight, 'The Blind Eye and the Strong Arm: The Colonial Archive and the Imbrication of Knowledge and Power in Mid-Nineteenth Century Java', *Asian Journal of Social Science*, vol. 33, no. 3, 2005, pp. 544-68.

of the native chiefs'.[224] Moreover, the hierarchy of *Priyayi* officials, on whom the Dutch had perforce to rely for the execution of their orders, had a command over the *wong cilik*, or common people, which was itself circumscribed by a variety of factors. Despite a propensity, particularly in the high offices of state in Batavia, to assume otherwise, the fact was that Javanese officials could not 'deliver' regardless of local circumstances. In short, there was nothing uniform about the extent to which the *Cultuurstelsel* was able to provide a solid agrarian underpinning for the expansion of sugar production which took place in the colony after 1830: on the contrary, outcomes varied considerably over both time and place.

The expansion of sugar manufacture throughout the island's eastern and central districts was indeed considerable. By 1850, some 30 000 hectares of peasant farm-land were being brought annually under cane for the factories working under Government contract.[225] The new industry's development was nonetheless a very uneven process. In the *Oosthoek*, sugar production of the kind prescribed by the architects of the *Cultuurstelsel* quickly took a firm hold during the course of the 1830s. High-ranking *Priyayi* did well from the *Cultuurprocenten* [Cultivation bonuses] with which the Indies Government sought to sweeten the labour both of its own officials and the Javanese power-holders through whom they worked. Peasant resistance (if that was indeed the proper word) certainly occurred, but it was minimised. Seasonal labour could be easily obtained from the nearby island of Madura, where the peasants themselves had always been more fertile than their fields. Moreover, a nucleus of manufacturers was already in place there by the late 1820s and — probably most significant of all — the extensive Chinese-Indonesian business networks of Surabaya and points east were evidently persuaded of the advantages to be gained from the new enthusiasm of the Indies Government for supplies of sugar.[226] For a couple of decades or more, Surabaya and the *Oosthoek* were the *Stelsel*'s star-performers.

Elsewhere, however, things went much less smoothly. In some parts of the *Pasisir* — notably the Pekalongan area already discussed — sugar was slow to take off. Not least, this was because other *Cultuurstelsel* commodities, above all the production of the organic dyestuff indigo, stood in the way, and played havoc with the kinds of accommodation on which the *Stelsel* depended. The problem was that state officials —

---

[224] AV, Pekalongan, 1863 [unpaginated], AD, Pekalongan, no. 6.

[225] Creutzberg, *Export Crops*, Table 7, p. 71.

[226] The indispensible account of developments in the mid-century *Oosthoek* is Elson, *Javanese Peasants*, passim.

at the centre of, and sometimes in, the Residency itself — appear to have entertained grossly unrealistic expectations about the agricultural potential of Pekalongan. It was something about which the then *Resident*, CFE Praetorius (and subsequently Director of Cultivations), cautioned the Batavia authorities in a defensive letter written to the Governor-General in August 1835:

> [In Pekalongan] up to now, circumstances operate against rather than for the Stelsel ... People consider Pekalongan suitable, yes perhaps even the most suitable of the coastal Residencies for all sorts of crops, rice not excluded. Neither the one nor the other notion seems to me well grounded.[227]

It was not until the 1860s, three decades after the inauguration of the *Stelsel*, that sugar began to flourish in Pekalongan Residency. There were several explanations, some of them aired at the time. High-ranking *Priyayi* and their Chinese-Indonesian associates — their interests hurt in this part of Java by developments that appeared to promise them little in return — proved 'recalcitrant' and found themselves at loggerheads with successive *Residents*, of whom there was a quite exceptionally large turnover in the mid-century decades.[228] One of them characterised Pekalongan's leading Chinese merchant, *Nonya* Oei Tay Lo (in one of the several Dutch versions of her name), as 'stubborn and grasping' in the extreme, qualities of which the Dutch were themselves fine judges.[229] This was a problem, because she appears to have dominated the commercial-financial world of Pekalongan Residency in the 1830s and perhaps in the following decade as well. *Nonya* Oei Tay Lo was reputed to control the trade in rice, both there and elsewhere in the *Pasisir* west of Semarang, and was the major creditor of both the Residency's leading *Priyayi*, the *Bupati* of Pekalongan and his counterpart further east in Batang, who was said to be 'in her lead strings'. She also owned at least two ships.[230] Crucially, moreover, her family held the Indies

---

[227] Resident Praetorius to GG 28.8.1835/946, ANRI, Asip Cultuurs, no. 46.

[228] For the *Residents*, see 'Stamboeken Indische Ambtenaren', MK. During the mid-century decades, Tegal had nine *Residents* and great continuity of office, notably Pieter van der Poel (1824-33), DA Varkevisser (1836-46) and JA Vriesman (1846-57). Pekalongan had some fourteen *Residents*, only one of whom, FH Doornik (1837-43), lasted any length of time; the rest stayed no more than two or three years, with the exception of GJP van der Poel (1852-57) — but he was seriously ill in the last two or so years of his tenure. Astonishingly, one *Resident* came back (or was sent back) for more: MH Halewijn (1828-31 and 1844-46) — though he was said to have enjoyed a particularly close and friendly relationship with the *Bupati* family of Batang.

[229] Vitalis, 'Report Pekalongan ... 1834', pp. 35-6, NA, Collectie Baud, 460.

[230] Vitalis, 'Report Pekalongan ... 1834', pp. 35-6, NA, Collectie Baud, 460; S van Deventer,

Government's opium farm for the area — the management of which would have underpinned their stranglehold on local trade as well as the lucrative business of selling the drug itself.[231] Matters seem to have come to a head in Pekalongan late in the 1840s, when the two incumbent *Bupati* were replaced by more malleable but perhaps less effective successors.[232] What happened to *Nonya* Oei Tay Lo is not clear.

Even so, it is worth stressing that histories of contest occurred as incidents in a system that worked towards, and generally achieved, a degree of accommodation between the parties concerned — *Residents, Bupati*, Chinese business people — which was fundamental to the rise of sugar in the mid-century decades. In Pekalongan itself, the NHM's Wonopringgo sugar factory, managed in the 1850s by the formidable Thomas Edwards (whom we met in the preceding chapter), was a case in point: 'accommodation' was manifest in a degree of understanding between the factory's management and the local *Priyayi*, led in this case by the Javanese District Head or *Wedana*. Before Edwards arrived at Wonopringgo in 1852, it had already been noted that the 'native chiefs' were regular visitors to the factory — and were accompanied on occasion by their wives and children, suggestive of a social as well as a purely functional dimension to the relationship.[233] Subsequently, the factory made 'loans' to the *Wedana* — though not without drawing so stony a response from company headquarters in Amsterdam that no further mention of the loans appeared in the correspondence.[234]

It was indicative of the continuing relationship of accommodation between the Wonopringgo factory and the local Javanese power-holders, moreover, that Edwards

---

Bijdragen tot de Kennis van het Landelijk Stelsel op Java, Zaltbommel, Joh. Noman & Zoon, vol. 2, 1865-1866, pp. 704-5; AV, Pekalongan, 1831, Bijl. F, AD, Pekalongon, no. 2 shows Oeij Tailo as owning two ships, one of 97 tonnes and the other of 150 tonnes; 'Aantekeningen ... Reise GG ad interim [JC Baud] Mei-Augustus 1834' [unpaginated], NA, Collectie Baud, 462; AV, Pekalongan, 1834 [unpaginated], NA, Collectie Baud, 391 shows that virtually all the Government farms of markets [*pasar*] and stalls [*warong*] are held by either Oei Tay Lo or Oei Ponggoan.

[231] The Opium farmer was identified in 1847 as 'Oeij Tankoie', and he was fined 4000 guilders for his *overtreding der pachtvoorwaarden*. See 'Civeel Teregtzetting Landraad Pekalongan, 16.3.1847', in AD, Pekalongan, no. 58.

[232] For instance, the 'PV, Pekalongan, 1858', p. 11, in AD, Pekalongan, no.1/5 noted that the *Bupati* of Pekalongan at that time had spent a long time in Sumanep, was in effect a stranger to the Regency and (not surprisingly, perhaps) showed 'little energy'.

[233] Rapport JC Teengs, 27.6.1850, in Factorij to A'dam, 24.7.1850/ 29.

[234] Factorij to A'dam, 24.10.1857/597 & 7.5.1859/737.

greeted the transfer in 1861 of a 'well-disposed' District Head — a 'cultivated [*beschaafd*] fellow', it was said — with great dismay in his reports to his employers. Dismay rapidly turned to relief, however, when it transpired that his successor came from the same family as the previous District Head and that 'he seems to be as sound and just as energetic a man as his predecessor'.[235]

By definition, accommodation was a two-way process. Edwards was well aware of this. A case in point related to his requisition of 'Government Coolies', the corvée labourers who formed the backbone of the workforce employed in and around the factory itself during the sugar Campaign, supplied through the intermediary of the *Wedana*. Edwards knew and accepted that a percentage of them would be retained by the Wedana for the *Wedana*'s own use. Edwards was likewise fully aware that if he made too heavy demands, for example, for the carting of firewood to the factory, it would be met by a reduction of co-operation from the District Head in relation to other facets of Wonopringgo's operations: 'Every favour of this sort given is an excuse for bad plantation', he remarked to his employers, because he would be informed that '… the cane planters are busy cutting wood and therefore cannot attend to the plantation …'[236] Most revealing of all, it looks as if Edwards was forced to back off when he tried to get the *Wedana* to interfere in person in a dispute with some cane-carters hired by the factory. Instead, he appears to have had to follow the *Wedana*'s advice that to do so would be quite contrary to the usages of the carefully organised hierarchy of provincial Java. '[I]t's no use in me talking directly with ordinary people', Edwards was apparently told. '[Instead] I'll tell one of my *lurahs* [village heads] to talk to the people.'[237]

In short, as these particular examples from one sector of the expanding industry suggest, the provision of labour to the sugar industry was subject to a variety of constraints. Commandeering by the state was far from a straightforward exercise, and

---

[235] Factorij to A'dam, 16.3.1861/940 & 2.5.1861/951.

[236] [Extract] Edwards to Factorij, 4.2.1854/742, in Factorij to A'dam, 25.2.1854/271.

[237] The [faulty] 'malay' text as reproduced by the NHM's Batavia *factorij* in a letter about the incident forwarded to company headquarters in Amsterdam reads: '*Saya rasa voor tjoemah bestjara sama orang ketjil. Saya poenia orang ketjil nanti loeroeh saya poenje parinta sadja*'. I am indebted to Professor Anton Lucas of The Flinders University of South Australia for the suggested reconstruction of the text to read (translated in the text, above): '*Saya rasa percuma bicara sama orang kecil, saya punya orang kecil nanti lurah saya punya [akan] perintah saja [orang kecil itu]*'. See Factorij to Directeur Cultuures, 31.1.1857/48 in Factorij to A'dam, 11.3.1857/533.

accommodation as well as coercion was the order of the day. So, too, as we have seen, was the permeation of systems of servile labour with cash payment and an increasing variety of different labour forms based on inducement as well as constraint. Devices for provisioning the industry with labour, moreover, were only one aspect, albeit a very important one, of the dynamics of the sugar industry's attempts to dominate rural Java. Equally critical was a degree of reconstruction of the peasantry as a whole.

Sugar and the Making of a Colonial Peasantry

There has been a tendency in the existing literature to envisage the rise of sugar in Java in the mid-nineteenth century primarily in terms of the adaptation for new purposes of old arrangements for exploiting the island's agrarian resources. In tandem, Java has often been viewed as a relatively unproblematic — albeit somewhat singular — case of 'sugar-with-peasants'. Neither position, however, seems quite right, and the present argument — hardly novel but well worth reiterating — is that existing arrangements for securing commodity production in rural Java formed only one of the bases for the huge expansion of the sugar industry which took place in the middle decades of the nineteenth century.

Sugar and peasants, in fact, did not simply *find* each other in Java in the mid-nineteenth century. In a crucial, though asymmetrical sense, they *made* each other, to an extent that seriously undermines any lingering suggestion that the industry expanded from the 1830s onward simply, or predominantly, by exploiting relations of production in the countryside which it left essentially undisturbed. In fact, a variety of factors were involved, prime among these the forging of an internally differentiated colonial peasantry out of what was previously a somewhat more amorphous mass of rural cultivators and labourers. Although the organisation of large-scale sugar production did indeed take on a form heavily influenced by the existing rural political economy of rural Java, it also evolved in ways with a pronounced dynamic of their own. In short, the 'symbiosis' of peasantry and sugar production needs to be unpicked with some care.

The essential argument here is that some (but by no means all) elements of the rural working population of Java in the mid-nineteenth century became more 'peasant-like' than had earlier been the case. In consequence, these workers were more easily subordinated to some (at least) of the requirements of the industrial project in sugar. In this context 'peasant-like' refers, above all, to what one participant in a now global debate has described as 'the creation out of a series of much more varied and flexible social formations of a more homogeneous society of petty arable producers working predominantly with family labour'.[238]

This concept of 'peasantisation' (the jargon is ultimately unavoidable) contrasts, of course, with any notion that there is something immutable, even primordial, about peasantry. Instead, it asserts that specific forms of peasantry emerged in tandem with capitalist expansion, commodity production and settled agriculture. *Inter alia*, colonial peasantries came into existence 'when the state set out to fix people in their locations so that they might be taxed and controlled better'.[239] In the case of Java, the Dutch sociologist Jan Breman has strongly argued that by the mid-century a series of developments can be seen at work, which had the effect of tightening the bond between sections of the cultivators and the land. Such developments made them more readily taxable and — in the circumstances of the State Cultivations organised by by the Indies Government in the mid-nineteenth century — 'corvée-able' by the state and its agents.[240]

In consequence, colonial Java is an excellent example of the way in which peasantry was not a trans-historical phenomenon but one formed and re-formed over time in particular and varying social and economic constellations. Peasantry was less a 'pre-capitalist survival' than a corollary and part-creation of capitalist modernity and of the colonialisms within which capitalism was encompassed. 'Capitalism is a system only obscured by the phenomena it produces', the sociologist Henry

---

[238] CA Bayly, 'Creating a Colonial Peasantry: India and Java c. 1820-1880', in Mushirul Hasan et al., *India and Indonesia from the 1830s to 1914: The Heyday of Colonial Rule*, Leiden, Brill, 1987, pp. 93-106, here p. 93. For an expansion of Bayly's views, see the section on 'The Consolidation of the Indian Peasantry', in Bayly, *Indian Society and the Making of the British Empire*, Cambridge, Cambridge University Press, 1988, pp. 138-45.

[239] DA Washbrook, 'Progress and Problems: South Asian Economic and Social History c. 1720-1860', *Modern Asian Studies*, vol. 22, no. 1, 1988, pp. 57-96, here pp. 80-1. In addition to the work on South Asia cited above, the avowedly eclectic approach to the issue of peasantisation adopted here owes something to the seminal writings of Frederick Cooper, e.g. 'Peasants, Capitalists and Historians: A Review Article', *Journal of Southern African Studies*, vol. 7, no. 2, 1981, pp. 284-314; and Jack Lewis, 'The Rise and Fall of the South African Peasantry: A Critique and Reassessment', *Journal of Southern African Studies*, vol. 11, no. 1, 1984, pp. 1-24.

[240] Jan Breman, *Control of Land and Labour in Colonial Java*, Dordrecht, Foris Publications, 1983, pp. 17-18; Breman, 'Village Java and the Early Colonial State', *Journal of Peasant Studies*, vol. 9, no. 4, 1982, pp. 189-240.

Bernstein has argued, and '… some of the phenomena of capitalism resemble those of pre-capitalist formations … which is the basis of (mistaken) articulationist notion of the "persistence" or "conservation" of pre-capitalist social relations and forms'.[241] Obfuscated as its development might be by a preference among colonial officials for a quasi-feudal terminology (for example, *Herendienst, Cultuurdienst*), a specifically *colonial* peasantry was in the process of formation. This peasantry served — in however contingent, contested and imperfect a fashion — the purposes of capitalist commodity production in general and the industrial project in sugar in particular.

To be sure, there are important counter-arguments here. Discussion of the subject has certainly advanced some considerable way since Clifford Geertz's celebrated hypothesis in the mid-twentieth century about the 'Agricultural Involution' of late colonial Java. The relevant aspects of Geertz's multi-faceted hypothesis were articulationist *avant le lettre*, in so far as they postulated that the industry represented an amalgam of Western capitalist enterprise with Eastern pre-capitalist land and labour embodied in a largely homogeneous, classless peasant society.[242] More recent research (much of it in archives) has begged to differ.[243] It has drawn attention to the extent of landlessness and wage labour, the emergence of entrepreneurial groups among the peasantry, and to the consolidation of peasant elites of substantial landholders. Nonetheless, otherwise divergent accounts remain largely at one in maintaining that the cultivators' long-standing status as *peasants* was certainly impacted upon but not undermined in the mid-century decades by the requirements of the expanding sugar industry. Explicitly or otherwise, these accounts seem to assert the long-standing existence of peasantry and its essential mid-century continuity.[244]

---

[241] H Bernstein, 'Capitalism and Petty Bourgeois Production: Class Divisions and Divisions of Labour', *Journal of Peasant Studies*, vol. 15, no. 2, 1988, pp. 258-71, here p. 261.

[242] E.g. Clifford Geertz, *Agricultural Involution: The Process of Ecological Change in Indonesia*, Berkeley & Los Angeles, University of California Press, 1963, pp. 97-8.

[243] See in particular Ben White, '"Agricultural Involution" and its Critics: Twenty Years after', *Bulletin of Concerned Asian Scholars*, vol. 15, 1983, pp. 18-31; RE Elson, 'The Cultivation System and "Agricultural Involution"', Working Paper no. 14, Centre of Southeast Asian Studies, Monash University, Melbourne; Elson, 'Clifford Geertz, 1926-2006: Meaning, Method and Indonesian Economic History', *Bulletin of Indonesian Economic Studies*, vol. 43, no. 2, 2007, pp. 251-63.

[244] Robert Van Niel, for example, despite his great sensitivity to mid-century change and development, was clearly loath to abandon the idea that a key factor in the consolidation of the sugar industry was that it changed relatively little as far as the peasantry was concerned. In phrases reminiscent of Geertz, he contended that 'local arrangements eventually made by

Even so, the idea that sectors of Java's rural working population ended the nineteenth century a good deal more 'peasant-like' than they had entered it is a persuasive one. An ostensibly crucial factor in this evolution was the imposition of a state land tax, the so-called *Landrente*.[245] Initiated in 1813 but evolving in piecemeal fashion for much of the century, it had major long-term implications for the structured evolution of rural society. It had the potential for creating a situation in which peasant households had to supplement their income with 'off-farm' labour in order to meet the increasingly monetary character of the state's fiscal demands. In 1830, however, when the *Cultuurstelsel* was introduced, the *Landrente* was still in a rudimentary stage of its implementation, a quasi-monetary tax that for many cultivators still amounted to little more than a 'traditional' delivery of part of their harvest. In short, the *Landrente*'s role in mid-century peasantisation may be somewhat overdrawn. The system of crop-payment or *plantloon*, instituted under the auspices of the *Stelsel* itself, on the other hand, had an altogether more immediate and significant impact.

In many parts of the lowlands of Central and East Java, *Cultuurstelsel* production was characterised in its early years by what colonial contemporaries styled '*en masse*' recruitment of the rural workforce in the general vicinity of the sugar factories. Workers were marshalled into large gangs and marched off the sugar fields under the supervision of local Chinese-Indonesian *mandur* [foremen] and sometimes made to work there for days at a time. This proved ineffective, however, and by the mid-century, virtually everywhere in the colony's sugar districts, the basis for cane cultivation had become the individual cultivator household. Workers were thus ordered in increasingly regulated villages [*desa*], and under the control of the village headmen or *lurah*, which proved a much more satisfactory formula for working the fields, distributing 'incentives' and sheeting home responsibility for failure.[246]

Whether the *desa* organisation was fundamentally a colonial creation or more properly viewed as a mid-century consolidation of an entity with a long prior history

---

the peasants [prevented] … the collapse of Javanese housekeeping arrangements … [T]hese *adjustments* and others made the System bearable [emphasis added]'. See Robert Van Niel, 'The Effect of Export Cultivations in Nineteenth Century Java', *Modern Asian Studies*, vol. 15, no. 1, 1981, pp. 25-58, here pp. 44-5.

[245] The authoritative discussions are in Hugenholtz, 'Landrent'; and Hugenholtz, 'Landrente Belasting'.

[246] See Elson, *Village Java*, pp. 42-98; Knight, 'The Peasantry and the Cultivation of Cane', pp. 49-66.

need not detain us here.[247] Either way, it formed a crucial stage in the 'peasantisation' of agrarian Java. Cultivators became increasing bound to the soil, not only through their settlement in villages, but also through the system of *plantloon* devised quite specifically to anchor work in the sugar fields in the peasant household. One leading authority on the subject has a wonderfully revealing quotation from the *Resident* of Kediri (East Java) in 1833 about the need to incorporate hitherto itinerant elements into the resident working population: 'we can only expect useful work from them once they are settled and cultivating'.[248]

Plantloon hence became a vital feature of the colony's sugar districts where — by the mid-century — it was being paid on a routine basis to individual heads of farming households in return for their work in the cane fields. At one stroke, it both 'recompensed' them for their household's labour and consolidated whatever bonds already existed between the household and the tilling of the soil. Since the agent of payment was the *lurah*, crop-payment further served to underscore his control over the village unit. These developments took place, moreover, within the context of an increasingly 'agrarian' discourse on the part of the state's bureaucracy.

This discourse, framed in terms of a categorisation of rural life, amounted (in Shahid Amin's pregnant phrase) to a 'cataloguing of the countryside' which made it — notionally at least — amenable to uniformity and record keeping.[249] Over time, at least, this 'cataloguing' had a clear potential to impact on the character of peasant society itself. None of this, of course, is to ignore the agency of Javanese peasants and *Priyayi* elites in forging the mid-century basis on which the sugar industry was able to establish itself. Developments depended heavily not only on coercion but on the apparent perception among certain strata of the peasantry that what was happening served their own interests as well as those of state and industry.

Nonetheless, the *consolidation* of a colonial peasantry that took place in Java in the middle decades of the nineteenth century under the auspices of the *Cultuurstelsel* was a multi-faceted process. More was involved than the tying of cultivators to the soil and their organisation into *lurah*-dominated villages. A concomitant facet was the increasing economic differentiation among the peasantry. Some elements of the

---

[247] See, notably, Breman, 'Village on Java', passim cf. Elson, *Village Java*, pp. 29-35.

[248] Elson, *Village Java*, p. 296.

[249] Shahid Amin, 'Cataloguing the Countryside: Agricultural Glossaries from Colonial India', *History and Anthropology*, vol. 8, nos. 1-4, 1994, pp. 35-53.

peasantry benefited more than others from the cultivation of cane and the commercial opportunities — the hire of ploughing teams and other beasts of burden, for example — which the expansion of the industry brought in its wake. Others were pushed toward the margins of subsistence by the same process. This was a development possibly accelerated (the point remains controversial) by the deleterious impact of long-term cane cultivation on the agricultural cycles in which it was embedded. Whatever its causes, this was the very antithesis of the 'homogenisation' of the rural population in socio-economic terms which the *Cultuurstelsel* was once widely held to have promoted.

Skewed access to resources in the lowlands of rural Java had long meant that some peasant households had far greater access to land, credit, water, tools, seeds and cattle than others. Developments in the middle decades of the nineteenth century, however, accentuated this situation markedly: there were ever more individuals and households for whom labour (rather than land) provided the essentials for subsistence. In consequence, a potentially 'industrial' workforce was in the making, which the sugar industry was able to exploit — in both field and factory — on an essentially seasonal basis. It is immaterial whether such workers were indeed 'proletarians': the essential point was that they could be treated as such, and taken on and laid off at will. However designated, they were an important constituent in the creation of industrial production.

Conclusion: Peasantry and the Industrial Project

The arrangements devised under the auspices of the *Cultuurstelsel* for raising cane through the utilisation of 'peasant' resources moved Java from the fringes toward the front rank of the international sugar economy. Most world-class cane sugar industries emerged or expanded during the course of the nineteenth century through the creation of Caribbean-style plantations utilising either slaves or indentured labour. In Java, however, under the direction of the Indies state and under the aegis of the *Cultuurstelsel*, the agrarian base of the industry evolved on quite different lines. In place of plantations as such, there took place a large-scale commandeering of peasant land and labour, in tandem with a system of concessions for processing cane into sugar granted to several score of formally designated contracting manufacturers. At the same time, the appropriation of village land and labour for expanded commodity production created what was, in effect, a specifically colonial peasantry of landholding farmers (themselves increasingly differentiated into 'big' peasants and a mass of petty cultivators) and functionally landless workers.

None of this sits easily, of course, with an increasingly threadbare scenario that posits the industry's exploitation of a persisting, largely homogeneous 'peasantry'. Instead, it underlines the extent to which the subordination of land and labour to the requirements of the large-scale production of sugar cane was predicated on a growing differentiation among Java's rural population.

The Industrial Project's Escape from the Constrictions of Peasant Production

These several developments highlighted not only the difference between Java and the leading sugar industries of the New World but also the differences between Java and other parts of contemporary Asia. The agrarian contexts in which cane had been grown in Java early in the nineteenth century — as in other, contemporary pre-industrial centres of sugar production in places as far apart as the Indian subcontinent, Formosa and southern China — were fairly diverse. In the *Ommelanden* around Batavia, as we have seen, a quasi-plantation form of production evolved during the seventeenth and eighteenth centuries. Further east, however, production was organised predominantly on the basis of cultivation of cane by 'peasant' farmers as part of a broader, multi-crop agricultural regime. In tandem with merchant capital provided by Dutch colonial and Chinese-Indonesian interests, the growers were often closely associated with the rudimentary milling of cane and the production of sugar, more or less *in situ*. Units of production were small and decentralised. The arrangement offered a way of producing crude sugar which combined minimal capital outlay and maximum flexibility in response to market fluctuations.

As elsewhere in nineteenth-century Asia, that is to say, the incremental and piecemeal implementation of the industrial project in sugar manufacture in Java (see below) had to take place in the context of a persisting pre-industrial production of the commodity. In the short run, at least, this had the capacity to undercut its more 'advanced' counterparts. It was one of the factors — not, of course, the only one — which made so very hazardous the take-up of new industrial technologies and consequent adaptation of the industry to their structural requirements. In this context, the *Cultuurstelsel*'s achievement was remarkable. As nowhere else in nineteenth-century Asia, it contrived over time to subordinate agrarian resources to the industrialised manufacture of sugar in ways that resolved (for a time at least) the potential contradictions between 'peasant production' and the requirements of the new international sugar economy that grew out of the industrial revolution. It was managed, as we have seen, through a mixture of coercion and accommodation, impacting on both *supra*-village elites and those powerful groups within the now consolidated 'village' whose formation formed a crucial part of the creation of a colonial peasantry.

What took place in rural Java during the middle decades of the nineteenth century, that is to say, proved to be a crucial step in the suppression of those tensions between pre-industrial, 'peasant' production and the claims of factory-made sugar which were apparent throughout the major sugar-producing regions of Asia in the nineteenth and early twentieth centuries.[250] In Java, moreover, another development was at least as critical. Commodity rice production, the long-standing staple of the lowlands of Central and East Java, was made subservient to the cultivation of cane. In this sense, during the middle decades of the nineteenth century, the *Cultuurstelsel* and the arrangements surrounding it managed to do something that was not achieved elsewhere in Asia until considerably later, if at all.

Of course, none of this would have counted for much had not other factors been present. One such factor was the extent to which the Dutch colonial presence in Java in the mid-nineteenth century — a far more intense presence than any such presence elsewhere in the region — facilitated the emergence, as we have already seen, of a Creole Prometheus on the colonial frontier (in the sense of the adoption and adaptation of technology and science). But industrial projects of this kind also cost money and pre-supposed the existence of institutions and of moneyed men — and women — who were prepared to underwrite them.

It is to that aspect of the rise of sugar in Java in the mid-nineteenth century that we can now turn. There can be no dispute that the large-scale commandeering of labour and the requisition for cane of some of the island's best farm-land played a highly significant part in the reconstruction of Java's sugar industry, which had begun with the inauguration of the *Cultuurstelsel* in 1830. Nonetheless, the relationship turns out to have been a highly complex one. In the broad term, the stereotypical

---

[250] For illuminating discussions of this problem in the East Asian context, see Mazumdar, *Sugar and Society in China*, pp. 295ff. For South-East Asia see Bosma, *Asian Sugar Plantation*, pp. 1-10.

Stelsel inputs created the *potential* for Java sugar's mid-century trajectory — but they did not ensure it.

5 The Money Trail: State, *Suikerlords* and Bourgeoisie

In the mid-1880s, when most sugar manufacturers in Java were *in extremis* on account of a sudden and dramatic fall in world sugar prices, an apologist for the industry published a book in Amsterdam under the polyglot title of *Suikerlords* [Sugar lords].[251] It was a spirited defence of Java's sugar manufacturers and traders, whose purportedly profligate behaviour over the preceding years was widely blamed for the financial predicament in which they now found themselves. Yet the book was no mere polemic, since it drew on the author's extensive experience of the Indies over the preceding twenty or more years, and came from the pen of a man who was well-known and respected in Dutch business circles. He had been the founder, a few years earlier, of the Koloniale Bank, an enterprise that became one of the major pillars of the Java sugar industry for the next half-century of its colonial-era existence. The title that Jan Hudig had chosen was deliberately ironic. Indeed, the whole point of his account was to establish the solid bourgeois rather than quasi-'Asiatic' or seigniorial credentials of the Indies sugar manufacturers who had dominated the Java industry over the last few decades. It was to their formidable accumulation and investment of capital that he now he sought to draw attention (and to which we shall return later in the chapter).

Despite the efforts of Hudig (and, until recently, very few others), the colonial or 'Indies' bourgeoisie of nineteenth-century Java have enjoyed a mixed history. Indeed, according to some accounts they scarcely figured at all. Rather, the bourgeoisie were judged to have been marginal to projects for large-scale commodity production in the

---

[251] Jan Hudig Dzn, *Suikerlords*, Amsterdam, PN van Kampen, 1886.

colony, since such projects continued to be masterminded by the Indies state through the middle decades of the nineteenth century. This judgement is simply wrong. Between the 1840s and 1880s, Java sugar had been transformed (as we have seen) by an industrial project, grounded in the state's commandeering of land and labour and, initially, by the state's direct provision of finance. Contrary to some lingering notions about the dynamics of capital in Java in the mid-nineteenth century, however, this industrial project was closely linked to the spawning of a bourgeoisie, without whom it would scarcely have reached the stage of development that it did.

Nonetheless, it would be a mistake to conceive of that bourgeoisie solely or exclusively as a 'colonial' one. Rather, it was one whose organic links to its counterpart in the Dutch metropolis played a key role in both its rise and its subsequent history. Allowing for the term's not entirely inappropriate pejorative connotations, the bourgeoisie was Janus-faced. Comprising people manufacturing and trading sugar and other commodities — and their associates in the Indies Government service — it was a bourgeoisie that looked both to the Netherlands *and* to the Indies. What are usefully termed 'Empire Families' played an important part here.[252] At an elite level, such families bridged the notional divide between centre and periphery. Their high colonial status was defined by the sojourns they and their kith and kin made back and forth between the Indies and Holland, and by the ties they carefully nurtured in the metropolis (mainly through education and marriage).[253]

Empire Families and their associates, moreover, had an economic as well as social significance. In this context, as in others, once-fashionable notions of the 'isolation' of the Indies in the mid-nineteenth century need to be discarded.

---

[252] The concept has been most fully explored in the context of British India in the opening decades of the twentieth century, where Empire Families were said to have displayed a number of key characteristics. These included, first and foremost, 'a ... bourgeois identity [that] became predicated on travels to, and formal education in, Britain ...'. Hence Empire Families embraced people who identified themselves as '... sojourners in the [Indian] subcontinent who maintained a secure foothold in the metropole'. In this context, 'repetitive journeys between, and alternating residence' in, colony and patria proved 'crucial to creating and stabilising ... middle class status'. See Elizabeth Buettner, *Empire Families: Britons and Late Imperial India*, Oxford & New York, Oxford University Press, 2004, pp. 9-13.

[253] See, in particular, Ulbe Bosma, 'Sailing through Suez from the South: The Emergence of an Indies-Dutch Migration Circuit, 1815-1940', *International Migration Review*, vol. 41, no. 2, 2007, pp. 511-36; Ulbe Bosma, *Indiëgangers: Verhalen van Nederlanders die naar Indië Trokken*, Amsterdam, Bert Bakker, 2010.

Metropolitan capital played a very minor role in establishing the industrial project in Java sugar. Instead, the industrial project was largely sustained during the mid-century decades by capital accumulated locally, in Java itself. Nonetheless, this accumulation and investment took place within a framework in which an ongoing nexus between colony and metropolis was a vital sinew of bourgeois existence in both locations. In one key respect, therefore, mid-century Java provides evidence for a wider critique of the notion (in so far as it retains any credibility) which posits metropolitan capital penetration as the key to 'plantation' development.[254] Nonetheless, such a revision does not run along the lines of asserting the exclusive character of bourgeois capital formation within the colony itself. Rather, it is based on a critique of the colonial-metropolitan binary per se.

This part-colonial, part-metropolitan bourgeoisie had a vital role to play in sustaining the industrial project in Java sugar. Somewhat differently constituted than their more purely domestically-based counterparts in contemporary Cuba, the bourgeoisie in Java were not, as were the Cuban bourgeoisie, the 'prime movers' in initiating the industrial project.[255] Initially, in the 1830s and 1840s, that role was taken by the Indies Government itself, albeit somewhat ambiguously (because it is not clear how committed the Government was to it). Nonetheless, from around the mid-century onward the activities of the Indies bourgeoisie in importing both machinery and the men to manage it — activities that mirrored almost exactly those of their Cuba counterparts — became the sine qua non of the industrial project's continuance in the Dutch colony.

Capital Formation in Java in the Mid-nineteenth Century

Capital formation took place in Java in the mid-nineteenth century on different lines than those experienced in most other major sectors of the evolving international

---

[254] For a recent and cogent argument about the importance of locally accumulated capital and the 'need to look more closely at the dynamics of capital formation in colonial sugar economies', and, in particular, about the need for a reappraisal of the idea that the social and economic history of 'plantation colonies' is invariably to be 'described and analysed in terms of metropolitan capital's penetration into the colonial world, and the attendant consequences of incorporation into the modern capitalist world economy', see Allen, *Slaves, Freedmen and Indentured Labourers*, pp. 2-8.

[255] For the contemporary situation in Cuba, see in particular Curry-Machado, *Cuban Sugar*, pp. 20, 35, 40.

sugar economy. For an understanding of the situation we need to go back to events that took place in the colony in the decades immediately following the collapse of the VOC at the close of the previous century. The import of these events was far-reaching. Very briefly, in the second decade of the nineteenth century, considerable tracts of land (notably in West Java but also in the *Oosthoek*) were alienated by the Company's successor regimes to colonial European and Chinese-Indonesian interests. At about the same time — particularly, though not exclusively, in the *Vorstenlanden* [Principalities] of Central Java — a significant number of colonial entrepreneurs emerged, chiefly engaged in the production of commodities such as coffee and, to a lesser extent, indigo and sugar. For a variety of reasons, however, both they and the owners of the newly created estates failed to prosper. In the *Vorstenlanden*, official Dutch hostility and the Java War (1825-30) temporarily interrupted the emergence of a European planter class. Elsewhere in the colony, neither estates nor planters made much headway in the production of commodities.[256] By the late 1820s, moreover, the mercantile sector of the colonial economy — which was made up of European, Chinese, Arab and Armenian trading firms who had established themselves in Java's main ports over the previous decade — was in deep trouble, caught up in the vicissitudes of global commodity chains (above all, cotton goods and coffee) over which it had minimal control.

The consequent failure of an incipient colonial bourgeoisie to establish itself in Java in the opening decades of the nineteenth century had important and long-term consequences. It meant that subsequent capital formation took place there in a different context, and on different lines, than that found in many other contemporary 'sugar colonies'. Global comparisons help make sense of this difference. Westward of Java, across the Indian Ocean in Mauritius (which was the mid-century location, as we have seen, of a technologically precocious industry that for a while clearly outpaced Java's), the formation of domestic capital took place around a nucleus of both landholding and labour ownership (in one form or another). To the north of the Indies, in the Philippines — where sugar production flourished on both Luzon and Negros — landholding and its associated peonage was again at the base of capital formation. In Cuba — Java's occidental coeval and after the mid-century the largest

---

[256] On the entrepreneurs and landowners of this period, see EMC van Enk, 'Britse Kooplieden en de Cultures op Java: Harvey Thompson (1790-1837), en zijn Financiers', Proefschrift, Vrije Universiteit Amsterdam, 1999; Knight, 'From Plantation to Padi-Field', passim; Bosma & Raben, pp. 109-44.

sugar exporter in the world — the ownership of African slaves as well as of land constituted the nucleus of bourgeois capital until late in the century.[257]

Java was different. In the so-called Government Lands (i.e. those parts of the island where the Dutch governed directly) along the island's Northeast Coast and in the *Oosthoek*, where the bulk of sugar production in the mid-nineteenth century took place, neither landownership nor direct control over labour constituted the main foundation for capital formation. The state itself laid claim to ownership of the soil and, at least after the return of the colony to the Dutch in 1816, was reluctant to alienate it. Nor was the state prepared to sanction the direct expropriation of the island's petty landholders in favour of a class of colonial sugar planters. In consequence, the nucleus around which colonial sugar capital began to form, from 1830 onward, was not the possession of latifundia or of servile labour. Instead, it revolved around the possession of sugar factories and — above all — of state contracts for the manufacture of sugar issued in association with the *Cultuurstelsel*.

At the core of this emergent bourgeois presence on the island were state sugar Contractors. Between 1830 and 1850, nearly 100 concessions to manufacture the commodity had been granted by the Indies Government, and by the end of that period there were around 180 individuals involved in owning or managing the factories concerned. The majority of such people were Europeans, generally from the Netherlands but also from the United Kingdom. Some were new or relatively new arrivals in the Indies, but others were individuals who had previous careers in the Indies and extensive ties to the Indies-born Dutch colonial community. Some belonged to what have already been described as Empire Families. A minority of Contractors, amounting to some 27 named individuals, were Chinese-Indonesians, who owned around a dozen of the colony's 'contract' sugar factories.[258] Some of

---

[257] For Mauritius, see Allen, *Slaves, Freedmen, and Indentured Labourers*; for the Philippines, see e.g. Larkin, *Sugar and Philippine Society*; McCoy, 'A Queen Dies Slowly'; Aguilar, *Clash of Spirits*; Michael S Billig, 'The Death and Rebirth of Entrepreneurism on Negros Island, Philippines: A Critique of Cultural Theories of Enterprise', *Journal of Economic Studies*, vol. 28, no. 3, 1994, pp. 659-78. For Cuba, see e.g. Bergad, *Cuban Rural Society*; Franklin W Knight, 'Origins of Wealth and the Sugar Revolution in Cuba, 1750-1850', *The Hispanic American Historical Review*, vol. 57, no. 2, 1977, pp. 231-53; Gert J Oostindie, 'La Burguesia Cubana y sus Caminos de Hierro, 1830-1868', *Boletin de Estudios Latinoamericanos y del Caribe*, vol. 37, 1984, pp. 99-115.

[258] For a Residency-by-Residency listing (circa 1856) of factories, their owners, general managers (*administrateurs*) and other interested parties, etc., see *SU*, Bijl. D.

them, at least, were members of families who (as we saw in an earlier chapter) had long been connected to the island's sugar industry.

The *Cultuurstelsel*, Bourgeoisie and Bureaucratic Polity

The close and long-term involvement of the Indies state in the expansion of sugar production and the formation of capital implied by the system of contracts has had a profound impact on the historiography of the era. An older orthodoxy, still apparently deeply entrenched though not unchallenged, maintains that under the impress of the *Cultuurstelsel* Java evolved into a kind of bureaucratic polity *avant le lettre*. Virtually by definition, it was a polity in which the state and its officials monopolised access to resources.[259] On this reading, bourgeois impulses were either stifled or, at best, relegated to the margins of society and economy. Such 'private' colonial entrepreneurial activity as did take place suffered from its 'pariah' status. One highly respected commentator has remarked (albeit only in passing) on what he perceived as a 'twenty-year struggle of the *Kultuurstelsel's beamtenstaat* against private colonial capital (1848-68).'[260] A parallel reading stresses that the ostensible bourgeoisie of sugar Contractors and the like which emerged within the confines of the *Stelsel* was, in reality, composed of people who were no more than the privileged clients of a bureaucratic state. In modern parlance, they were 'ersatz' capitalists. Expressed somewhat differently, in a manner redolent of the 'good old days' — the afore-mentioned *Tempo Doeloe* — of a fancifully remembered Netherlands Indies of

---

[259] For a classic statement, see JS Furnivall, *Netherlands India: A Study of Plural Economy*, Cambridge, Cambridge University Press, 1939, p. 121: 'the Culture System grew until it overshadowed and blighted the whole economic organisation of the country, and nothing remained but the Government as a planter on a superhuman scale, with the NHM as its sole agent'. More recent literature, heavily focused on the impact of the *Cultuurstelsel* on the society and economy of rural Java (e.g. Elson, *Village Java*), has done little to open up the subject, though much of the work of Robert Van Niel (*Java under the Cultivation System*, and *Northeast Coast*) and C Fasseur (*Colonial Exploitation*; and *Indischgasten*, Amsterdam, Ooievaar, 1996) is pregnant with implications.

[260] BRO'G Anderson, 'Old State and New Society: Indonesia's New Order in Comparative Historical Perspective', *Journal of Asian Studies*, vol. 42, no. 3, 1983, pp. 477-96, here p. 489 (the Germanic spelling in the quotation is Anderson's own invention). The concept of the colonial *beamtenstaat* — a state run by an autonomous bureaucracy, largely for its own purposes — was given wide circulation by Harry J Benda (e.g. 'The Pattern of Administrative Reforms in the Closing Years of Dutch Rule in Indonesia', *Journal of Asian Studies*, vol. 25, no. 4, 1966, pp. 589-605, here pp. 591-3). It reflects, however, a set of assumptions about the 'Indies state' which has a much older history.

the nineteenth century, they were *Suikerlords*, variously 'feudal' or 'quasi-Oriental' in character.

According to this scenario — which is, as we shall see, a highly disputable one — the historical consequences of these developements were far-reaching. In the 1870s, under pressure from the metropolitan legislature, the Indies bureaucracy was forced to relinquish some degree of its economic control, though many facets of the *Cultuurstelsel* were gradually phased out rather than suddenly terminated. Commercial crisis in the following decade, however, when the world price of sugar suddenly fell by nearly half — revealing that the industry required large-scale new investment if it was to survive — finally settled the issue. Given the way in which the *Stelsel* had purportedly worked against their interests, there was no substantial local, Indies bourgeoisie to take the place of the state, and the way was open for metropolitan Dutch financial and commercial interests to step in. In one form or another, these interests continued to hold sway until the transfer of power to the Indonesian republic at the end of the 1940s. In the wake of the *Cultuurstelsel*, in short, Java developed along the 'classic' lines of a colony where the dominant dynamic was provided by metropolitan capital, albeit with significant variations brought about by the uncommon strength of its state bureaucracy.

On none of these broadly complementary readings did the *Cultuurstelsel* leave significant interstices in which 'private' colonial capital might hope to develop and in which an Indies bourgeoisie might be expected to flourish. Yet flourish it did, and for a variety of reasons. A crucial one was that the state in which the bourgeoisie was situated was far less hostile to its evolution than has sometimes been imagined. To be sure, there were significant and heated disputes between sugar Contractors and the Indies Government. More often than not, these disputes centred on two things: firstly, on the state's unwillingness to continue commandeering labour on the industry's behalf — or, more precisely, on the scale that the industry expected — and secondly, on the conditions under which the Contractors could dispose of their output. The two things were often linked. When world sugar prices were buoyant during the 1850s, Contractors wanted to be able to freely dispose of their sugar rather than have to deliver it to the Government at a fixed price. At the same time, they were hostile to any quid pro quo that reduced their access to compulsory labour.[261]

---

[261] Well-documented examples are to be found in Fasseur, *Colonial Exploitation*, pp. 198-9; and R Reinsma, *Het Verval van het* Cultuurstelsel, Den Haag, Van Keulen, 1955, p. 65.

This was no mere paper war. In 1864, for example, commenting on the ongoing enactments by the metropolitan Government designed to 'reform' the relations between state and industry, the NHM's Batavia office (the *factorij*) observed — albeit with a certain degree of hyperbole — that for the majority of factories the latest regulation threatened a total 'annihilation of their enterprise' and that 'the future of the industry has never seemed darker than at present'.[262]

To focus exclusively or even predominantly on such antagonisms, however, is bad history. Far from being representative of a fundamental and unswerving hostility to the emergence of 'private capital' on the part of state officials, these disputes were an integral part of the dynamics of an emergent bourgeoisie. More specifically, we need to take cognisance of the 'half-formed' character of the Indies colonial bureaucracy of the mid-nineteenth century.[263] Rather than being an autonomous entity (as the *beamtenstaat* thesis would have it), this bureaucracy was an essentially porous one. As such, it was deeply permeated, as a number of historians have been quietly insisting in recent decades, by family and familiar relationships that bound together the interests of state officials with sugar manufacturers, estate-owners and partners in the colony's leading mercantile houses.[264] In this overall context, we also need to recognise that (contrary to lingering notions on this score) Java under the *Cultuurstelsel* was not a 'closed' colony shut off by Government monopoly to all but 'official' Europeans and state clients.[265]

The Indies State as Industry Financier

Compared to their counterparts elsewhere in the international sugar economy of the day, Java's sugar Contractors in the mid-nineteenth century were singularly fortunate. Their requirements for capital were significantly less than was the case in the New

---

[262] JVFB, vol. 39, 1863-4, pp. 35-45. For other contemporary comment on the difficulties facing the industry in the 1860s, see e.g. [Kamer van Nijverheid en Koophandel te Semarang], *Memorie over de Suikerindustrie in de Governments Residentien van Midden Java*, Semarang, Van Dorp, 1865; J Millard, *De Suikerindustrie op Java*, The Hague, Nijhoff, 1869.

[263] Sutherland, *Bureaucratic Elite*, pp. 16, 35.

[264] For notable examples, see Robert Van Niel, 'The Alfred A Reed Papers', *Bijdragen tot de Taal-, Land- en Volkenkunde*, vol. 120, 1964, pp. 224-30; Rush, *Opium to Java*, pp. 118-19, 147-9; Fasseur, *Indischgasten*, passim; Bosma & Raben, passim.

[265] For a cogent argument against this position, see Ulbe Bosma, 'Het *Cultuurstelsel* en zijn Buitenlandse Ondernemers: Java tussen Oud en Nieuw Kolonialisme', *Tijdschrift voor Sociale en Economische Geschiedenis*, vol. 2, no. 2, 2005, pp. 3-28.

World — and in other industry sectors elsewhere in Asia. The way in which the Java sugar industry functioned under the aegis of the *Cultuurstelsel* meant that would-be manufacturers did not have to stump up the money to buy a plantation, nor did they have to meet the capital costs of imported slaves or indentured labourers. Instead, their raw material came (as we saw in the previous chapter) from requisitioned peasant farm-land, and their workforce was amply available locally at minimal cost.

Nonetheless, the equipment used in manufacturing sugar had indeed to be paid for at fully commercial rates, and factories also required working capital to cover their annual running costs. The advanced steam-operated installations for the boiling house which both Lucassen and his erstwhile brother-in-law *Jonkheer* Otto Carel Holmberg de Beckfelt (both of whom we met earlier in this book) brought back with them to Java at the beginning of the 1840s are a case in point. Manufactured in France and Belgium by the celebrated firm of Derosne et Cail[266], together with freight and insurance, the total cost of the package would have been in the region of 150 000 to 200 000 guilders.[267] The costs of such apparatus, moreover, were far from being a once-off affair. Factories needed to be continually upgraded if they were to keep up with the industrial revolution in sugar manufacture which was going on worldwide from the late eighteenth century onward. The Lucassens, for example, faced bills for installing a major new milling system for grinding their cane at the end of the 1850s, and later still had to find the money for a Multiple Effect.

Initially, some percentage of these costs was met out of the public purse. During the first two decades of operation of the *Cultuurstelsel*, the provision of state capital to contracting manufacturers took the form of low-interest loans from the Indies Government's treasury. On this basis, between 1830 and the late 1840s, the Indies Government lent something in excess of 8.5 million guilders to nearly 60 sugar Contractors. The amounts of money involved varied very considerably. Some Contractors borrowed as little as 30 000 or 50 000 guilders, suggesting that the

---

[266] For Derosne et Cail, see Leidelmeijer, *Grootbedrijf*, pp. 150-5; and Curry-Machado, *Cuban Sugar*, pp. 37-8.

[267] Leidelmeijer, *Grootbedrijf*, pp. 166-7. Lucassen was initially provided with 120 000 guilders to buy Derosne et Cail apparatus at the beginning of the 1840s (and a further 130 000 to build his factory — a sum so large that it must have included the cost of other equipment, possibly the mills for grinding the cane). However, the state's advances to Lucassen eventually amounted to 550 000 guilders, which would suggest that he spent considerably more than the initial 130 000 guilders on equipping *both* his factories.

operations they sought to finance were very modest ones or, rather more probably, that they had other sources of finance. At the opposite end of the scale, four Contractors stood out in terms of the size of their loans, all over 400 000 guilders.

The list was headed by an Englishman, one William 'Jack' Stavers (mentioned earlier in the book), who was the front man for a small consortium of Dutch interests and to whom we shall return shortly. He and his associates received a massive 673 368 guilders to build the Koning Willem II sugar factory in East Java's Surabaya Residency. Next were Holmberg and Lucassen, who between them were in receipt of more than 1 million guilders (Lucassen got 555 000 guilders and Holmberg 488 000 guilders) for their adjoining factories near Tegal on the north coast of Central Java. The fourth and last of the 'big four' was one CFE Praetorius, who obtained a loan of 428 435 guilders in 1844 to upgrade the Phaiton sugar factory in the *Oosthoek*. Praetorius was the recently retired Director of Cultivations — the CEO of the *Cultuurstelsel*, one might say — who had begun a career as a Government official some two decades earlier, and might now look forward to a prosperous retirement. (In fact, he died two years later.) In all, the sugar industry accounted for more than four-fifths of the money dispersed by the Indies Government to foster large-scale commodity production during the formative phase of the *Stelsel*.[268]

In terms of developments elsewhere in the international sugar economy of the mid-nineteenth century, the provision of state finance on this scale was without parallel. In Cuba, the state authorities might assist the industry in all sorts of ways, not least by turning a blind eye to the continued, large-scale and 'illicit' importation of the black African slaves on whom the industry depended for its workforce. Nonetheless, direct financial subvention of the industry was unknown there, as was the case elsewhere in the New World and in those areas of Asia — notably the Mascerenes, Siam, Formosa, the Philippines and the Indian subcontinent — where the export production of sugar burgeoned during the mid-century decades. The unique importance to the Java industry of state finance embedded in the system of sugar contracts had, moreover, further ramifications that were of vital importance to the industrial project during its initial phase.

---

[268] The data in this paragraph are derived from 'Cultuurinrigtingen op Java ... tot Ultimo 1844', Exh. 1.2.1847/22. GG Rochussen estimated in 1845 that around 10 million guilders had been expended on loans to sugar, tea and tobacco Contractors (see Fasseur, *Colonial Exploitation*, p. 92, fn. 40). This reflected the fact that capital required to process tea and tobacco was relatively modest (as no expensive machinery was involved).

In particular, state finance bolstered the Java sugar Contractors at a time when the vagaries of the international price of the commodity might otherwise have brought the industrial project to its knees. For the first twenty or more years of their existence, the Contractors were (in effect) insulated from the impact of the world market. In addition to privileged, low-cost access to labour and raw material and to cheap finance from the public purse, they were guaranteed a fixed price for the sugar they delivered to the Indies Government's warehouses. This was no small matter. As one singularly acute scholar long ago pointed out, a fall in sugar prices in Amsterdam in the early 1840s meant that for several years — key years in the establishment of the industry — the Indies Government was paying its Contractors well over the market rate for the commodity.[269] It was not the only way, however, in which the emergent bourgeoisie of sugar Contractors and their associates were able to manipulate their relations with the colonial state.

Bourgeois Snouts in the Trough and the Progress of the Industrial Project

There can be no serious doubt that during the mid-century decades the snouts of the bourgeoisie were to be found firmly positioned in the trough. It was, after all, their habit! What is highly disputable, however, is whether this amounted to the behaviour of mere 'rent seekers' or wealthy sinecurists.[270] Much more convincingly, it is better designated in terms of the corruption and sheer graft naturally inseparable from successful capitalist entrepreneurship.[271] Patently, a significant number of *concessionaires* were not content merely to exploit their privileged access to the state to

---

[269] Fasseur, *Colonial Exploitation*, pp. 86-91. The Java industry was being heavily subsidised by the Indies Government (which had signed twenty-year contracts to obtain sugar at a fixed price). In 1841 sugar was sold in Amsterdam for little more than 50 per cent of what the Indies Government had paid for it, and in 1840-44 the Indies Government lost well over 8 million guilders on its sugar sales.

[270] The point needs to be underlined because of the propensity in contemporary 'liberal' polemic against the *Cultuurstelsel* to cast the Contractors in general in precisely that role. As part of a more extensive and heterogeneous critique of the *Stelsel* itself, which developed in Holland during the 1850s and 1860s, the Contractors came to be anathematised as wealthy sinecurists, '*bekleed met eene geheime macht in der staat en daardoor aan de minachting van het volk prijs gegeven*' ['clad with a secret power in the state and thereby deserving of popular contempt']. See Millard, *Suikerindustrie*, p. 58.

[271] For a notable general discussion, see RT McVey, 'The Materialisation of the Southeast Asian Entrepreneur', in RT McVey (ed.), *Southeast Asian Capitalists*, Ithaca, NY, Cornell University, Southeast Asia Program, Studies in Southeast Asian History, 1992, pp. 8-21.

guarantee a steady income from the sugar manufacturing. Instead, they were imbued with entrepreneurial ambitions, reflected in their taste, already demonstrated, for furthering the industrial project through the importation both of up-to-date machinery and of people qualified to operate and maintain it.

A remarkable case in point is what happened *chez* Lucassen after the family patriarch had repatriated to Holland at the beginning of the 1850s. Two of the Colonel's sons, the stepbrothers Theodore Nicolaas Reinier Lucassen (1830-1897) and Donald Francois Willem Lucassen (1837-1892), remained in Java to run the Tegal factories, thereby keeping things in the family, as was frequently the case throughout the industry. This was even though, as the family's chief financiers dryly observed, Donald Lucassen was a youth of very tender years with absolutely no experience of the sugar business.[272] What the two stepbrothers lacked in expertise, however, they made up for in 'connection'.

In this case, their 'connection' was much enhanced as a result of their father's second marriage (in 1832) to Susanna Pietermaat, a young woman who was singularly well-connected in the 'Old Indies World'. She herself was the daughter of a *Resident* (and, one suspects, a formidable absentee dowager after the Colonel's death in The Hague in 1854). It was the marital history of her sisters, however, which really counted. Indeed, they made such good marriages as perhaps to make her reflect on her own 'choice' of husband. One of her sisters married a future Governor-General and subsequently Colonial Minister (Pieter Mijer), thereby shoring up this Empire Family's interest in both 'home' and the colony in a laudably economic fashion. Not to be outdone, however, another sister wed a man who subsequently became a member of the Council of the Indies, the Governor-General's supreme advisory body.[273] As if this was not sufficient, among the Lucassen 'connection' in the Indies was yet another brother-in-law, Otto van Rees, the 'Coming Man' of the Indies bureaucracy (he was also related to Holmberg).[274]

The Lucassen brothers were to use this influence in Batavia to good effect in relation to the updating of their sugar factories in line with current global best practice. To squeals of outrage from The Hague, they persuaded the Indies Government to alter

---

[272] NFB, 5.12.1860/668.
[273] *NP*, vol. 12, 1921-22, pp. 390-2.
[274] For Otto van Rees, see Fasseur, *Indischgasten*, pp. 113-51.

their contracts so as to give them the free disposal of most of the sugar they produced (which had previously been delivered to the Government at a fixed price).[275] This was no mere windfall gain, however, for they promptly used the advantage they thereby gained as collateral for a substantial loan (from the NHM *factorij*) to enable them to buy new equipment.[276]

The classic example of the way in which the connection — and corruption — associated with the nexus between the state and the industrial project prevailing in Java sugar around the middle of the century might yet advance rather than retard the industrial project does not relate, however, to the Lucassens and their operations in Tegal. Rather, it relates to the great East Java sugar factory known as 'Koning Willem II' and to the nefarious dealings in The Hague which led to its establishment. The Government Contractor at the Koning Willem II factory — the man who held the concession to manufacture sugar there — was, as we have seen, William 'Jack' Stavers (1789-1864). Stavers was born to the east of the City of London in the dockland area of Rotherhithe.[277] Perhaps his upbringing there accounted for a certain lack of polish. Leastways, he was described by one acquaintance who had known him

---

[275] Exh. 20.10.1859/17 & Exh.Geheim 29.2.1860/54; NFB, 29.9.1858/409; NFB, 1.3.1859/449; NFB, 17.9.1859/512 & NFB, 17.1.1860/549; NHMR, 4796.

[276] This enabled them to buy a state of-the-art steam mill (costing 80 000 guilders) from the London firm of Robinson. Contemporaneously, Holmberg's son-in-law and successor, Hubertus Hoevenaar (see below), borrowed 360 000 guilders from the NHM, and — like the Lucassens — entered into long-term consignment contracts with them, under the terms of which they provided him with annual working capital. See NFB, 2.3.1860/57; NHMR, 4796.

[277] See the 'Journal' of his brother, Thomas Reed Stavers, at http://www.du.edu/~ttyler/ploughboy/trstaversjournal.htm (accessed 15 August 2014). For other information in the following paragraphs about Stavers, his career in Java and his connections in Holland see HG Nahuijs van Burgst, *Herinneringen van het Openbare en Bijzondere Leven (1799-1849) van Mr HG Baron Nahuijs van Burgst*, Utrecht, Gebroeders Muller, 1852, p. 13; see also the following documents from *Letter Books of John Palmer*, Bodleian Library, Oxford: John Palmer to William Stavers, 2.5.1825, Eng. Lett. c. 102, p. 68; John Palmer to Edward Watson, 13.11.1832, Eng. Lett. c. 122, pp. 398-400; John Palmer to Gillian Maclaine, 6.4.1833, Lett. c. 123, p. 387. See also Willem van Hogendorp to GK van Hogendorp, 28.2.1826, NA, Collectie Van Hogendorp, 91; IB, 26.8.1823/23 & IB, 28.12.1824/13, MK, 2779 & 2786; *Bataviasche Courant*, 22 June 1822/25 & 13 November 1824/11; VMK, 17.11.1826/56; Stavers to Nahuijs, 17.10.1823, Nahuijs Papers, vol. 8, no. 3, Leiden Universiteits Bibliotheek, MSS 616; IB, 17.1.1834/9, MK, 2846; 'Aantoning der op Java gevestigde Suiker Etablissmenten tengevolge van gesloten contracten met het Government', 11.9.1834, MK, 3203.

in Java in the early 1820s as

> a very kind, excellent hearted rough fellow, in whose house I have spent many a happy day. He was formerly an officer of cavalry here, and after the island was given to the Dutch, settled at the Native Capital of Solo [Surakarta], where he has made some money ...[278]

He may indeed have 'made some money' in the *Vorstenlanden*, but prior to becoming a sugar Contractor, Stavers's fortunes had been very mixed indeed. When the Java War broke out in 1825, the former cavalryman put his military experience to good use and performed sterling service for a suitably grateful colonial Government. Sometime after the war ended, however, he relocated to East Java, where, early in the 1830s, he became involved in the area's burgeoning sugar industry. It does not appear to have been an entirely happy experience. One contemporary letter speaks of

> poor Jack Stavers ... reduced to [overseer on] a sugar plantation after his enterprising, spirited and useful toils in various more distinguished courses of life. But he is well and in high feathers, you say ...[279]

Subsequently, however, he became embroiled in a dispute with the Indies Government which saw him banned from living in the area, and the close of the 1830s found him back in England, where a further venture, involving running a coastal steamer, appears to have met with little success. At this point, however, his luck changed.

Stavers's contacts in Holland — all dating from his and their days together in Java in the previous decade — included the influential and ambitious Colonel Nahuijs van Burgst, formerly the Dutch *Resident* at the Court of Yogyakarta and, subsequently, Surakarta (indeed, early in 1830, Stavers had been managing a plantation belonging to Nahuijs in South-Central Java).[280] Nahuijs was now retired and living back in the Netherlands, but he remained far from inactive in colonial circles. Indeed, there is some suggestion that he held out hopes of being appointed Governor-General. By the end of the 1830s, he and some of his friends were keen to get a stake in the profits of the *Cultuurstelsel*. What they needed, however, was a front man, since at least one of the would-be *concessionaires* was still on active service with the Indies Government

---

[278] Gillian Maclaine to John Gregorson, Salatiga, 29.5.1822, Gloucestershire Archives, Osborne-Maclaine, MSS D3330, Box 18.

[279] John Palmer to Gillian Maclaine, 6.4.1833, *Letter Books of John Palmer*, Bodleian Library, Oxford, Eng. Lett.c. 123, p. 387.

[280] Nahuijs to Merkus, 22.6.1830, in VMK, 13.5.1831/25-114.

and hence formally disqualified. They also needed somebody who was prepared to go out to Java and look after their interests. Stavers, down on his luck — but with a great deal of experience in Java, and known to be reliable — was their choice.

How this small coterie of well-placed individuals succeeded in obtaining a sugar manufacturing concession in the first place, however, was something else again. Along with Nahuijs, the repatriated sugar Contractor and merchant Johann Erich Banck was also involved.[281] Banck had made a great deal of money in East Java during the course of the 1830s and was what today would be called a 'white collar' criminal. Reviewing Banck's history a decade later, the Governor-General of the day was singularly unflattering, describing him as *een schurk* [a scoundrel] who had swindled the Indies Government and presumably anyone else who had the misfortune to be in his proximity. He had also played fast and loose with the funds of the Surabaya branch of the Javasche Bank (De Javasche Bank).[282] None of this disqualified him, however, from standing surety, together with Nahuijs, for the huge loan that was part of the contract that Stavers was eventually awarded. Nonetheless, the key person concerned in obtaining the contract, albeit covertly, was the Dutch nobleman RL Van Andringa de Kempenaer. As an officer in the Indies army, Van Andringa de Kempenaer had fought, like Stavers himself, in the Java War and was an associate of Nahuijs. Most important of all, however, he was one of a select group of individuals with inside knowledge — obtained during his Java days — about an affair that had once threatened to engulf the Dutch king, Willem II, while Willem was still the youthful heir to the throne some two decades earlier.

Whether there had actually been a plot to assassinate his father, and whether the young Willem was involved in this plot, is immaterial. What mattered was that Van Andringa de Kempenaer knew about it from one of the 'conspirators' who had

---

[281] For Banck's career, see Ulbe Bosma, *Koloniaal Circuit: De Migratie tussen Nederland en Indië 1816-1962*, Amsterdam, IISG, 2009, pp. 40-2.

[282] Rochussen to Baud, 26.6.1847 & Rochussen to Baud, 29.10.1847, in Jhr. Mr WA Baud, *De Semi-Officiele en Particuliere Briefwisseling tussen JC Baud en JJ Rochussen, 1845-1851*, vol. 2, Assen, Van Gorkom, 1983, pp. 262, 304, no. 3. Banck appears to have used the funds of the bank, of which he was local trustee, to finance his own business operations. See Baud, *Briefwisseling Baud-Rochussen*, vol. 3, p. 155, no. 4. Nonetheless, he declined to initiate a full investigation on the grounds that '… *zulks kan, onder de gegeven omstandigheden, alleen strekken om hem [Banck] te plaatsen in een donkere ligt dan in hetwelk hij reeds geplaatst is*' ['such an [investigation], under the prevailing circumstances, would only serve to depict Banck in an even worse light than is already the case'].

been exiled to Central Java in its wake. As a result, he is widely thought to have been blackmailing the newly enthroned monarch, who succeeded his father late in 1841, after the latter's characteristically impetuous departure from the throne and retirement to Berlin. Willem II was said subsequently to have lent Van Andringa de Kempenaer a large sum of money (at least 8000 guilders) to cover the latter's gambling debts, to be repaid from the profits of the sugar contract, a 50 per cent share in which was quietly transferred to him by Stavers soon after it was awarded by Colonial Minister JC Baud (without any reference to the Indies Government, which might normally have been expected to be consulted on such matters).[283]

The granting of the contract for the eponymously named sugar factory — it was indeed a nice touch to name it this way — was presumably one of the fruits of this endeavour. Nonetheless, the dealings that very evidently went into the making of the Willem II factory were by no means inimical to promoting the industrial project. Stavers and his backers secured state finance to the tune of a little under 700 000 guilders, but they put some, at least, of their windfall to work in establishing Willem II as one of the largest and best equipped factories in mid-century Java. Indeed, in all probability, only the NHM's Wonopringgo surpassed it. In the late 1850s, the factory had 800 *bau* of cane planted on its behalf (making it, on this measure, the largest such enterprise in Java) along with steam-operated equipment in its boiling house manufactured by Derosne et Cail in Paris and the Glasgow firm of Napier. Output in 1856 was something over 2000 MT, making it the highest-producing factory in the colony.[284]

The state's largesse (such as it was) came to an end in respect to sugar industry finance at the close of the 1840s. Having hitherto primed the pump of bourgeois capital accumulation by providing a substantial part of the capital flowing into the industry, the state stopped making capital loans to Contractors in 1847. A little over a decade later, it also stopped providing them with annual subventions of working capital.[285] Thereafter, industry finance was garnered outside the immediate orbit of

---

[283] On Van Andringa de Kempenaer and his involvement in blackmail, etc., see Baud, *Briefwisseling Baud-Rochussen*, vol. 1, p. 167, and the references therein; Fasseur, *Colonial Exploitation*, p. 187; WR Hugenholtz, *Het Geheim van Paleis Kneuterdijk: De Wekelijkse Gesprekken van Koning Willem II met zijn Minister JC Baud over het Koloniale Beleid en de Herziening van de Grondwet 1841-1848*, Leiden, KITLV Press, 2008, pp. 100, 111-12, 119.

[284] See *SU*, Bijl. E, G & H.

[285] Fasseur, *Colonial Exploitation*, pp. 92-3.

the Government treasury. By far the greater part of it, moreover, came from sources operating within the colony itself. Indeed, the most immediately striking thing about the investment in sugar in Java in the mid-nineteenth century was the extent to which it took place without a direct call on metropolitan capital. Holland was not a particularly wealthy country and its overseas investment flows tended to go elsewhere than Java. As a result, the colony's mid-century industry, though it certainly drew on metropolitan capital to a limited extent, was predominantly financed from capital accumulated in the colony itself.

Flagship of the Bourgeoisie: The NHM *factorij* as Industry Financier

By the late 1850s, arrangements for the provision of capital to the sugar industry had departed substantially from their initial moorings. The state took a back seat, and in its place a substantial amount of the finance available for the industrial project came from Batavia Branch Office — otherwise the *factorij* — of the NHM. Indeed, at one time or another in the 1850s and 1860s, the *factorij* financed (in one mode or another) almost 20 per cent of Java's 'contract' sugar factories. Nonetheless, the NHM's role is in need of some clarification. As a heavily capitalised commercial and (subsequently) banking corporation founded under royal patronage in the Netherlands in 1824, it could be regarded, at least in its mid-century manifestation, as essentially an arm of the metropolitan state and as strongly representative of metropolitan interests. In fact, however, neither of these suppositions is entirely correct.

Not for the first time on the colonial frontier, the tail often managed to wag the dog. This was certainly true of the dynamics of the relationship between the NHM's metropolitan headquarters and its Indies branch. Around the middle of the century, and even allowing for the newly minted speed of communication made possible by the development of the so-called Overland Mail route, the 'turnaround' time for letters to and from the Indies can scarcely have been less than twelve weeks, and could well have been much more. To be sure, the telegraph linked Amsterdam to Batavia (via Singapore) by the end of the 1860s, but this mode of communication remained both cumbersome and expensive, while the mail from Holland still took well over a month to reach Java. The result was that close or detailed management by Head Office was all but impossible. Local interests tended to override attempts in the centre to exert authority.

This aspect of the dynamics of the relationship between centre and periphery is only one part of the story. The other part concerns how we 'read' the NHM in relation to the state. It still remains possible to construe the role of the NHM as evidence that the Indies bourgeoisie was too under-developed to take over where the Indies Government had left off, and that in consequence the financing of the industry had to be taken over by a body intimately linked to the state. Yet this view risks misconceiving the real situation. Indeed, altogether more plausible is the view that the Batavia *factorij* was so effectively 'infiltrated' in the mid-century decades by local, colonial interests as to become, at least temporarily, the flagship (along with the Javasche Bank)[286] of the emergent Indies bourgeoisie.

During the period 1840-80, to cite some prime evidence for this thesis, the senior management of the *factorij* was overwhelmingly composed of individuals who had come out to the Indies as young men in junior positions and who had been absorbed through marriage and acquaintance into the Indies milieu — more specifically, into the ranks of the local bourgeoisie. Notably, only one *President* of the *factorij* during this period (the resonantly named Nicholaas van Taack Tra Kranen, 1859-66) was an 'expatriate' manager, sent out from the metropolitan Head Office — and his dispatch was a highly particular response to the murder of his recently appointed predecessor by a household servant.[287] For the rest, the *factorij*'s top personnel were people whose 'business culture' had been shaped pre-eminently by their experience in the colony and whose connections and loyalties were more likely to be rooted in the Indies than in Holland.

Take, for example, Jan Louis van Gennep (1820-1873), *President* of the *factorij* in the early 1870s. Born in The Hague, van Gennep arrived in the Indies in his twenties, and by the age of thirty-one he was the NHM's agent at Padang on the west coast of Sumatra. He evidently impressed his employers, because within a decade he was appointed as the firm's agent in Surabaya, the de facto commercial capital of the

---

[286] For a reassessment of the Javasche Bank's role in assisting the growth of the Indies bourgeoise, see Alexander Claver, *Dutch Commerce and Chinese Merchants in Java: Colonial Relationships in Trade and Finance, 1800-1942*, Brill, Leiden and Boston, 2014, passim. It should be noted, however, that the bank's statutes prohibited it from becoming a direct investor in the sugar industry or any other agricultural ventures. This would not appear to have stopped it from lending money to firms that *were* direct investors.

[287] See the genealogy of the leading personnel of the NHM Factorij Batavia, 1826-1884, researched by Peter Christiaans (see Christiaans, forthcoming). On the murder of Jan Constantin Teengs in June 1859, see Factorij to A'dam, 20.6.1859/176.

Indies. It was there that he met and married his wife, the Indies-born Anna Paulina Morrees (1826-1863), scion of an elite colonial family long-established in the colony. By 1867, he had been transferred to Batavia, where he was one of the small group of top executives at the *factorij*, before being promoted, finally, to the position of CEO. He died while on leave in Holland some three years later.[288]

Consistent with this local identification was the *factorij*'s vigorous advocacy during the 1860s of the interests of Java's colonial sugar factories against attempts by the metropolitan Government to alter the terms on which the industry interacted with the state.[289] Equally indicative was the *factorij*'s behaviour toward its Java clients. In the mid-1870s, for example, the *factorij* extended further credit to bail out Donald Lucassen — one of the late Colonel Lucassen's two sugar-manufacturer sons — at his Tegal factory, ignoring the protest telegraphed from the corporation's Amsterdam office (on 11 October 1876) that 'we do not approve transaction entered into regarding Doekoewringin'.[290]

What the Lucassen case is also indicative of, however, is the extent to which, during the 1850s and 1860s (there was some falling-off towards the end of the latter decade), the *factorij* had developed extensive financial links with the sugar industry. Some of its investment took the form of working capital, provided on an annual basis and in return for consignment of that year's output. Altogether more important, however, were the capital loans that the *factorij* made to individual producers — like Donald Lucassen — secured in the form of mortgages on their factories. A rough calculation would be that by the end of the 1860s, the NHM *factorij* had invested nearly 6.5 million guilders in the sugar industry in this form. NHM investment was at its strongest in the sugar belt along the north coast of Central Java but fairly weak in the rich sugar districts of East Java. There and elsewhere — notably in the *Vorstenlanden* — the finance needed to support the industrial project came from different sources.[291]

---

[288] *NP*, vol. 9, 1918, pp. 122-3.

[289] See, e.g., JVFB, vol. 39, 1863-64, pp. 35-45.

[290] NHMR, 4796-4797. Part of the problem was that Donald Lucassen's mother (Susanna Lucassen-Pietermaat) had a mortgage on the factory for 145 000 guilders — and an outstanding claim for 15 000 guilders in interest.

[291] For a succinct preliminary discussion of sugar finance, see Fasseur, *Colonial Exploitation*, pp. 92-4.

The Sugar Industry and the Indies Merchant Houses

The emergence of an Indies bourgeoisie was based not simply on the manufacture of sugar but also on trade in sugar and other commodities. It is one of the persistent myths about Java in the mid-nineteenth century that until the *Cultuurstelsel* itself was formally dismantled from about 1870 onward, the NHM (as the agent for the sale of the *Stelsel*'s output) effectively monopolised the trade in Java's main commodities. In fact, nothing could be further from the truth.[292] The emergent bourgeoisie was closely associated not only with the NHM but also with the growth of merchant houses at Batavia and the other major ports of Semarang and Surabaya. In turn, this growth was fueled from around the mid-century onward by profits from the trade in sugar and other colonial commodities. The figures from the Indies Government's trade statistics tell their own story. By 1860, in terms of value, mercantile firms other than the NHM accounted for 46 per cent of the Netherlands Indies' total export trade, and for some 65 per cent of the export value of Java sugar itself. A decade later, in 1870, the comparable figures were 51 and 72 per cent.[293]

As far as Java's contract sugar factories were concerned, the immediate point of connection with the growing colonial mercantile community of the island's three major ports was the insistence of the Indies Government on *borgen* [guarantors] for the contracts that the *concessionaires* entered into. Some of these guarantors were people of little substance or, somewhat surprisingly perhaps, other Contractors. A goodly number of them, however, were partners in the colony's European mercantile houses. The substantial Batavia firm of Paine Stricker & Co was an example.[294] Two of the firm's partners — Alfred A Reed, a businessman born in New England, and the Dutchman EW Cramerus — were guarantors for a quasi-contract sugar factory in the north coast of Central Java, whose output they no doubt acquired in return.[295]

---

[292] G Roger Knight, 'Rescued from the Myths of Time: Toward a Reappraisal of European Mercantile Houses in Mid-Nineteenth Century Java, c. 1830-1870' (forthcoming).

[293] The relevant data (and an authoritative commentary) are in WL Korthals Altes, *Changing Economy in Indonesia (12A), General Trade Statistics 1822-1940*, Amsterdam, Royal Tropical Institute, 1991, pp. 13ff., 142-6. Others have touched on the point, e.g. Vincent JH Houben, 'Private Estates in Java in the Nineteenth Century: A Reappraisal', in Thomas J Lindblad (ed.), *New Challenges in the Modern Economic History of Indonesia*, Leiden, Programme of Indonesian Studies, 1993, pp. 47-66.

[294] Knight (forthcoming).

[295] AA Reed (on whom see Van Niel, 'Alfred A Reed') and the Dutchman EW Cramerus

For such people, the attraction of standing as guarantor lay in the possibility of favourable access to the Contractor's 'free disposal' sugar — the part of the factory's output which the manufacturer was not obliged to deliver to the Indies Government's warehouses. The percentage of free disposal sugar on the local market stood at around 25 per cent circa 1850, and thereafter increased significantly, in tandem with the Government's backing away from the overall package of support which it had hitherto provided (which included capital loans, working capital and unlimited access to semi-servile labour).[296] Indeed, by 1860 around half of the output of Java's contract factories took the form of free disposal sugar, as was likewise the case at the end of the decade.[297] Standing as a guarantor for a particular sugar Contractor, moreover, also appears to have been part of a wider arrangement in which merchant houses in the colony acted as middlemen for overseas principals with a stake in the industry. The very solid and long-lived Batavia merchant house of Reijnst & Vinju, for example, stood as surety for the Contractors at several East Java sugar factories in which their 'correspondents' in Holland, the great Rotterdam firm of Van Hoboken, also had an interest.[298]

Arrangements of this kind were not without their hazards. Early in the 1860s, in particular, a wave of bankruptcies among colonial merchant houses and their clients threatened the whole edifice of mercantile credit to the industrial project. The biggest collapse was that of the firm of Schimmelpenninck & Co, whose operations in Batavia and Surabaya embraced mainly sugar and tobacco, and whose clients included a prominent — and very well-connected — sugar Contractor, Anton baron

---

were guarantors for the Lemahabang factory in Tegal Residency. (See 'Kultuurinrigtingen NI 1861', Exh. 29.1.1863/5). Both men were partners (together with ARJ Cramerus) in Paine Stricker & Co., Batavia correspondents (1845-67) of the well-known Amsterdam firm of Van Eeghen & Co — see J Rogge, *Het Handelshuis Van Eeghen*, Amsterdam, Van Ditmar, 1949, pp. 206-66. Paine Stricker had interests in other sugar factories in Cirebon and Krawang, where Reed and Cramerus were *borgen* for the Sindanglaut and Sindang Blender sugar factories in the former Residency and for the Wonosepie factory in the latter. See 'Kultuurinrigtingen NI 1852 & 1853', Exh. 17.3.1854/4 & 21.3.1855/15.

[296] At the beginning of the 1850s, around 25 per cent of the sugar produced by contract manufacturers was 'free disposal', i.e. they could sell it on their own account rather than deliver it to the Government. See Fasseur, *Colonial Exploitation*, pp. 91-2.

[297] Creutzberg, *Export Crops*, Table 7 — comparison of lines 3 and 7.

[298] Van Hoboken was initially associated in two East Java sugar factories with JE Banck (see above) and took them over from him in 1853. See Baud, *Briefwisseling*, vol. 1, p. 126, and the references therein.

van Oldruitenborgh.[299] Among other major businesses that went to the wall at this time was the firm of Ommeren Rueb. Operating in Batavia for more than twenty years, it had been regarded as one of the 'most solid' of Java's European mercantile houses. Willem van Ommeren had been on the board of directors of the Javasche Bank, the colony's main financial institution, and both he and his partner, William Rueb, came from substantial merchant families in Rotterdam.[300]

A major contributory factor to the firm's collapse was the sudden death of one of their major clients, Johannes Herderschee, in May 1862. Herderschee's career in mid-century Java is important on a number of counts. As well as exposing debts reportedly approaching 3 million guilders — the lion's share of which was said to be owed to Ommeren Rueb — Herderschee's post-mortem insolvency also sheds considerable light on the financing of commodity production in general.[301] It also has something to say about the dynamics of the *beamtenstaat* in which commodity production was purportedly embedded.

Johannes Eliza Herderschee was born in Amsterdam in 1813 and arrived in the Indies during the 1830s. Shortly before his death, he had come to prominence — at least among people who knew and cared about these things — through his role in the so-called Simbang Affair. The Affair revolved around the recruitment of labour for work at Herderschee's big sugar factory — a non-contract operation — at Simbang in the Pekalongan Residency on the north coast of Central Java. At least according to his own account, the Affair pitted the factory owner against the Indies Government's *Resident* there, one FHJ Netscher. Perhaps more than coincidentally, Thomas Edwards, while *administrateur* at Wonopringgo, had himself clashed with Netscher only a few years earlier. The Affair ended in the *Resident*'s discomfiture and premature retirement to Holland — hardly an indication of the all-consuming *beamtenstaat* alluded to earlier, in which the interests and agenda of an essentially homogeneous and autonomous officialdom supposedly enjoyed an unquestioned dominance.

The background to the Simbang Affair, moreover, reinforces an altogether broader conclusion about sugar capital in Java in the mid-nineteenth century, in so far

---

[299] Knight (forthcoming); Fasseur, *Colonial Exploitation*, pp. 169-72; NFB, 11.2.1863/ 827.
[300] JVFB, vol. 38, 1862-3, pp. 20-5.
[301] FHJ Netscher, *Regt en Onregt of de Toestand der Gewestelijke Besturen in Indie tegenover de Particuliere Industrie*, The Hague, HC Susan, 1864, pp. 41-3.

as it reveals the debateable nature of attempts — both at the time and subsequently — to juxtapose 'private' capital with the operations of the state's *Cultuurstelsel*. In fact, the putative divide between the two was at least as porous as it was contested and, in so far as the emergent bourgeoisie and their promotion of the industrial project were concerned, notions of a 'state' as opposed to a 'private' sphere are somewhat overdrawn. The world of Contractors working for the Indies Government was not self-contained or autonomous; nor was it fundamentally in conflict with 'private' capital. Instead, state ('contract') and non-Government (aka 'private') enterprises in sugar (and other commodities) largely complemented each other, and individuals and firms moved easily — and profitably — between them.

Established during the 1830s as a commodity trader in Batavia (where he married Johanina Clasina Kool in November 1834), Herderschee appears, even then, to have been an individual of some substance and connection, for he belonged to the 'The Star in the East' Freemason's Lodge and was an officer of the City Guard or *Schutterij*. Suggestive, furthermore, of well-rounded bourgeois interests is the fact that he was a member of both the Batavia Society of the Arts and Sciences, one of the oldest such foundations in the colonial 'East', and of the recently founded Netherlands Indies Society for Industry.[302] Evidently, he prospered. During the course of the following twenty years he came to own the Simbang factory on the north coast of Central Java and another in the *Vorstenlanden*.[303] It was there, in Central Java, that during the mid-century decades a significant number of entrepreneurs established a substantial sugar industry that exploited the area's cheap, semi-servile labour. The Javanese aristocracy of the Princely Courts sought to profit from this situation by leasing their landholdings to European planters with whom they also mingled socially.[304]

Herderschee was obviously at home in this world, as well as in the so-called Government Lands down on the coast, where he also had a presence within the contract system established under the *Cultuurstelsel*. His brother's wife was a daughter of the 'notorious' Contractor Louis Vitalis, owner of the Sragie sugar factory, located, as was Herderschee's own, in Pekalongan Residency. Vitalis was notorious on account

---

[302] Respectively, the Bataviaasch Genootschap van Kunsten en Wetenschappen, and the Nederlandsch-Indische Mij. van Nijverheid. See *IN*, vol. 7, 1994, p. 205.
[303] NHMR, 4796.
[304] See Bosma, 'Sugar and Dynasty', pp. 73-94.

of his decades-long battle with the Indies bureaucracy of which — as an Inspector of Cultivations — he had once been a senior member. He was likewise notorious for his role as a prominent absentee proprietor who had retired to live in Paris once the factory was operational. Herderschee's connection with Vitalis, however, was not simply that of family. At one time or another, according to his own account at least, he both helped finance Sragie and even, at one time, managed operations there.[305]

Herderschee's capital seems to have come from a number of sources. He had a relatively small loan (160 000 guilders) from the Widows' Pension Fund for Officers in the Netherlands Indies Army. Another 700 000 guilders or more of his capital represented the investment in his business of a number of individuals living in the colony. The bulk of the funds available to him, however, came in the form of credit extended by Ommeren Rueb, said to amount to 1.7 million guilders.[306] In short, he was evidently a well-connected — as well as persuasive — capitalist entrepreneur of some standing, whose interests embraced both the state contract system and the 'private' business and investment world that grew up alongside and in conjunction with it. Hardly surprisingly in the circumstances, the crisis of 1862-63, in which Ommeren Rueb and Herderschee were so deeply implicated, caused a deal of havoc in the small community of Indies merchants and the manufacturers and planters with whom they associated.

Notwithstanding this, the secular trend was toward the growth in investment in sugar by the cream of Java's mercantile bourgeoisie. One of the key companies was the Maclaine Watson 'group', consisting of a trio of firms based in Batavia (Maclaine Watson), Semarang (McNeill & Co) and Surabaya (Fraser Eaton & Co). All three were founded within ten years of each other and their interests, commercial and plantation, sprawled across Java. The founder of the Batavia house, Gillian Maclaine (1798-1840) had married very well indeed into official and 'old' landowner circles in the colony, and one of his successors in the business, his cousin Donald Maclaine of Lochbuie, did even better: among his in-laws were a Governor-General and the *President* of the NHM *factorij*.[307] The Maclaine businesses were big in the 'private'

---

[305] *De Zaken van het Land Simbang Nader Toegelicht (Uitegeven door de Kommissie van Liquidatie des Boedels van Wijlen den Heer JE Herderschee)*, The Hague, Nijhoff, 1866, p. 72. On the Herderschee family's relationship to Vitalis, see *IN*, vol. 1, 1934, p. 16.

[306] NHMR, 4796; Netscher, *Regt en Onregt*, pp. 41-3.

[307] Donald Maclaine (1816-1863) married Emilie Vincent in Batavia in 1844. Subsequently, her sister Elizabeth (who died young) married Governor-General (and subsequently leading

sector, and at one stage had investments in the *Vorstenlanden* — that is to say, outside the sphere of the state's own operations in commodity production. At the same time, however, they were also heavily involved in the *Cultuurstelsel*, as themselves the owners of contract sugar factories and as the financiers and guarantors [*borgen*] of other Contractors.[308] By the 1880s, they were very big indeed in sugar, and in 1884 it was reckoned that the Maclaines and their associates in Semarang and Surabaya were reliably reckoned to have bought around 40 per cent of the colony's total sugar crop, much of it from factories 'in which they had an interest'.[309]

How much 'colonial' money was invested in the industrial project? The well-placed contemporary whom we met at the beginning of this chapter, the Koloniale Bank's Jan Hudig, estimated (in the wake of the crisis of the mid-1880s) that 100 million guilders had been invested in the colony's export agricultural sector in the decade or so prior to 1884, and that as much as 75 per cent of that money had come from within the Indies.[310] His larger argument was that the so-called *Suikerlords* had ploughed the 'greater part' of their profits into improvements to existing factories, into building new factories, and even into agricultural ventures outside the immediate range of the industry itself.[311]

Metropolitan Investment: The 'Big Five' of the Period 1860-84

The Indies bourgeoisie did not stand alone in making investments such as those described by Hudig, and they cannot be viewed in isolation from, and juxtaposed with, those of their metropolitan counterparts. Indeed, quite the contrary: it had long been the case that Dutch metropolitan commercial and financial networks had worked together with the colonial bourgeoisie. In turn, this constituted an important

---

Dutch parliamentarian) Jan Jacobus Rochussen; another sister married CA Granpré Molière, partner [*lid*] and subsequently *President* [CEO] of the NHM *factorij* in Batavia; and a brother married Anna Catherina Hofland, daughter of TB Hofland, one of the colony's richest landowners and sugar manufacturers. See *IN*, vol. 2, 1988-9, p. 50; *IN*, vol. 16, 2003, pp. 1-7.

[308] In the 1850s, for example, one of the partners in Fraser Eaton was also co-owner of a sugar factory in Kediri in East Java (*SU*, Bijl. D); for Fraser Eaton, Maclaine Watson & A McNeill & Co as *borgen* in a number of factories in Surabaya and the *Oosthoek*, see 'Kultuurinrigtingen op Java 1852', Exh. 17.3.1854/4. In West Java, Maclaine Watson owned at least one major sugar factory, in Cirebon Residency: see NHMR, 4976.

[309] JVFB, vol. 59, 1884, p. 7.

[310] Hudig, *Suikerlords*, p. 28.

[311] Hudig, *Suikerlords*, pp. 16-23.

dynamic of bourgeois capital formation in colonial Java between the 1850s and the 1880s. Back in the 1850s, for instance, several of the Java firms that acted as guarantors for sugar contracts were closely connected to commodity traders in the Netherlands. The well-known Rotterdam firm of Van Hoboken and the Amsterdam firm of Van Eeghen were cases in point. From the early 1860s, following in the wake of the commercial crisis in Java discussed earlier, the connections became more institutionalised. Financial and mercantile capital came together, for example, in setting up the Nederlandsch-Indische Handelsbank [Netherlands Indies Trading Bank] and the Credit en Handelsvereeniging 'Rotterdam' [The Credit and Commerce Association 'Rotterdam'], better known as Internatio.[312] In consequence, there were increasing inflows of metropolitan capital into Java sugar during the 1870s and early 1880s.

This was well ahead, that is to say, of the sugar crisis of 1884, which has often been seen as the critical date for the onset of such investment. As Hudig argued, however, the extent of this metropolitan investment should not be overestimated. Nor was 1870 — the date of the legislation in the Dutch Parliament which laid the legal groundwork for the dismantlement of the *Cultuurstelsel* and hence notionally 'opened up' the colony for 'private' investment — anything like the watershed historians have sometimes assumed it to have been. As one authority has remarked, 'there was absolutely no question of private [metropolitan] entrepreneurs taking Java by storm after that year'.[313] Conversely, they and their associates had already been there for decades.

For several of these early 'metropolitan' investors, moreover, the experience of investing capital in agricultural speculations in Java was hardly a happy one. Internatio, one of the original metropolitan investors from a decade earlier, appears to have burnt its fingers as a direct investor in sugar factories in the 1870s. The firm subsequently confined itself to the modest provision of working capital and associated consignment

---

[312] NP van den Berg, *Munt-, Crediet- en Bankwezen, Handel en Scheepvaart in Nederlandsch Indië: Historisch-statistische Bijdragen*, The Hague, Nijhoff, 1907, pp. 115-30. On the Handelsbank in particular, see WL Korthals Altes, *Tussen Cultures en Kredieten: Een Institutionele Gescheidenis van de Nederlandsch-Indische Handelsbank en Nationale Handelsbank, 1863-1964*, Amsterdam, Nederlands Instituut voor het Bank, Verzekerings-en-Effectenbedrijf, 2004.

[313] C Fasseur, 'Purse or Principle: Dutch Colonial Policy in the 1860s and the Decline of the Cultivation System', *Modern Asian Studies*, vol. 25, no. 1, 1991, pp. 33-52, here p. 42.

contracts.[314] The Handelsbank had a significant enough portfolio of sugar and other agricultural investments by the time of the 1884 crisis for it to come within a hair's breadth of disaster.[315] Like Internatio, however, the Handelsbank had held back from any major investment in the building of new factories or the renovation of old ones. It had 'relations' with some thirty factories, and nearly 13 million guilders invested in *cultuurrelaties* [plantation investements] in general, though these consisted (so it would appear) of working capital-consignment contracts.[316]

On the capital investment front, only the Koloniale Bank and the NHM were more ambitious. In the early 1880s, the NHM *factorij* owned, or largely controlled, a string of sugar factories along Java's Northeast Coast.[317] The total value of such capital investments (by that date the firm had reduced its involvement in purely consignment contracts) amounted to something in excess of 3 million guilders.[318] In comparison with its smaller rivals, this figure might seem on the low side: however, the *factorij* had become cautious in its agricultural investments by the early 1880s — which is no doubt one of the reasons that it escaped the crisis of 1884 with relatively little damage. Meanwhile, the newly arrived Koloniale Bank, established in 1881, had become involved in financing five new factories and in working on

---

[314] The amount of sugar involved in such contracts was fairly inconsiderable: as late as 1883 it amounted to around 12 300 MT, less than 4 per cent of Java's total output. The information relating to Internatio's investments in sugar in the years prior to 1885 comes from Jaarverslagen Internatio, 1863-1887, Gemeente Archief Rotterdam, Archief van de Internationale Crediet-en-Handelsvereeniging 'Rotterdam' (Internatio), Inventaris no. 76. I am grateful to Drs Jasper van de Kerkhof for kindly supplying me with this information.

[315] Van den Berg, *Muntwezen*, pp. 212-14; Kortes Altes, *Tussen Cultuures en Kreditien*, pp. 99-143.

[316] JCF Schor (Directeur Koloniale Bank, 1940-45), 'Gedenkboek Koloniale Bank' [MSS], NA, Archief Koloniale Bank, 2.20.04/883, pp. 91-4; *Jaarverslagen NI Handelsbank, 1865-1884*, NA, Archief Nederlandsch-Indische Handelsbank, p. 190; Van den Berg, *Muntwezen*, pp. 203-5.

[317] That is to say, the *factorij* directly owned some factories, such as Wonopringgo (Pekalongan) and Kemantran (Tegal), whereas in the case of others such as Kalimatie (Pekalongan) the owners were so deeply in debt to the *factorij* that the latter exercised de facto control over them.

[318] This is calculated on the basis of information about the book value of its own sugar factories (950 000 guilders) and loans to other manufacturers in JVFB, vol. 57, 1882, pp. 55-8; & JVFB, vol. 59, 1884, p. 71. Given the somewhat fragmentary nature of the evidence, it may be that this figure (of capital sugar investments only) somewhat understates the *factorij*'s total commitment.

exclusive capital-consignment arrangements with four more. Its total investment in sugar by 1884 amounted to the better part of 6 million guilders.[319] The last of the 'new arrivals' — its founders had already been operating in Java for a decade — was the Handelsvereeniging Amsterdam [Commercial Assocation 'Amsterdam'], though its investments remained modest — a little over 1 million guilders in 1884 — until the late 1880s.[320]

A Financial Enigma: The Place of Chinese-Indonesian Capital

Not only the colony's European mercantile houses and, towards the end of our period, metropolitan trading houses and financiers were engaged in providing capital to industrial projects in sugar. Back in the 1830s, for example, when the shady Surabaya businessman Johann Erich Banck and his partners, the Hofland brothers, needed money to finance their operation in sugar on behalf of the Indies Government, the people to whom they turned belonged to the Chinese-Indonesian communities that had flourished in the city and the adjacent *Oosthoek* districts since the mid-eighteenth century or earlier. Apart from the Dutch, Indies-Dutch and British components of the emergent bourgeoisie, that is to say, there was also a Chinese-Indonesian one (and, although harder to discern in present evidence, an Arab and an Armenian one). The role of such capital, probably locally or regionally generated, was a significant factor in the mid-century promotion of the industrial project. Given the importance of Chinese capital, in particular, throughout the nineteenth-century Nanyang in China's southern seas, this could hardly have been otherwise. The problem is to trace the capital and access its relative importance.

Until late in the century, opium farm revenues and the profits of the trade in Java's interior to which the farms gave de facto access are generally considered to have formed the basis for capital accumulation among the Chinese-Indonesian element of the colony's nineteenth-century bourgeoisie.[321] Prior to 1830, the Chinese had run the great bulk of the island's sugar industry, and their capital was not easily displaced thereafter, nor found to be dispensable. Among the sugar Contractors, as we have

---

[319] The exact sum was 5 712 000 guilders (with another 1 621 000 invested in coffee plantations). See Schor, 'Gedenkboek', pp. 18, 73.

[320] Claver, *Dutch Commerce and Chinese Merchants*, pp. 88-9; Alexander Claver, 'The Colonial Flow of Trade, Credit and Information: The Chinese-Arab Clientele System of Van Beek, Reineke and Co/HVA (1870s-1880s)', *Itinerario*, vol. 26, no. 2, 2012, pp. 113-21.

[321] Rush, *Opium to Java*, pp. 83-107.

seen, there was a minority Chinese-Indonesian presence during the *Cultuurstelsel*. Chinese interests also had capital invested with European Contractors.

This was where Banck and the Hofland brothers came into the picture.[322] Around the mid-century, it was reliably reported that the Hoflands — who were East Java sugar Contractors and also the proprietors, as we have already seen, of the huge P&T estate in West Java — owed 'great sums of money' to the recently deceased Chinese merchant Kwee Yang Ho. The latter's family also owned several contract factories in East Java, dating from the early years of the *Stelsel*.[323] The Hoflands' long-term business associate, Johann Erich Banck, was likewise heavily involved.[324] Banck had begun business in Surabaya in the mid-1820s[325], and evidently put the close ties he had subsequently developed with the Chinese-Indonesian business community in East Java to good use in exploiting the possibilities opened up by the introduction of the *Cultuurstelsel* in that part of the colony. *Inter alia*, he subcontracted a concession he had obtained from the Indies Government for the delivery of large quantities of sugar to nearly a score of local Chinese sugar makers throughout the *Oosthoek*. Perhaps most important of all, he was the long-time business partner of the 'Captain China' of Surabaya, the Goan Tjing, the most powerful Chinese-Indonesian businessman in the area. He and Banck owned the large Tjandi sugar factory just outside the city, an enterprise that was still in operation a century later.[326]

---

[322] On the Hoflands, see Bosma and Raben, pp. 126-7 and (for their East Java dealings in the 1830s) Van Niel, *Northeast Coast*, pp. 368-70.

[323] See 'Extract Kontracten … Vervaardigen en Verzending Stoomtoestellen tot het Kooken van Suiker', NA, NHM, 7999, file 588. For the Kwee family, and for their factories in East Java in the mid-1850s, see Claudine Salmon, 'The Han Family of East Java: Entrepreneurship and Politics (18th-19th Centuries)', *Archipel*, vol. 41, 1991, pp. 53-87, here p. 84; SU, Bijl. D.

[324] Banck was the Contractor for two large factories in Pasuruan Residency. He was born in Schleswig in 1797 and died in The Hague in 1857. For more information about his connection with the Goan Tjing, mentioned shortly, see *SU*, Bijl. D; Tjoa Tjwan Phing & JJ Moolenaar, *125 Jaren Tjandi, 1832-1957*, Surabaja, Fuhri & Co, 1957, pp. 15-22.

[325] From the beginning of 1824, Banck was a member of the firm of Jessen Trail & Co (Junior) of Surabaya (*Bataviasche Courant*, 24 January 1824/4), founded by Josias Jessen & David Trail four years earlier (*Bataviasche Courant*, 30 September 1820/40). Following David Trail's death on 5 June 1824 (*Bataviasche Courant*, 19 June 1824/25), the firm was continued as Jessen & Co, with Banck as a partner (*Bataviasche Courant*, 11 December 1824/50). The firm was dissolved as of 31 October 1827, and Banck continued in business as Banck & Co (*Javasche Courant*, 20 October 1827/99).

[326] For the Tjandi [Candi] sugar factory, see Tjoa & Moolenaar, *Tjandi*, pp. 15-22. After the Goan Tjing's death, the arrangement was continued with his heirs, who included the Boen Bee

Chinese-Indonesian interests also owned or financed 'backwoods' sugar-making operations in Java's 'Government Lands' and, in addition, were notably active in the substantial sugar industry that grew up in the *Vorstenlanden* of Central Java from the mid-century onward, outside the purview of the *Cultuurstelsel*. What is also worth noting — in light of a subsequent, late colonial 'archive' that tended to denigrate Chinese enterprise — is evidence that around the mid-century, Chinese-Indonesian factory owners were as keen to industrialise manufacture as their Dutch counterparts were. Around 1850, for example, a number of Chinese sugar Contractors in the *Oosthoek* utilised their local Dutch business connections to order Vacuum Pans for their factories from Western European manufacturers.[327]

It is possible, nevertheless, to overstate the degree of Chinese-Indonesian involvement in ownership of the industry. After the mid-century, it may well have been in decline, not least perhaps because of a certain amount of official hostility toward the Chinese presence in the industry. After 1837, for instance, no further Government contracts were given to Chinese-Indonesians. To be sure, regulations like this were easily circumvented, not least because of the enduring ties that existed between European Contractors and Chinese-Indonesian capitalists. The case of the Pagongan sugar factory just outside the north Java coastal city of Tegal (discussed in the following chapter) was presumably just one instance of an altogether wider phenomenon of Chinese-Indonesian sugar interests maintaining a de facto presence inside the contract system despite de jure attempts to curtail their activities.

Nonetheless, the overall position of Chinese capital in the industry may indeed have been weakened by the Indies' state's hostility. One well-respected authority remarked, for example, that 'in the 1870s and 1880s nearly half the private sugar mills

---

and the Boen Kee (both designated as *Lieutenant der Chineesen*) and who were all domiciled in Surabaya. The existence of a family ancestral temple in Surabaya in the 1880s is noted in Claudine Salmon, 'Ancestral Halls and Funeral Associations, and Attempts at Resinicization in Nineteenth Century Netherlands India', in Anthony Reid (ed.), *Sojourners and Settlers: Histories of Southeast Asia and the Chinese*, Sydney, Allen & Unwin, 1996, pp. 183-214, here p. 186. In the early twentieth century, members of the family were still associated with the Tjandi sugar factory. By 1911 it had become a big, up-to-date enterprise run by a limited liability company. See also Salmon, 'The Han Family'.

[327] See '[Extract] Kontracten ... Vervaardigen en Verzending Stoomtoestellen tot het Kooken van Suiker', NHMA, 7999, file 588.

in Java were Chinese owned' — a remark that is open to serious misinterpretation.[328] The 'private sugar mills' referred to here exclude all the (former) contract factories, at that date still by far the most important and productive sector of the industry. Nor does the reference to the number of mills convey the necessary vital information about productive capacity and output. An informed guess would be that many — though by no means all — such mills were backwoods outfits of relatively small capacity.

All the same, in a field well worth further investigation, we should not draw rash conclusions. In particular, the Oei Tjiong Ham Concern, the greatest 'Chinese' business operating in late colonial Java, was famously the operator of large, well-equipped and productive sugar factories in several parts of Java. Its proprietor in the late nineteenth and early twentieth century, Oei Tjiong Ham himself, (1866-1924)[329] was undoubtedly a leading member of an Indies bourgeoisie that was, and remained until the end of the colonial era itself, a markedly cosmopolitan one. Even so, the European sector of the bourgeoisie is 'privileged' in regard both to surviving documentation and to its position in a colonial state run by Dutchmen who were often kith and kin. As a result, this sector inevitably stands out in any attempt to illuminate the role played by Indies people of wealth and connection in establishing and furthering the industrial project in Java sugar during the middle decades of the nineteenth century.

---

[328] Rush, *Opium to Java*, p. 102: that is to say, the factories to which Rush refers were those set up outside the parameters of the *Cultuurstelsel* from about 1870 during the period of its slow dismantlement. Regrettably, Onghokham's richly suggestive treatment of the subject, 'Chinese Capitalism in Dutch Java', in Onghokham, *The Thugs, the Curtain Thief and the Sugar Lord: Power, Politics and Culture in Colonial Java*, Jakarta, Metafor, 2003, comes devoid of any substantiating documentation.

[329] On the Oei Tjiong Ham Concern, see Yoshihara Kunio (ed.), *Oei Tiong Ham Concern: The First Business Empire of Southeast Asia*, Kyoto, Center for Southeast Asian Studies, Kyoto University, 1989; and, in particular, the invaluable ongoing reconstructions of his and his subsequent family history being carried on by the Dutch scholar Peter Post, e.g. 'Chinese Business Networks and Japanese Capital in Southeast Asia 1880-1940: Some Preliminary Observations', in RA Brown (ed.), *Chinese Business Enterprise in Asia*, London, Routledge, 1995, pp. 154-76.

The Discreet Charms of a Bourgeoisie: The Holmbergs and the Hoevenaars

Figure 10: The successful *Suikerlord*: Jonkheer OC Holmberg de Beckfelt.
Source: Koninklijk Instituut voor Taal-, Land- en Volkenkunde, Leiden, no. 47A58

Jonkeer Otto Carel Holmberg de Beckfelt died in Brussels on Christmas Eve in 1857.[330] The city was no doubt an altogether more convivial spot than the grim confines of The Hague to which the Dutch Royal Court had removed after the secession of the 'Belgian' provinces in the 1830s. Its more worldly society may also have had a particular appeal to a man sixty-three years old who had recently wed a young woman forty years his junior, and whose new wife was a coachman's daughter at that.[331] Holmberg has more claim to our attention, however, than his taste for inter-generational liaisons — something that in any event would have been the object of rather less prurient attention in his day than in ours. In the first place, he belonged indisputably to an Empire Family. Indeed, the Holmberg clan had an established connection of colonial service dating back to

---

[330] The information on Holmberg and his family in this and the following paragraphs comes from *DNL*, vol. 50, 1932, pp. 300-7; *NAB*, vol. 12, 1914, pp. 342-5; *NAB*, vol. 40, 1942, pp. 594-7; *NAB*, vol. 93, 1995, pp. 368-75. Holmberg was the scion of a noble Swedish family, a branch of which had relocated to Holland in the mid-eighteenth century. His father, Niclas Holmberg (1742-1818) — an old East India hand who had risen to the position of VOC *koopman* [merchant] at Surat, prior to returning to Europe in 1774 — had held a post in the household administration of the last Dutch *Stadhouder*, Willem V, as *Raadsheer in het Hof van Justitie en de Rekenkamer van het Graafschap* Culembourg. (He was subsequently *Burgomeester* there 1804-09). The foothold thus gained in Dutch Royal circles stood his son in good stead after the Orange restoration of 1814.

[331] J Kortenhorst, 'Eduard Douwes Dekker in den Haag', *Jaarboek Die Haghe*, vol. 51, 1969, pp. 69-98, here pp. 88-9. The young woman was Elisabeth van der Meyde, born in The Hague, 5 December 1834. She married Holmberg in The Hague on 16 April 1856.

the 1760s. Otto Carel's father had been in the employ of the VOC before returning to Holland in 1774, and two of his elder brothers, Nicholaas Anthony Holmberg (1779-1821), and Mr Frederick George Holmberg (1787-1817), had held official positions in Java.

Born in 1794 in the deeply rural Dutch province of Brabant, Otto Carel Holmberg himself had sailed to Java as a young — and by the looks of his portrait — rather dashing Hussar in 1817.[332] Once there, he married an even younger woman, the sixteen-year-old Henriette Smissaert, who was the daughter of a *Resident*, and was hence near the pinnacle of official colonial society on the island.[333] Like Holmberg, moreover, she was the scion of a family with deep roots in the Indies and well-maintained connections in the Netherlands. Holmberg's father-in-law, Anthony Hendrik Smissaert (1777-1832), had been born in Java. Like many similarly placed individuals, however, he had been educated in Holland, where his patrician family — in addition to ties with the Indies which went back several generations — was well established in the province of Utrecht. On returning to the colony from Europe in 1802, Smissaert held a series of official positions, culminating in his promotion in 1823 to the post of Dutch *Resident* at the Sultan's Court at Yogyakarta. His subsequent mishandling of the delicate political situation there caused many of his contemporaries to blame him for the outbreak of the so-called Java War two years later. Smissaert's consequent dismissal and quite literal removal from office — he was bundled into a carriage and sent down to Semarang by an exasperated superior — continued to rankle with him down to his death seven years later.[334]

---

[332] Holmberg was a page to King Louis Bonaparte (1807) and subsequently to Napoleon himself (1810). As a First Lieutenant, he had seen active service during the closing phases of the Napoleonic wars, and had been captured by the Russians at the Battle of Leipzig in 1813. He was subsequently repatriated, and by 1814 was a First Lieutenant with the newly formed *Oost-Indische Hussaren* in the restored Kingdom of the Netherlands. On Holmberg's military career, see 'Extract uit de Stamboek der Heeren Officieren van het Nederland'sch Oost-Indische Leger', in VMK, 9.12.1841/9.

[333] For the family history, see *IN*, vol. 3, 1990, pp. 12-13 & MP Smissaert, *Het Geslacht Smissaert*, Utrecht, Kemink en Zoon, 1882, pp. 84-6. The copy of this book in the Koninklijk Biblioteek in The Hague has a MSS, 'Genealogie', enclosed. For Hendrik Smissaert's intimate social (and indeed sexual) intercourse with members of the Javanese elite at the Court of Yogyakarta, see Houben, *Kraton and Kumpani*, pp. 107-8, and for an extended discussion of his appointment to Yogyakarta and the subsequent outbreak of the Java War, see Carey, *The Power of Prophecy*, pp. 518ff.

[334] Documentation on Smissaert's removal from office and his subsequent petitions for restitution is in VMK, 9.11.1829/46 & VMK, 19.10.1830/21.

Henriette Smissaert produced five children in fairly quick succession during the 1820s, by which time her husband had switched from military to Government service. Once there, he became a *Resident* — the same rank held by his father-in-law — in a matter of a very few years. Influence 'back home' no doubt worked very much in his favour: the family had made itself useful to the House of Orange in the late eighteenth century, and Holmberg had evidently nurtured the connection. His first posting, to Pekalongan on the north coast of Central Java, was not an entirely happy one. In 1828, caught up in a major altercation with his deputy, which required investigation by the state's top legal official, Holmberg was officially reprimanded.[335] Curiously, it did him no real harm. His connections again must have come into play, and it may also have helped that he was a Freemason. It should cause no surprise, therefore, that his next posting was a somewhat better one, as *Resident* of the Preanger, in the coffee-rich hill districts of West Java.[336]

His wife — from whom he had separated some two years earlier — died at sea in August 1832, and his children (all girls) were brought up in the Netherlands.[337]

---

[335] Holmberg became embroiled in a fierce dispute there, involving his Assistant *Resident* and the Residency Secretary. There is a lingering suspicion that Henriette was also implicated. On his way back from official business in Semarang, the colony's *Procurer Generaal* was ordered to investigate, and on the basis of his report, the Secretary was dismissed, the Assistant transferred and Holmberg himself censured by Commissioner-General Du Bus, whose 'displeasure' [*misnoegen*] with the *Resident* was minuted in the official record. See IB, 21.4.1828/17, MK, 2515.

[336] IB, 20.6.1828/ 9 & 10, MK, 2517.

[337] Henriette's youngest child, Clara Elisabeth Holmberg de Beckfelt, was born at Cianjur (Preanger) on 28 August 1829; see *NA*, vol. 40, 1942, pp. 596-7. The couple would appear to have separated some time after that. In March 1832, Henriette was referred to in official documents as Holmberg's '*gesepaareerde huisvrouw*' ['separated housewife'] to whom 100 guilders a month would be paid from Holmberg's salary, beginning in the month following her departure for the Netherlands. See IB, 19.3.1832/1, MK, 2545. In April of that year, Anthony Smissaert, Henriette Holmberg's father, began a return journey to Holland after a visit to Java during which he had made a final, futile attempt to 'clear his name' in respect to the events in Yogyakarta some seven years earlier. Henriette joined him on the voyage, which was prolonged by the need to circumnavigate the British Isles in order to evade a British blockade of the Channel to Dutch shipping (London and The Hague were currently at loggerheads over the Belgian bid for independence). For Henriette, the delay proved fatal, for she died on board the ship *Cornelia Sara* on 13 August 1832, off the north coast of Scotland. Quite possibly there was sickness on board, because Smissaert himself died in The Hague a few weeks after landing. Smissaert and his family had been given free passage to the Indies, apparently departing early in 1830. (See VMK, 9.11.1829/46 and VMK, 19.10.1830/21.)

Holmberg himself, however, remained in Java in his official position for another six years. At some time during this period, we must assume that his thoughts turned to exploiting his connections in the Netherlands to transform himself into an incipient member of an emergent Indies bourgeoisie of sugar manufacturers, traders and financiers. It was in pursuit of this that he sailed to the Netherlands in 1838. Ostensibly, he was on leave for health reasons. In fact, however, he took advantage of his connections at Court not only to lobby for a peerage but also to apply for a Government contract to manufacture sugar back in Java.

His family's old links with the House of Orange must again have stood him in good stead, for the Dutch monarch, Willem I, awarded him both the peerage and the contract. Alternatively, maybe Holmberg was just singularly persuasive, particularly in so far as he came up with a scheme (as did his friend and erstwhile brother-in-law Theodore Lucassen, whom we met in an earlier chapter) to take back to Java a ship-load of up-to-the-minute apparatus for making sugar. The king, susceptible in this respect, was always on the look-out for people who promised to modernise his decrepit realm. Holmberg was not the only contender for this particular contract, but he was clearly the better placed. In communicating the decision to the Indies Government, the Minister of Colonies took care to include a verbatim extract from the letter he had received from the king's private secretary, urging his Majesty's 'personal interest' in the matter.[338]

Empire Families were predicated on the cementing of ties back home as well as in the colonies, and in this respect Holmberg behaved in exemplary fashion. Indeed, he rounded off a successful stay in the Netherlands by marrying his eldest daughter to *Jonkheer* Ludolph van Bronkhorst, private secretary to the Prince of Orange, who was heir to the Dutch throne. Another daughter later married Arnoldus Gallois, at that time an official in the service of the Indies Government and, subsequent to his return to Holland, Administrator of the Royal Domains for King Willem II. At this point, Holmberg's business affairs became inextricably bound up with those of another of his sons-in-law, Hubertus Hoevenaar. As we saw in a previous chapter, Hoevenaar

---

In mid-1832, again at the state's expense, he took passage back to the Netherlands on the ship *Cornelia Sara* (captained by a Captain Leeuwrijk), departing Batavia — together with Henriette — on 1 April 1832. See VMK, 14.9.1832/23 & *Javasche Courant*, 3 April 1832/40.

[338] The details of how Holmberg obtained his sugar contract are to be found in Exh. 24.6.1840/19; Exh. 6.7.1840/20 & Exh. 16.7.1840/5.

had arrived in Java as a young man in the early 1840s as part of an entourage of the pioneering sugar manufacturer, Colonel Theodore Lucassen. Hoevenaar had been the leading individual in settling up the new steam-operated sugar factory that Lucassen was contracted to build — but had subsequently fallen out with the Colonel and switched his allegiance to Holmberg, one of whose daughters he promptly married.

Unlike either of his patrons, Hoevenaar was knowledgeable in the ways of steam, steel and sugar — and became a great deal more so during the twenty years or more that he spent in Java before retiring to Holland in the mid-1860s. The executives at the NHM's Batavia *factorij* — not people much given to high praise in this context — awarded him the rare accolade of 'known to us as a skilled sugar maker'.[339] Hoevenaar, moreover, was evidently a very astute man of business. Theodore Lucassen, who demonstrably came to loathe his former protégé, might have put it rather differently.[340]

The details of Hubertus Hoevenaar's subsequent business dealings after his break with Lucassen remain, somewhat appropriately, murky. It looks very much, however, as if he forged relations with his newly acquired father-in-law's associates in Court circles in the Netherlands to consolidate his own position as a leading Indies sugar maker. Hoevenaar became deeply implicated in the convoluted dealings over the Pangka sugar factory, near Holmberg's (and his) factories in Tegal. The Indies Government and the Dutch Contractor at Pangka, van Vloten (perhaps more than coincidently a lawyer), became involved in an acrimonious struggle over labour that culminated in the termination of the contract, a protracted court case and, finally — after many twists and turns — the downfall of a Colonial Minister. At one stage or another, Hoevenaar held power of attorney for van Vloten, was *administrateur* of Pangka and subsequently lease-holder of the factory (which was used to process cane grown elsewhere) and, later still, its part-owner. For good measure, he was also the brother-in-law of the two men (van Bronckhorst and Gallois) who finally extracted a new contract for the factory from a reluctant Dutch Colonial Office.[341]

---

[339] NFB, 26.9.1860/627.

[340] It is demonstrable due to a document by Lucassen, headed '*Weldaden met Ondank Beloond*' ['Good Deeds Repaid with Ingratitude'], in which he lists his vividly remembered slights and grudges, which may or may not be accurate. Categorically, however, it establishes the fact of the complete breakdown of his relations with Hoevenaar. I am very grateful to Dr Margaret Leidelmeijer for kindly providing me with a copy of this document (which is in private hands in the Netherlands).

[341] Fasseur, *Colonial Exploitation*, pp. 198-202, 223-30.

Figure 11: A rare glimpse inside a nineteenth-century Java sugar factory: Pangka, North-Central Java, 1870s. Note the record keeper seated at his table and the (shadowy) presence of Javanese women operating the centrifuges in which half-dry sugar was spun into crystalline form.
Source: Koninklijk Instituut voor Taal-, Land- en Volkenkunde, Leiden, no. 10751

The end result of twenty years of wheeling and dealing was that Hoevenaar became owner of a small clutch of sugar factories — they became known in the business world as the 'Hoevenaar Concerns' and continued to operate under that name until the Second World War — and had a stake in several others.[342] After

---

[342] In addition to his late father-in-law's two factories (i.e. Adiwerna and Djatibarang), he was at one time or another in the mid-century decades the owner or part-owner of the nearby Pangka sugar factory (where for some years prior to that he had been the lessee) and of two factories in neighbouring Cirebon Residency (Soerawinangan and Sindang Laut). For some years, he was also the owner of the Lemahabang factory in the western part of Tegal. Hoevenaar was at various times *administrateur* of Pangka (prior to its temporary closure in 1851), lessee

Figure 12: The industrial project in Java in the closing decades of the nineteenth century: the Pangka sugar factory, North-Central Java c. 1890.
Source: Koninklijk Instituut voor Taal-, Land- en Volkenkunde, Leiden, no. 10750

initially working for his father-in-law, Hoevenaar, some time around 1860 after his father-in-law's death, took over these factories, buying out the other heirs in the process. In order to finance this, he borrowed 360 000 guilders from the NHM's Batavia *factorij*, and entered into long-term consignment contracts with the firm, under the terms of which they provided him with annual working capital.[343]

---

of the factory and then co-owner with Willem Jacob Hendrik van Rijck (1827-1880). The latter was married to Hoevenaar's stepsister Melanie (after her death in 1881, he married Hoevenaar's daughter Clara) and subsequently bought out his brother-in-law's interest in Pangka. See *SU*, Bijl. D ; NFB, 15.3.1859/451; *DNL*, vol. 29, 1911, p. 312. Hoevenaar must have taken over Soerawinangan (previously owned by LA Saportas) in 1863. At the end of that year the NHM, his financiers at Djatibarang and Adiwerna, were initially strongly resistant to his proposal to move to Soerawinangan to supervise in person the operation of the factory. See NFB, 12.12.1863/889. Hoevenaar became owner of Lemahabang at the end of 1855, having bought it at auction from the bankrupt TC Boogaardt, and in the following year was listed as *administrateur* there (*SU*, Bijl. D). The significance of the latter (see below) was that it brought him into contact with one of the colony's leading import-export businesses, the Batavia house of Paine Stricker & Co., a firm with good connections both in Holland and the East Coast of the United States.

[343] For the loan — apparently to enable him to buy out his co-owners in Djatibarang and

A decade later, however, he was evidently sufficiently financially independent of the NHM and was able to switch his allegiance to the Nederlandsch-Indische Handelsbank[344], one of a number of firms, both metropolitan and colonial, which began to supply capital — albeit in a modest way — to Java's sugar factories from about 1860 onward. As late as 1884, two years prior to his death, Hoevenaar was part of a consortium granted a concession for the laying of a railway along Java's north coast from Semarang to Cirebon, linking virtually all the area's sugar factories to the main ports.[345] Meanwhile, back in the Netherlands he developed banking interests both in the town of Eindhoven, in the south-east of the Netherlands near to what became (as we shall see) his country seat at the village of Geldrop, as well as in Rotterdam, the commercial and shipping metropolis of the southern part of the country.

Empire Families and their Metropolitan Connections

Colonel Theodore Lucassen, Hoevenaar's erstwhile patron, would presumably have been gratified that two of his granddaughters married sugar industry executives in Holland, but — perhaps even more gratifyingly for a rising bourgeois — that others married into the French aristocracy. Moreover, one of his sons, the last child of his Indies-born first wife, obviously managed to squeeze enough money out of his sugar factory to retire to Mentone, in the South of France, one of the classic havens of *La Belle Époque* of the bourgeoisie. He died there in 1897, having survived his equally Indies Dutch wife by almost two decades.[346]

Judged by social as well as by economic criteria, however, Hubertus Hoevenaar himself, together with his wife Anna Holmberg, were even riper exemplars of a newly emergent Indies bourgeoisie that was at once colonial and metropolitan. Hoevenaar himself died in 1886, twenty years after retiring to patria and transforming himself into a country gentleman with a seat at Geldrop in Brabant, in the south-east of the Netherlands, not so very far from where his family originated. Anna Hoevenaar, however, survived her husband by almost two decades, and died in The Hague in

---

Adiwerna — see NFB, 2.3.1860/571.

[344] NHMR, 4796.

[345] HP Hoevenaar of Geldrop was one of five partners granted a concession for laying a railway from Semarang to Cirebon. (At the end of 1884 they were asking for more time because they had still to come up with the guarantor money.) See JVFB, vol. 59, 1884, p. 17.

[346] *NP*, vol. 5, 1914, pp. 269-77; & *NP*, vol. 53, 1967, pp. 168-78.

Figure 13: A bourgeois dream: the Hoevenaar 'castle' at Geldrop in the Netherlands unchanged from the late nineteenth century.
Source: *Kasteel Geldrop* by Reval. Creative Commons Attribution-Share Alike 3.0-2.5-2.0-1.0. Wikimedia Commons, http://commons.wikimedia.org/wiki/File:Kasteel_Geldrop.jpg#mediaviewer/File:Kasteel_Geldrop.jpg

1905, full of years and very far indeed from her birthplace in one of the more remote parts of Java's Northeast Coast.[347]

The *casteel* [castle] at Geldrop, where the widow Hoevenaar appears still to have lived almost up to the time of her death, had been made over into a dignified but hardly grand country house by the couple's efforts after their return from the Indies in 1866. Prior to that, it had been a semi-ruinous set of buildings inherited by Hoevenaar from a distant relative, complete with the title of *Heer* [squire] of Geldrop. Judging by a plaque on the renovated building's outer wall, this was a feudal designation (obsolete as it was) of which Hoevenaar was rather proud. He and his wife were presumably proud, too, of the 'English' garden and park they created around their

---

[347] Gemeente Archief, Den Haag, Death Certificate 432, 9.2.1905, shows that, '*wonende te Geldrop*' ['living at Geldrop'], 'Anna ... Hoevenaar geboren [born] Holmberg de Beckvelt' died in The Hague at 10.30 on the evening of 7 February 1905. The witnesses were Jacob Cromer, thirty-two-year old *bedienste* [servant], and sixty-one-year-old Engelbertus H, '*zonder beroep*' [without profession], both of The Hague.

casteel, complete with an Orangery and a stud for breeding horses (only the shooting rights were missing, held by an adjoining and unaccommodating landowner).[348]

Along with the marriage of two of their daughters into the Dutch aristocracy (one of the sons-in-law, Mr HNC *baron* van Tuyll van Serooskerken, was on the board of the family firm)[349], Geldrop and its grounds formed part of a bourgeois dream that was far from being confined to the Netherlands. It was also the dream, however, of Empire Families, in so far as it consolidated 'back home' the constantly renewed ties between colony and metropolis which dated back (in this case) to the late eighteenth century — and were to continue into the twentieth. These ties were to become of key significance in saving the industrial project in sugar when it was threatened with annihilation during the course of the 1880s.

The Indies Bourgeoisie, Capital and the Sugar Crisis of 1884

The Indies bourgeoisie did not stand alone. Indeed, quite the contrary. The Empire Families to which they generally belonged provided an organic connection to the metropolis, while at the same time Dutch metropolitan commercial and financial networks had long worked together with the colonial bourgeoisie. Indeed, the two groups were intimately linked.[350]

The career of Jan Hudig, author of *Suikerlords* and founder of the Koloniale Bank, demonstrates the point well enough. Born in the Netherlands in 1840 into an old-established Rotterdam merchant family, as a sixteen-year-old he had served an apprenticeship in Van Hoboken's dockyard in Rotterdam and spent three years in England before arriving in Batavia in 1864. His acquaintances there included the

---

[348] On the family and its country house, see Eugene Franken, *Hubertus Paulus Hoevenaar: Kasteelheer en Ondernemer* (forthcoming). See http://www.eugenefranken.nl/hoevenaar.htm (accessed 15 August 2014).

[349] *HCHO*, 1899, p. 618. In 1899 the Directors were M Boek and DC Eibergen-Santhagens and Board Members were Mr HNC *baron* Tuyll van Serooskerken, J van Hasselt, MJE Henny, T van den Ben and (the family's lawyer) HWF Ligtenbergen.

[350] For evidence of the substantial overlap between the 'colonial' and 'metropolitan' bourgeoisie of the era, see Claver, *Dutch Commerce and Chinese Merchants*, passim; Korthals Altes, *Tussen Cultuurs en Kredieten*, pp. 53-63, 89-98; Jan Rutger van Swet, 'President in Indie en Nederland: Mr. N.P. van den Berg als Centraal Bankier', PhD Diss, Universitiet Leiden, 2004, pp. 51-216; NP van den Berg, 'Uit de Tijd van de Oprichting en de Eerste Jaren van het Bestaan der Nederlandsch-Indische Handelsbank', *De Indische Gids*, vol. 35, no. 2, 1913, pp. 987-1003.

young NP van den Berg, agent of the newly established Handelsbank (and later its *Directeur*); the *President* of the Javasche Bank, CFW Wiggers van Kerchem; and the head of the firm of Reijnst & Vinju, A van Delden. Hudig himself was employed in various agricultural ventures, mostly coffee, and he lived — very much in the Indies style — with a Chinese-Indonesian woman, Tjan Joe. Revisiting Holland in 1874, he married a Dutch woman, MH van der Waarden, and then returned to Java the following year. In 1878 he was again in Holland, where he took the position of *Secretaris* of the NHM in Amsterdam. Resigning the following year, he travelled once again to the Indies, where he lived as a guest for a time of JTh Cremer — who was then well on his way to making a fortune as a tobacco planter, which was to carry him into the upper echelons of the Dutch business and political world. In 1880, sickness forced Hudig back to Holland, where in the following year he founded the Koloniale Bank.[351]

Hudig was far from being an isolated figure, however. It was people like him, with a foot in the two worlds of Indies entrepreneurship and Netherlands capital, who were indicative of the community of bourgeois interests in colony and metropolis which would see the industry through a period in its history potentially disastrous for the Indies bourgeoisie and the industrial project they had promoted over the preceding decades. This was the period, in the middle months of 1884, when, like comparable industries worldwide, Java sugar was hit by a precipitate fall in the international price of sugar which reduced its sale price by as much as 40 or 50 per cent.

We shall return to this crisis and its impact on the industrial project shortly. Before doing so, however, it is important first to review the development of industrialised sugar production on Java in the decade or so prior to the crisis.

---

[351] Schor 'Gedenkboek' pp. 1-11; *NP*, vol. 50, 1964, p. 260. For an extended account of Hudig's career, see Claver, *Dutch Commerce and Chinese Merchants*, pp. 105-9. On Hudig and his Rotterdam background, see also Gene M Moore (ed.), *Conrad's Cities: Essays for Hans van Marle*, Amsterdam, Rodopi, 1992, p. 107.

Part III

Metamorphosis

6 Metamorphosis: Machinery, Science and the Manufacture of Sugar in Java on the Eve of the Crisis of the Mid-1880s

In July 1870, the fifty-year-old Jan Louis van Gennep, *President* [CEO] of the NHM's Batavia *factorij*, left Batavia by coastal steamer to begin a tour of inspection of his company's investments on the island's Northeast Coast.[352] On his way back, he travelled inland through the *Vorstenlanden* of South-Central Java. Late in the month, having arrived by rail on a recently opened section of the line being built from the *Vorstenlanden* down to the coast at Semarang, he stayed for some days at the Court-city of Surakarta (Solo).[353] The city, the seat of the *Soesoehoenan*, head of one of South-Central Java's two ruling families, was also at the centre of a considerable belt of plantation activity that had begun there several decades earlier, in which coffee, indigo and sugar were well to the fore.[354]

Commensurate with his important position in colonial circles in the Indies, van Gennep, an old Indies hand who (as we saw earlier) had been in Java for over a quarter of a century, evidently spent some time with the *Resident* Tobias, the Dutch representative at the *Soesoehoenan*'s Court. Indeed, he may well have stayed with

---

[352] JL van Gennep was born in The Hague on 25 April 1820, married (in Sourabaya, 1845) the Ambon-born Anna Paulina Morrees (1826-1863) and died in The Hague on 10 December 1873.

[353] JL van Gennep, 'Cultuurondernemingen op Java, 1870', Reisverlagen en Rapporten no. 70, NHMA. The railway between the Principalities and Semarang, first projected circa 1860, had been partially completed in February 1870. See Houben, *Kraton*, p. 289. It closed in 2000.

[354] Houben, *Kraton*, pp. 257-304; Bosma, 'Sugar and Dynasty', pp. 73-84.

Figure 14: Prince Mangkunegara IV, Javanese aristocrat and owner of the Colomadu sugar factory near Surakarta in South-Central Java.
Source: Koninklijk Instituut voor Taal-, Land- en Volkenkunde, Leiden, no. 7831

the *Resident*, and it was presumably Tobias who suggested that he might visit the Colomadu factory at Malangjiwan, a few kilometres to the east of the city. This enterprise was unusual in that it was the only industrial sugar factory in the colony owned by a Javanese, having been established almost ten years earlier by the Solonese aristocrat, Pangeran Adipati Ario Mangkunegra IV, in whose Principality it stood. What made Colomadu even more unusual, however, was that it also boasted the first 'Triple Effet' apparatus — the sine qua non of 'modern' sugar manufacturing from the 1860s onward — to be installed anywhere in the colony.[355] Within the three interconnected, pressurised tanks of the Triple Effect, cane-juice from the mills was both cleansed and concentrated before being pumped to the Vacuum Pans, where it was further reduced into a mix of quasi-crystalline sugar and molasses. Its advantage, along with offering a much more fail-safe method of operation than had previously been available to sugar manufacturers, was that it worked on the basis of the recirculation of steam-heat between the various phases of its operation, thereby greatly reducing the factory's expenditure on fuel.

It did so, of course, at a price. Triple Effect apparatus did not come cheap. Indeed, because of both its size and expense, it had originally been considered as best

---

[355] It was, van Gennep reported ('Cultuurondernemingen op Java, 1870'), the only one in Java at that time '*die volgens het zoogenaamde systeme van Triple Effet werkt, met gebruik van het "acide carbonique"*' ['that operated according to the so-called Triple Effet system, with the use of "carbonic acid"'].

suited to sugar refineries rather than colonial factories producing raw sugar. Just how big an investment it represented can be gauged from the fact that (in 1881) the NHM paid some 40 000 guilders (including freight and insurance) for a Triple Effect for one of its factories on the north coast of Central Java[356], whereas the entire Colomadu operation — almost a decade prior to the installation of its Triple Effect — appears to have cost around 100 000 guilders when first built in 1861.[357] Mangkunegara IV (1809-1881), however, was reckoned to be a very rich man, with an annual income said to be as much as 1 million guilders, and was also likely to have been a business associate of another very rich man, the 'Captain Chinese' at Semarang, Be Biauw Tjoan (1824-1904), one of the leading businessmen in the colony.[358]

The Pangeran had presumably purchased his 'Triple Effet' on the advice of his *administrateur*, the German-born Johann Robert Kampf (1822-1897), a sugar engineer who had worked closely with Thomas Edwards at Wonopringgo less than a decade earlier (and who was later associated with the beet sugar industry in the Netherlands).[359] Maybe it came from French ateliers, like the magnificent chandeliers

---

[356] JVFB, vol. 56, 1881, p. 52.

[357] A useful ally of the Dutch at the Surakarta Court, Mangkunegara IV had been advanced 100 000 guilders by the Indies Government to build Colomadu (the sum was to be repaid over five years in coffee delivered from Mangkunegara's estates). See Houben, *Kraton*, p. 301.

[358] I infer this relationship from the fact that when, early in the 1880s, Hermanus van Blommestein, proprietor at this date of both Kalimatie and Wonopringo, was in financial difficulties, his NHM creditors thought that he could turn for help both to Mangkunegara IV and to Be, with both of whom he was said to be 'on terms of the greatest friendship'. See [Extract] Factorij to A'dam, 22.7.1881, 'Dossiers Cultuurzaken ... Wonopringgo & Kalimatie', NHMA, 7945. On Be Biauw Tjoan, see Rush, *Opium to Java*, pp. 77-8, 93-6.

[359] Indeed, Edwards had proposed him to the *factorij* as his successor when he left Wonopringgo in 1862. See Factorij to A'dam, 7.9.1860/877 ('die daartoe bijzonder door den Heer Edwards is aanbevolen'). Instead, Kampf took himself to the *Vorstenlanden* and the employ of Mangkoe Negoro IV. Johann Robert Kampf was born in Prussia (Cleve) on 7 November 1822; in Pekalongan, on 5 March 1860, he married Maria Louisa Neumman (who was born in Pekalongan on 16 November 1839, and who was the daughter of Maur Neumman, born in Germany, no date, merchant at Pekalongan, and of Jacoba Carolina Greuder, born in Pekalongan, no date). Kampf died on 22 September 1897 in Lemelerveld (the Netherlands). Lemelerveld — in Overijssel — was the location of NV Overijsselsche Beetwortelsuikerfabriek [Overrijssel Beetsugar Factory Ltd], established in 1865 (nl.wikipedia.org/wiki/Lemelerveld). This can scarcely have been a coincidence: it looks as if Kampf returned to Europe at some stage to work there.

Figure 15: The audience hall or *pendopo* of Mangkunegara IV's palace.
Source: Koninklijk Instituut voor Taal-, Land- en Volkenkunde, Leiden, no. 3374

in the *pendopo* [audience hall] of the Pangeran's palace. However this may have been, the whole enterprise so impressed van Gennep — the factory was '*inderdaad een uitmutende inrighting*' ['in point of fact a quite outstanding set-up'] — that he strongly recommended his company establish financial and commercial ties with Mangkunegara.

Something of the factory's impact on van Gennep can be grasped from an early photograph of Colomadu, taken in the late 1860s by the celebrated Batavia commercial photographers, Woodbury & Page. It may show *administrateur* Kampf — whom van Gennep extolled for his *kunde en ijver* [knowledge and energy] — dressed in whites, standing under the factory's massive portico: what it certainly makes clear is how formidable an enterprise Colomadu indeed was. To the left, a free-standing building houses the factory's boilers (evidenced by the towering chimney), while to

Figure 16: The Colomadu sugar factory in South-Central Java c. 1865. One of the most technologically advanced Java factories of its day also had the distinction of being the sole factory operating in the colony at that time that was owned by a Javanese.
Source: Koninklijk Instituut voor Taal-, Land- en Volkenkunde, Leiden, no. 26962

its immediate right an impressively fronted (and presumably recently whitewashed) tile-roofed, stone or brick building would have housed the apparatus for processing the cane-juice once it had come from the mills. To its right again, is an open-sided, high-roofed and well-ventilated pavilion, presumably the place where the sugar was given its final drying — and packing.[360]

The Myth of the 'Dark Ages' of Sugar Manufacture in Java in the Mid-nineteenth Century

Mankunegara's pioneering advances at Colomadu notwithstanding, one of the things which has bedevilled our understanding of the history of sugar in nineteenth-century Java has been a lingering notion that the industry had to wait for the dismantlement of the *Cultuurstelsel* and the sugar crisis of 1884 before it could be technologically modernised. In one form, indeed, a now-fading orthodoxy has insisted that it took the crisis to shake the industry out of its purported 'lethargy' and institute a period of far-reaching technological and scientific innovation, directed by metropolitan capital,

---

[360] Steven Wachlin, with a contribution by Marianne Fluitsma & Gerrit Knaap, *Woodbury & Page: Photographers Java*, Leiden, KITLV Press, 1994, p. 127.

which signalled Java sugar's emergence from 'the dark' ages.[361] In fact, nothing could be further from the truth.[362]

There existed, to be sure, a body of contemporary opinion which loudly asserted that the Java sugar manufacturers of the mid-nineteenth century indeed lagged behind other sectors of what was rapidly becoming an international sugar economy.[363] Some of these assertions, moreover, appear well-founded. For example,

---

[361] This orthodoxy was reflected early in the twentieth century in a self-serving depiction of the 'bad old days', which had preceded the industry's 'modernisation' at the hand of the companies who presently owned it. A ripe example is to be found in the commentary of one leading industry apologist of the 1920s, who asserted that integral to the way in which sugar production was organised under the auspices of the *Cultuurstelsel* was a whole series of obstacles to the' progress and development' of the industry while 'the [prevailing] uncertainty about the future makes it risky to invest capital in machines etc.' (See Tichelaar, 'De Expoitatie eener Suikerfabriek', pp. 209, 216, 219.) Unfortunately, this 'orthodoxy' has found its way into modern literature. Hence, for example, Aard J Hartveld, in his otherwise invaluable — and widely cited — University of Wageningen doctoral thesis, commits himself (quite unnecessarily) to the argument that the sugar crisis of the mid-1880s was the vital turning point in manufacturing technology in Java sugar. Viz.: 'Around 1884 declining prices for Indonesian sugar on the international market *caused drastic technological changes in the sugar industry* ... In order to retain their market position, the mill owners had to invest in new processing technology that improved the quality of their product and the efficiency of their mills ... Both cultivation techniques and technology of sugar refineries [i.e. mills] underwent considerable changes. New crushing equipment and modern refinery technology had to be applied ...' (emphasis added). See Aard J Hartveld, 'Raising Cane: Linkages, Organisations and Negotiations in Malang's Sugar Industry, East Java', Proefschrift, Landbouw Universitiet Wageningen, 1996, p. 47. The geographer Jock Galloway's essay on 'The Modernisation of Sugar Production in Southeast Asia, 1880-1940', *The Geographical Review*, vol. 95, no. 1, January, 2005, pp. 1-24 likewise carries the strong implication that such 'modernisation' only began in Java in the 1880s, though the author's graph (fig. 5, p. 9) makes it clear that by 1880 Java (in contrast to the rest of the region) was already producing a very substantial amount of 'modern' centrifugal sugar (as indeed, it had been for some decades) which was, virtually by definition, the product of 'advanced' factories.

[362] Leidelmeijer *Grootbedrijf*, passim, had done much to explode the myth as early as the 1980s. For a futher pioneering critique, see Bosma, 'Sugar and Dynasty', pp. 89-92.

[363] Writing late in the 1860s, John Millard (*De Suikerindustrie op Java*, p. 15ff.) argued that uncertainty about the future of the Contract system and the system itself (not least the vacillating policy of successive colonial administrations vis-à-vis the 'free disposal' of the sugar that the Contractors produced — pp. 59-61) militated against the uptake of technological innovations. Yet Millard (himself the one-time *administrateur* of a Java sugar factory) was careful to qualify his remarks. The situation was one in which the manufacturers, he noted *'de onmogelijkheid verkeren de resultaten der wetenshap geheel toe te passen'* ['were in a position where it was impossible to apply scientific findings *in their entirety*; emphasis added]'. Millard

the NHM (who had reason to know) complained that the relatively low grades of sugar specified in the Government's sugar contracts were a disincentive to investment in improved manufacturing apparatus.[364]

Over time, however, things changed. From the 1850s onward, in particular, most manufacturers were allowed to dispose (albeit erratically) of increasingly substantial amounts of their output on the open market. In turn, this undoubtedly created more enthusiasm for improved equipment. As Thomas Edwards, *administrateur* of the NHM's Wonopringgo sugar factory, remarked to his employers in 1856, '[the island's manufacturers] have already given evidence by the general adoption of steam machinery that they are ready to spend their money freely when a fair chance of a profit can be shown'.[365] For example, three years later (as we have seen) the owners of the Kemanglen and Doekoewringin sugar factories (located like Wonopringgo on the north coast of Central Java) were able to negotiate the 'free disposal' of all the sugar they produced. They promptly used the potential advantage gained thereby (since sugar prices were on the rise) as collateral for a substantial loan to enable them to buy new equipment.[366] This was not an isolated instance. As we have seen in the foregoing chapters of this book, and as we will futher discover in the pages that follow, notions of the 'backward' nature of Java's sugar industry during the decades extending from the 1840s to the 1880s simply do not stand up to examination.

How then to account for a 'black legend'? First and foremost, it has to be concluded that a contemporary critique of the 'backwardness' of the mid-century Java industry is hard to distinguish from a general polemic directed against the *Cultuurstelsel* by opponents in Holland. In part, moreover, this stemmed (as we

---

roundly rejected any suggestion that the manufacturers were '*niet op de hoogte van hun vak*' ['not on top of their business'].

[364] See, for example, the NHM *factorij*'s observations in the mid-1840s that Derosne equipment in the mid-1840s produced sugar of higher quality than was stipulated in Government Contracts (Factorij to A'dam, 31.12.1845/246). Leidelmeijer *Grootbedrijf* (pp. 170ff.) likewise draws attention to the disincentive to technological advance inherent in the poor reception that Derosne 'steam' sugar got from the Dutch refiners. Worldwide, however, this does not always seem to have been the case. French refiners appear to have paid 'remarkable' prices for 'Derosne' sugar from French colonies in the Caribbean — see Tomich, *Slavery in the Circuit of Sugar*, p. 205.

[365] Edwards to Factorij, 2.8.1856/1036, enclosed in Factorij to A'dam, 9.8.1856/480.

[366] This enabled them to buy a state of-the-art steam mill from the London firm of Robinson. See NHMR, 4796.

have seen) from a refusal in the metropolis to legitimate the Creole technology that developed on the colonial frontier. For subsequent commentators and historians, however, acceptance of the 'legend' appears to stem from misunderstandings about the complexity of the ongoing and essentially incremental nature of technological advance in manufacture throughout the international sugar economy during the middle decades of the nineteenth century. In particular, the fact that many of Java's factories boasted a variety of equipment, some of the latest design and some belonging to an earlier era, was — very emphatically — not evidence of 'regressive' tendencies. Rather, it was perfectly in line with the situation of such industries worldwide. Improvement, it is worth reiterating, was incremental and continuous, rather than sudden and total. In Cuba itself, despite its deserved reputation as the *ne plus ultra* of industrial progress in cane sugar manufacture, 'mixed' systems incorporating both the new and the old were the order of the day, and patchy, uneven technological development was totally characteristic of all the more advanced sectors of commodity sugar manufacture worldwide.[367]

In short, just as elsewhere, the industrial project in sugar was a piecemeal affair in Java in the mid-nineteenth century: new-fangled and obsolete machinery and techniques rubbed shoulders. In the late 1860s and 1870s, however, the arrival of Multiple Effect apparatus in one of its several forms — since, along with 'Triple Effet', there were the alternative possibilities of 'Double Effet' and 'Quadruple Effet'— was the single most important development in the technology of sugar production since the appearance of the Vacuum Pan a quarter of a century or more earlier. The Multiple Effect heralded the arrival of continuous process manufacture, which began with the milling of cane and ended only in the Centrifuge and the packing shed. The adoption of continuous process technology — along with its associated science — not only took the guesswork out of manufacture but also, at least as importantly, created a basis for expanded productive capacity.[368] Its adoption in Java, along with other major new appurtenances of industrialised manufacture, was hence an index to

---

[367] See e.g. M Moreno-Fraginals, *The Sugar Mill: The Socio-Economic Complex of Sugar in Cuba, 1780-1860*, New York, Monthly Review Press, 1976, pp. 81-175; Curry-Machado, *Cuban Sugar*, pp. 23-30; for Louisiana, see JA Heitmann, *The Modernisation of the Louisiana Sugar Industry, 1830-1910*, Baton Rouge, Louisiana State University Press, 1987, pp. 48ff.; and for Martinique, see Tomich, *Slavery in the Circuit of Sugar*, pp. 191-7.

[368] See e.g. the suggestive comments on this score in *Griggs, Global Industry, Local Innovation*, pp. 186-7.

the technologically evolved state of significant numbers of Java's sugar factories in the decade or so before the crisis of the mid-1880s.

The Indices to Progress: The Multiple Effect, Grinding Mills and Boilers circa 1870-84

Initially, few other manufacturers followed Mangkunegara IV's initiative in installing Multiple Effect apparatus at Colomadu. Was Surakarta, despite the large amounts of sugar being manufactured in the Principalities by the 1860s and 1870s, too 'remote' from Java's main colonial production areas? Had its 'Triple Effet' not come up to expectations? Was the expense still considered too great? For whatever reason, prior to 1877 very few sets of such apparatus appear to have been installed on the island. Thereafter, however, the colony's manufacturers, faced with a secular decline in sugar prices which had set in a decade earlier, took up the Multiple Effect with alacrity. As well as improving the quality and quantity of sugar produced, through removing many of the hazards attendant on rule-of-thumb methods in open cleansing and evaporating pans, Multiple Effect apparatus also brought very substantial savings in the costs of fuel. In 1881, for example, the NHM's Batavia *factorij* reported to Amsterdam that it was buying a 'Triple Effet' for its Kemantran sugar factory on the north coast of Central Java, arguing that it would effect a big reduction in the present 'huge' costs of firewood. Indeed, it was reckoned that firewood had been costing Kemantran around 22 000 guilders a year for the previous six years; and a net annual saving of 17 000 guilders was anticipated from the installation of the new apparatus.[369]

In this latter respect, moreover, it must be assumed that the industry's decades-long timber consumption had taken its toll on easily reachable woodlands. Indeed, it was around this time that some manufacturers began to invest in the purchase of leases on areas that were suitable for 'farming' timber.[370] To be sure, by reducing the number of (skilled) manual operations in the boiling house, the Multiple Effect also promised significant savings on wages. Nonetheless, reduced fuel bills were critical. By the mid-1880s, when the industry was hit by a sudden and dramatic fall in the

---

[369] JVFB, vol. 56, 1881, p. 52.

[370] E.g. *HCHO*, 1888, pp. 255-6 shows that the Lucassen family had no other business interests in Java apart from their sugar factories — the only exception being a joint interest in two *erfpachtpeerceelen* [long-leasehold properties] in Brebes Regency (Tegal Residency) which produced firewood [*brandhout*], fish and sometimes coconuts.

price of sugar, it can be estimated that as many as one-third of the colony's sugar factories were already equipped with the Multiple Effect in one of its several forms. In the sugar belt that ran along the north coast of Central Java, for example, the Wonopringgo factory installed a 'Quadruple Effet' from the leading French firm of Fives Lille in 1879.[371] Elsewhere on the north coast, in the adjoining Tegal Residency, Kemanglen and Doekoewringin, which were smaller operations and were still in the hands of members of the family who had built the factories some forty years earlier, installed similar though rather less grand apparatus a couple or so years later. Other factories soon followed suit.[372]

Nonetheless, the installation of Multiple Effect apparatus was only one dimension — albeit a crucial one — of developments in Java's colonial sugar factories during the 1870s and 1880s which set the industry apart from its erstwhile Asian counterparts and underscored its global importance. Critical advances in machine technology and 'sugar' science were evident throughout the manufacturing process that turned raw cane into sugar. In 1884, for example, when the Dutch owner-manager of the Kalibagor sugar factory in South-Central Java published a short account of his enterprise, he remarked on a number of things. One was a recent and significant improvement in the grinding of cane consequent on the installation over the previous decade of two steam-operated sets of mills.[373] Steam power, as was widely recognised, created the potential for a more efficient extraction of juice because it allowed a greater degree of pressure to be brought to bear on the cane. In some locations, steam power had been adopted in the 1850s or even earlier.

---

[371] 'Overzicht van de Installatie van Wonopringgo' [c. 1905], File 'Wonopringgo', in NHMA, 7945.

[372] See the listing of sugar-manufacturing equipment in the *KV*, 1875-1882. The detailed listing stops in 1882, however, and in any event is demonstrably incomplete prior to that date. In some key sugar districts, the number of Multiple Effects in use prior to 1884 was very high. For example, in Pekalongan-Tegal (the north coast area of Central Java, which accounted for around one-tenth of Java's sugar exports), around two-thirds of the factories were so equipped when the crisis broke. See the information relating to the sugar factories in the *KV*, i.e. Pagongan (*KV*, 1881); Adiwerna (*KV*, 1879); Doekoewringin (*KV*, 1882); Kemanglen (*KV*, 1880); Djatibarang (*KV*, 1881); Pangka (*KV*, 1878); Kalimatie (*KV*, 1878). Other similarly equipped factories were Balapoelang (*JV, NI Handelsbank*, 1882, vol. 10, NA Handelsbank); Kemantran (JVFB, vol. 57, 1882, p. 49); Maribaia (JVFB, vol. 58 1883, pp. 51-2); Klidang (JVFB, vol. 58, 1883, pp. 51-2).

[373] JWA van Soest, *De Suikeronderneming Kalibagor*, Semarang, Bisschop, 1884, p. 21-4.

Even so, as late as 1869, more than half of the nearly 100 sugar factories working on Government contract in Java were still operating exclusively with water power; some 27 had auxiliary steam engines (generally for when water ran short) and only 11 relied exclusively on steam power for grinding their cane.[374] By the mid-1880s, however, steam had become increasingly common, both because of the efficiencies it offered and because the Indies Government became increasingly concerned about the detrimental effects on peasant farming of the diversion of water to the sugar factories' mill-race. According to the colonial authorities in Java, in 1871 there had been 362 stationary steam engines working in the sugar industry in Java, whereas by 1881 the number had almost tripled to 998 (it stood at 1232 ten years later).[375] To be sure, some caution is needed in interpreting these figures, not least because some steam engines were undoubtedly auxiliary to water-wheels in the grinding of cane, and others were used to provide steam for Vacuum Pans and Multiple Effects (as well as to run Centrifuges). Even so, the increase is impressive — and almost enough in itself to dispose of the myth of technological 'backwardness' prior to the crisis of the mid-1880s.

In some parts of the Java industry, the change-over to steam milling was slow. In the important sugar-producing region centred on the Residencies of Pekalongan and Tegal on the north coast of Central Java, in particular, it was not until the 1890s that the switch from water power as the motive force in grinding cane was complete. Given the particular circumstances in which the industry operated, however, this was a rational response to environmental circumstances rather than an indicator of inherent 'backwardness', evaluation of development risks in the mid-nineteenth century being distorted here by a New World perspective that pays no attention to differing local circumstances. As far as the Java manufacturers were concerned — although the peasantry in the locality of the factories presumably saw it rather differently, since it was their irrigation systems that were thereby impacted upon — water was a 'free'

---

[374] The position in the colony as a whole in 1869 was that 57 of the factories operating on Government contract (i.e. at that stage about 80 per cent or more of Java's industrial sugar factories) used exclusively water-wheels; 27 had auxiliary steam engines and 11 worked exclusively with steam engines. See *KV*, 1870.

[375] The data, based on the *KV* of the relevant years, is in Table 1, 'Use of Steam Power in Manufacturing Industry, 1870-1940,' p. 46 of W.A.I.M Segers, *Manufacturing Industry 1870-1942*, vol. 8 of P. Boomgaard (ed.), *Changing Economy in Indonesia*, Amsterdam, Royal Tropical Institute, 1987.

resource. In particular, for those factories located near the island's central mountain ranges, rainfall was often sufficient to replenish streams and rivers, even in the 'dry season'. If not, an auxiliary steam engine might well be — and often was — installed. Sticking with water power made good economic sense, since it avoided the necessity for costly purchases of firewood or (imported) coal. The essential point, however, was that, unlike the industry's situation in the Caribbean, where in many places watermills were simply not a practical alternative (it was either cattle-mills, windmills or steam)[376], they *were* precisely that in Java, where in many areas water was ostensibly in plentiful supply.

Moreover, quite emphatically, the relative slowness with which sections of the industry moved from water to steam did not preclude the installation of new and more powerful grinding mills, together with the adoption of new and improved milling techniques. In respect to the latter, by the early 1880s the practice of double-crushing the cane was beginning to be adopted at a number of Java factories. At the Kalibagor sugar factory, for instance, with its two mills, the arrangement was for the cane to be passed initially through the bigger, more powerful one, and subsequently for the cane remnants to be ground again [*herperst*] in the second, smaller mill.[377] What happened at Kalibagor was indicative of developments of this kind elsewhere in the industry.[378] Indeed, there is substantial evidence from the mid-1870s of a continuous, ongoing installation of new machinery related in one way or another to the grinding of cane. Inventories of equipment, including the dates of installation, preserved for a number of factories on the north coast of Central Java, for example, reveal just how much new equipment in this category was put into place there in the decade prior to the sugar crisis of 1884-45 and the subsequent 'reconstruction' of the industry.

In 1882, for example, the Kalimatie factory in Pekalongan Residency, owned by the second generation of the Dutch colonial family who had built it some forty years earlier, was equipped with a new mill (of the *Rousselot* type patented a decade earlier) from the Liverpool firm of Fawcett Preston in the United Kingdom.[379]

---

[376] Tann, 'Steam and Sugar', p. 65.

[377] Van Soest, *Kalibagor*, p. 24.

[378] *KV*, 1886 records double crushing of the cane as being adopted at a number of factories, including Kalimatie. *KV*, 1888 says some factories were even crushing cane thrice.

[379] For this and other information in this paragraph, see (except where separately noted) PA van Blommestein to Factorij, 4.3.1879 & 6.10.1885; 'Overzicht van de Installatie van Wonopringgo' [n.d., c. 1908]; 'Beschrijving van de Installatie Kalimatie' [c. 1908],

Fawcett Preston had also supplied a *middelmolen* [middle mill] for Kalimatie in 1874, which had subsequently been complimented, five years later, by a *voorpersmolen* [preliminary mill] from the French firm of Fives Lille.[380] Other apparatus from Fives Lille and Fawcett Preston — notably sets of *vlampijp-bouilleur ketels*[381] [steam boilers of significantly improved efficiency] — were installed in this and neighbouring factories at various dates between 1875 and the early 1880s.

There were, of course, factories that prior to the crisis were shockingly run-down and inefficient. Anton *baron* Sloet van Oldruietenborgh's once-resplendent Poerwodadi factory in Madiun Residency was one of them.[382] Nonetheless, there is no reason to suppose that developments at Kalimatie were exceptional, nor that they were confined to one part of the colony. Further east, in Surabaya Residency, for example, the Djombang factory could boast by 1884 an assortment of new equipment from the celebrated Nottingham firm of Manlove, Alliott & Co in the United Kingdom, including a new (steam) mill[383], while to the west of Kalimatie, in Cirebon Residency, a new steam mill had been installed at the Soerawinangan sugar factory some three years earlier, prior to the Campaign of 1881.[384]

NHMA, 7945. 'Fawcett Preston Engineering was founded in 1758, by George Perry, as the Liverpool branch of the Coalbrookdale Foundry at Ironbridge. It became an independent Liverpool company and built up an international reputation, particularly for sugar machinery …'. See http://www.nationalarchives.gov.uk (accessed 15 August 2014).

[380] The engineering firm of Fives Lille emerged (between 1861 and 1865) from the merger/combination of several pre-existing French enterprises. Its sugar machinery division, founded in 1870, was the successor of the mid-century Derosne et Cail companies, already famous in the middle decades of the nineteenth century for the manufacture of machinery of this kind. See fr.wikipedia.org/wiki/Fives-Lille.

[381] The full name is *Vlampijpbouilleurketel* (my thanks here to Margaret Leidelmeijer and Aart te Velde): around the boiler there were small pipes, through which hot combustion gases were forced. In this way it was possible to heat the boiler more quickly thanks to the larger heating surface that the arrangement of pipes brought in its train. See QAD Emmen, *Rietsuikerfabrieken op Java en hare Machinerieën*, 4th edn, vol. 2, Tegal, De Boer, 1930, pp. 356-62 and the illustrations/diagrams therein.

[382] See the file on 'Poerwodadi voor 1888' in NHMA, 7944.

[383] See 'Particulariteten omtrent de Sf. Djombang', 22.11.1884, in NHMA, 7966. Manlove Alliott had been established in 1837 and (in 1914) the company described itself as 'Engineers, Colonial and General. Specialities: Engines, Boilers, Sugar Machinery, Oil Mill Plant, Power Laundry Plant, Centrifugal Machines, Refuse Destructors. Employees 400'. See en.wikipedia.org/wiki/Manlove,_Alliott_%26_Co._Ltd.

[384] Fokker to Factorij, 21.2.1881, 'Inspectie Rapporten over Eigen en Andere Ondernemingen, 1879-1900', NHMA.

Of important developments in sugar milling in the third quarter of the nineteenth century, only machines for shredding the cane before it was ground — which hence facilitated the work of the mills — appear to have been absent from the Java industry prior to 1885. Such machines (the 'Ross Cane Cutter' prominent among those in use) were certainly in use in Java's industrial sugar factories in the final decade of the century, but one leading authority reported their presence there as *in de laatste tijd* [only very recent]. They were used in combination with the increasingly wide-spread practice of macerating partially milled cane with water or cane-juice in order to obtain a considerably increased juice extraction.[385] Again, it looks as if in Java, as elsewhere, maceration as a wide-spread manufacturing process only dated from the period after the sugar crisis of 1884, when sugar makers worldwide became increasingly desperate to increase the efficiency of their operations.

Even so, this was emphatically not a sign of some newly discovered interest in technological advance in the factory. Quite the contrary: the situation in this respect after 1884 had deep roots in ongoing developments over the preceding decades which stretched back into the middle years of the century. International comparisons are important here, and a singularly revealing one is between Java in the 1870s and early 1880s and the burgeoning sugar industry to its south in north-eastern Australia's Queensland. As recent scholarship has demonstrated, contemporary Queensland lagged substantially behind Java in terms of the installation of the Vacuum Pan, which only arrived there in the 1870s, almost forty years after its first 'pioneering' appearance in Java. (As we saw in an earlier chapter, Java's industrial sugar factories were already extensively equipped with Vacuum Pans by the late 1850s — and such Pans had begun to be installed twenty or more years before that.) Likewise with Multiple Effect apparatus: though its first appearance in Australia dated from 1878, it only began to be installed there in any numbers almost a decade later, and hence somewhat later than in Java. However, for reasons that perhaps had to do with the availability of firewood as well as with the greater efficiency of cane-grinding, 'sugar mills relying on steam power to drive the crushing rollers were very common in Australia during

---

[385] Griggs (*Global Industry, Local Innovation*, p. 191-2) notes that they were beginning to be used in the technologically rapidly advancing sugar industry of colonial Queensland at about the same time. For example, CSR (probably the most progressive of the Australian sugar owners) installed a shredder at one of its Queensland factories in 1889. The 'Ross' cutter itself was only patented in 1896. See http://www.vintagemachinery.org under EW Ross & Co, Fulton NY & Springfied OH, USA (accessed 15 August 2014).

the late 1860s and 1870s'[386], whereas, as we have seen, their installation in the Java industry was altogether less pronounced.

Other comparisons show Java in an even better light. As we saw in an earlier chapter, some Multiple Effects, for example, may have been installed in a few locations (probably refineries) in the Indian subcontinent late in the nineteenth century, but elsewhere, in Mauritius, the Phillippines and East Asia, they were notable for their absence from raw sugar manufacture until the opening decades of the following century. The weight of evidence, in short, is that Java sugar in the decade or so prior to the crisis of the mid-1880s was no laggard in respect to the technology of manufacture, and it compared well with other contemporary industries elsewhere in Asia and adjoining regions.

Science in Field and Factory

Technology, of course, was not everything. Improved machines did much to make the grinding of cane more efficient, either directly through the installation of better, heavier mills or through significant improvements in the efficiency of the boilers powering the mills in cases where steam had supplanted water power. Even so, a greater expression of juice from the cane brought potential problems in its train. In particular, it meant that the juice now contained a greater percentage of impurities that might adversely affect the final quality of the sugar. It was at this point that the 'sugar chemist' — already present in the industry — became ever more vital to the success of the entire operation. In the case of the Java industry, dating from the 1850s, there was a recognition in official circles (the industry being primarily in the Indies Government's orbit until the 1870s and 1880s) that the chemistry of sugar manufacture needed to be investigated. At this time, the Dutch colonial authorities, both in The Hague and in Java itself, sponsored the work of several chemists whose concerns were with what happened both in the cane field and in the factory. Their work (despite some discontinuities) formed the basis for developments that saw the Java industry brought firmly into the sphere of applied chemistry during the middle decades of the nineteenth century.

Of particular importance here was the work of the Utrecht University's Professor GJ Mulder, scientific advisor to the Dutch Colonial Office (whom we

---

[386] Griggs, *Global Industry, Local Innovation*, pp. 175-94. The quotation comes from p. 179.

met in the previous chapter in the context of his clash with Thomas Edwards), and his erstwhile disciple PFH Fromberg, who carried on major research in the Indies Government's Landbouwchemisch Laboratorium (Chemical-Agricultural Laboratory) at Buitenzorg (present-day Bogor) in West Java in the 1850s and 1860s. As well as his prominent role in field science, he oversaw experiments in Java in the most effective handling of cane-juice during its clarification and reduction into a viscous liquid.[387] This pioneering Dutch work was important, above all, because it addressed questions relating to sugar cane — a subject of minimal interest, of course, to the savants of the German beet sugar industry that had otherwise rapidly become the front-runner in matters relating to sugar science. German research was heavily focused on the conversion of liquid sucrose into sugar and, needless to say, was little concerned with the milling of sugar cane. The work done by Mulder, Fromberg et al., dealt, however, with the Java-specific cultivation of cane — and, very prominently, with issues concerned with the expression of cane-juice in the grinding mill (and to some extent with its subsequent treatment along the production line).

To be sure, there were disputes among the savants and their Government backers as to whether scientific investigation should focus on the cultivation of cane rather than the manufacturing process. Fromberg was of the former persuasion, arguing in essence that the manufacturers themselves could be relied upon to operate efficiently in their own sphere (as Edwards had indeed asserted). Mulder, though, was a keen (not to say ferocious) advocate of the need to understand the chemistry of the milling of cane and to improve thereby the whole process of juice extraction.[388] Despite such disputes — which appear to have contributed to the shutting-down of the Indies Government's Buitenzorg laboratory in 1860, two years after Fromberg's death — there is no lack of evidence that the middle decades of the nineteenth century saw a deal of Dutch scientific expertise brought to bear on the problems facing the Java sugar industry in both field and factory. It was an important forshadowing of what was to come.

---

[387] GJ Mulder (1802-1880) was one of the most outstanding chemists of nineteenth-century Holland, and a man with an international reputation. His academic career had begun in Rotterdam (1828) and continued at the University of Utrecht (1840). He acted as advisor to both the NHM and the Dutch Colonial Office, and it was on his advice that the Landbouw-Chemisch Laboratorium [Laboratory for Agricultural Chemistry] was established in the Indies in 1851 (at Buitenzorg/Bogor, in West Java) with PFH Fromberg at its head. For an account of Mulder's and Fromberg's careers, see Leidelmeijer, *Grootbedrijf*, pp. 195-8, 202-3.

[388] Leidelmeijer, *Grootbedrijf*, pp. 209-29.

From around 1860 onward, as one student of the North American cane sugar industry has remarked:

> [c]hemical analysis transformed the ... sugar factory by rapidly supplying answers to problems that had previously perplexed the operator ... Management increasingly relied on analytical data to control processes ... Exact weights and volumes were now a crucial parameter of plant efficiency and product quality.[389]

In this context, moreover, European beet sugar industries — particularly those of newly Imperial Germany — largely set the pace. This was reflected in the fact that German know-how and personnel became increasingly evident in Java. The early career of Samuel Cornelis van Musschenbroek (1857-1914), subsequently a leading figure — indeed, perhaps *the* leading figure — in Java's sugar industry, was a prime case in point. Born and educated in the Netherlands, he had initially arrived in Java to work in a sugar factory newly acquired by distant relatives. Subsequently, however, early in the 1880s, he took himself to Germany and spent almost two years studying the chemistry of sugar — as well as observing the formidable political clout of a well-organised industry. He came back to apply both lessons in the Dutch colony. He was one of the driving forces behind the establishment in Java in the mid-1880s of the research stations that were eventually fused into the Java industry's world-famous *Proefstation* [Research Institute] in Pasuruan, in the heart of the East Java sugar belt.[390]

In the decade before the formal establishment of resarch stations, however, chemists were already active in Java's more advanced sugar factories, creating in the process the embryo of the well-staffed and elaborately equipped factory laboratories that later became so characteristic of the Javanese sugar industry. Dates varied: at Kalibagor, for instance, it was 1884 before the cane-juice was routinely subjected to chemical analysis by a chemist. Significantly, the chemist concerned was said to be employed in other sugar factories in a neighbouring Residency.[391] Likewise, in the less 'remote' sugar factories owned or managed by the NHM in the north-coast sugar belt of Central Java, a German chemist (a Dr Ostermann) was already employed at the beginning of the 1880s — and possibly even earlier.[392] It was no accident, therefore,

---

[389] Heitman, *Louisiana Sugar Industry*, pp. 27-9.

[390] Leidelmeijer, *Grootbedrijf*, pp. 235-6; G Roger Knight, *Commodities and Colonialism: The Story of Big Sugar in Indonesia, 1880-1942*, Leiden & Boston, Brill, 2013, pp. 98-111.

[391] van Soest, *Kalibagor*, pp. 20-1.

[392] Extract letter [Superintendent] Steven Everts to Factorij Batavia, 15.1.1881/30, NHMA, 7936. Dr L Ostermann subsequently played a key role in the establishment of the Proefstation

that in 1885 the pioneering Proefstation West Java [Research Station West Java] was established in this same area or that it was 'under the direction of a chemist and a specialised physicist — both Germans'.[393]

Donald Lucassen and the Diffusion Process for Extracting Sucrose

What also excited the attention of Java's sugar industrialists in the early 1880s, was a way of processing cane which might offer better extraction rates than did conventional milling. This was the system of diffusion.[394] Adapted to cane processing from the beet sugar industries of northern Europe, where slicing the beets and submerging them in water was the standard way of extracting their sucrose through osmosis, it involved the mechanical chopping-up of the cane stalks before their submersion. The resultant sucrose-rich liquid — singularly free of the impurities that grinding the cane invariably brought to cane-juice — was then drained off and heavily reduced before being processed in the normal manner through the Multiple Effect, Vacuum Pan and Centrifuge. To some industry leaders it seemed — possibly — the way of the future. Among them was Donald Lucassen, second-generation owner of a sugar factory on the north coast of Central Java. (His father was the Colonel Lucassen whose pioneering activities we explored earlier in this book.) The younger Lucassen had been born in Java, lived there for much of his life and was to die there — in the East Java town of Malang — in 1892.[395]

His long stay in Java (contrary to many stereotypes) evidently did nothing to stifle his bent for improvement. In 1888 he encountered a fellow-manufacturer from Louisiana in the workshops of the firm of Fives Lille, great French fabricators of Multiple Effect apparatus — and of equipment for the diffusion process. The American, Harvey Wiley, was convinced by Lucassen 'that the diffusion cells designed and fabricated by the ... Fives Lille Company were superior to those of its competitors'. Wiley evidently thought highly of his new acquaintance, whom he correctly identified as 'an

---

West Java [Experiment Station West Java], was *Directeur* of the *Mestfabriek* [Fertiliser Factory] *Semarang*, a firm that both produced and imported fertiliser for sugar factories, and became co-owner of a sugar factory in the Principalities. See Leidelmeijer, *Grootbedrijf*, pp. 238-9.

[393] JVFB, vol. 60, 1885, p. 14.
[394] See e.g. Heitman, *Louisiana Sugar Industry*, pp. 52, 59-62.
[395] Donald FW Lucassen was born in Batavia in 1837, died in Malang in 1892 and was the owner of Doekoewringin. He was married to Adriana Casparina Minetta van Benthem van den Bergh (born in Zaltbommel in 1839, died in Heemstede in 1916).

Figure 17: Donald Lucassen: a leading figure in the on-going modernisation of the Java industry in the 1870s and 1880s.
Source: Koninklijk Instituut voor Taal-, Land- en Volkenkunde, Leiden, no. 8061

influential planter from Java who was instrumental in the Javan diffusion tests on sugar cane'.[396] Indeed, early in the decade, Lucassen had formed part of a small commission set up in Java to investigate the potential for diffusion in the island's sugar factories.[397] One factory in Cirebon Residency (Djatiwangi) had experimented with diffusion as early as the mid-1870s[398], and Lucassen himself appears to have installed some quantity of diffusion apparatus at his Wonopringgo sugar factory late in the following decade — as, indeed, his presence at Fives Lille implied.

In fact, however, diffusion was not the way of the future, at least not in Java. One authoritative report on the situation in the colony in the 1890s noted the potential of this adaption of beet sugar technology to the processing of cane, 'without it having gained general acceptance'. Diffusion certainly got more sucrose out of the cane than did grinding, but it needed more skilled workmen if it was to succeed, and a great deal of fuel was consumed in boiling down the resultant, much diluted cane-juice.[399] One verdict, passed early in the twentieth century, was

---

[396] Heitman, *Louisiana Sugar Industry*, p. 143.

[397] Its members consisted of GMW Zuur (owner of Djatiwangi), Lucassen, Steven Everts (Superintendant of Sugar Factories for the NHM) and JS Bowles (co-owner of Kadhipaten). See John Millard, *Riet en Bietsuiker in Verband tot de Suikerindustrie op Java: Voordracht ter Aanprizing van eene Proef met Diffusie op Java*, Gravenhage, Couvee, 1884, pp. 44-5. For Zuur (born in Leiden in 1831, died in Bandung in 1911) and his career, see http://www.myheritage.nl/æ/djatiwangi-suikerfabriek-djatiw (accessed 15 August 2014).

[398] Millard, *Riet en Bietsuiker*, p. 44.

[399] Prinsen Geerligs, *Korte Handleiding*, pp. 25-6.

that '… as yet [diffusion] has not yet met with general approval, and has even turned out a complete failure in most cases'.[400]

The Metamorphosis of the Java Sugar Factory

These several developments, touching on the milling of cane, the possibilities for the supplanting of milling by diffusion and, arguably most important of all, the introduction into the factory of Multiple Effect apparatus of one kind of another, reflected — and were reflected in — the unique metamorphosis of the Java sugar factory during the course of the nineteenth and early twentieth century. The Wonopringgo factory that Thomas Edwards had managed in the 1850s remained operational on the same site until it finally closed down more than three-quarters of a century later in 1933, at the height of the inter-war depression that came near to annihilating the entire Java industry. Whether Edwards would have readily recognised the final successor to the enterprise of the 1850s, however, is a moot point, since in the intervening years it had undergone a great increase in physical size and appearance, with an interior totally redesigned and re-equipped. Yet its location had not changed, and the changes that had taken place over the decades were incremental rather than radically and dramatically transformative. Moreover, Wonopringgo's owners and/or financiers were and remained the NHM, the Dutch company into whose hands it had come in the 1840s.

These elements of continuity — or at least some of them — were common to much of the Java industry. The point is most readily illustrated, not from the history of Wonopringgo itself, but from that of a factory some fifty kilometres away, in the same 'sugar belt' that had grown up on this part of the north coast of Central Java during the middle decades of the nineteenth century. The 1920s (the leap forward in time here is justified by the purpose of the present argument) was a period of unparalleled prosperity for colonial sugar capital. Among the industry's predominantly Dutch owners, the new-fangled aerial photography — an invention that dated only from the First World War — was much in vogue as a way of showing off and recording their achievements. One such photograph is particularly revealing. It shows the Pagongan factory on the outskirts of the town of Tegal, on the north coast of Central Java. Pagongan had started out, a hundred years or so earlier, as a simple cattle-operated mill of the kind that had existed throughout the coastal districts of Central and East

---

[400] Prinsen Geeligs, *Cane Sugar*, pp. 107-13.

Java prior to the inauguration of the *Cultuurstelsel* in 1830. Almost two decades later, at the end of the 1840s, its fortunes had changed and it began to evolve into a recognisably modern sugar factory.

The basis of the transformation was the fact that the van Blommestein family, who already operated one such sugar factory further east along the coast, near the small town of Batang, was successful in securing a Government contract for Pagongan as well.[401] The family's prior history was crucial to what happened next. The family patriarch, Hermanus van Blommestein, had held the position of harbour-master at Semarang prior to becoming a sugar Contractor for the Indies Government in the late 1830s. This position involved the collection of port duties and the like, and would have brought him into close contact with the town's large Chinese-Indonesian mercantile community. The connection served his family well later in the century when Hermanus's son, Adriaan van Blommestein, found himself in financial difficulties. Most immediately, however, it led the family in the 1850s to transfer the contract at Pagongan (de facto if not de jure) to a number of associates, among them the leading Chinese-Indonesian businessman in the town of Tegal itself. Identified in Dutch transliteration as one Tan Siong Kang, he was (presumably) a scion of the Tan business dynasty from Semarang.

Not only Chinese money was involved in Pagongan, however, since one of the guarantors of the Pagongan contract — and hence presumably a stakeholder of some kind — was the Semarang-based firm of Dorrepaal & Co. By the late 1840s, the firm was already on the road to becoming the biggest single financier of the sugar industry in the whole of Central Java.[402] The NHM *factorij* was also an interested party. Pagongan was one of that small minority of factories operating in the early days of the *Cultuurstelsel* with 'free disposal' of all the sugar it produced. That is to say, its owners could sell their sugar freely on the open market, rather than having to deliver it to the Indies Government at a fixed price. This enabled Pagongan's owners to

---

[401] The key references to the mid-century situation at Pagongan discussed in this and the following paragraphs are to be found in the voluminous file on the factory and its history in VMK, 8.4.1870/17 & NFB, 6.3.1858/364. The contract between Tan and the NHM stipulated that Tan would consign output for 1858, estimated at 5000 piculs to the *factorij*, in return for a loan of 36 000 guilders, payable in Tegal in monthly amounts. Ostensibly at least, Pagongan was taken over in 1863 by A Beijer & JC van der Palm (NFB, 6.3.1858/364). On Tan specifically, see chapter 4, above.

[402] On the genesis of the firm, see Bosma & Raben, pp. 119-21.

Figure 18: Like Topsy, she 'just grow'd': the Pagongan sugar factory, North-Central Java, from the air in the 1920s, showing its mid-nineteenth-century core.
Source: Courtesy of the author

consign the factory's output to the NHM, in return for working capital and possibly more substantial and long-term finance. Trust was obviously not paramount in the arrangement. As part of the deal, Tan Siong Kang had to hand over to the NHM's local agent a key to his Tegal warehouse, where Pagongan's sugar would be stored.

The upshot of all this manoeuvring was that the factory was substantially re-equipped with, among other things, a steam engine running its grinding mills — something of a rarity in this part of Java in the mid-nineteenth century. This was the beginning of a series of developments that can be viewed from the air, as it were, in the 1920s photograph. Hidden away in the centre of this (by then) middle-size sugar factory of the late colonial era was what we can safely identify as the 'original' Pagongan. This was the one built by Tan Siong Kang and his associates around the middle of the nineteenth century on the site of the original cattle mill. Thereafter, the factory, like Topsy, 'just grow'd'. At a rough guess, by the 1920s the factory's footprint had increased tenfold — the photograph shows big 'new' sheds (dating from 1905) at the front and older ones on each side. They virtually conceal the earlier building. Meanwhile, Pagongan's output had grown accordingly: in the 1850s, it produced around 300 MT (5000 piculs) of sugar annually, whereas by the time the photograph was taken it was approaching 9000 MT.[403] In short, on the same site, and without any serious discontinuity of operation, Pagongan — now owned by a big Dutch conglomerate, the Javasche Cultuurmaatschappij — had been transformed from a cattle mill into a fully industrialised manufacturing unit.

In global terms, this was a highly unusual if not unique development — certainly among major producers for the international market. Worldwide, the evolution of industrial manufacture during the course of the nineteenth century posed serious problems for many existing producers. The old 'estate-cum-factory' unit — with its notionally finite capacity for expansion — was placed under threat, and either dissolved into larger units of production or remained as a major impediment to further progress.[404] Factories needed to be relocated and radically restructured in relation to their agrarian context in order to meet the requirements of the industrial project in sugar. Writing of the situation that faced the Cuba industry in the second half of the nineteenth century, one of its foremost historians argued that the development of fully industrialised production was dependent on the appearance of

> a new kind of mill ... a separate phenomena, requiring such a radical transformation that it could not grow out of the narrow foundation of the old type ... [The latter] was simply liquidated. The big sugar industry was a separate phenomenon, springing from new concepts and using none of the elements of the old mill. All that went before ... had to be demolished and a new factory built.[405]

Elsewhere, the converse happened. In the case of the 'French' Caribbean, its leading historian contends that

---

[403] Figures from NFB, 6.3.1858/364 & *ASNI*, vol. 39, no. 1, 1931, p. 92.

[404] For a preliminary discussion, see Ulbe Bosma & G Roger Knight, 'Global Factory and Local Field: Convergence and Divergence in the International Cane-Sugar Industry, 1850-1940', *International Review of Social History*, vol. 49, no. 1, April 2004, pp. 1-26.

[405] Moreno-Fraginals, *The Sugar Mill*, p. 83. This was perhaps a somewhat exaggerated account, but it is noteworthy that Laird Bergad, in his richly documented study of Matanzas province, remarks that in the 1880s '[o]ver and over again the story is similar. Old mills [*Ingenios*] were abandoned or fell into disrepair, production plummeted or ceased, debts accrued and properties were auctioned to the highest bidder' (*Cuban Rural Society*, p. 295).

the existing estate system froze the framework for organising land, labour and the technology of sugar manufacture. It was difficult for already existing plantations to increase significantly the scale of their operations or to modify their technical and social organisation ... the re-organisation of production was inhibited and the existing constraints on production were reproduced and strengthened.[406]

The contrast with Java was pronounced.[407] One of the singular features of the Java sugar industry — Pagongan was no exception — was that its factories enjoyed a literal continuity of existence for a century or more, up to and beyond the end of colonialism itself. A quite remarkable metamorphosis from proto-industrial (and in some case from pre-industrial) sugar manufacture to the fully industrial modern sugar factory took place there within the physical framework of production which came into existence in the 1830s and 1840s. Factories changed hands and a significant number of new ones were added, particularly in areas subsequently 'opened up' for sugar after the initial period of expansion in the mid-nineteenth century. Nonetheless, the network of factories established under the auspices of the *Cultuurstelsel* remained in place, added to here, subtracted from there, until the inter-war depression of the 1930s — and beyond. One great survivor was the Sragi factory in Pekalongan, dating in its original form from the late 1830s. It was still in production on the same site at the time of writing in the early twenty-first century.

This metamorphosis of the Java sugar factory was made possible by the agrarian dimension in which the industry came to be located in the middle decades of the nineteenth century. Java, in this context as in others, took a singular path. By international standards, the sugar industry that developed in Java during the middle decades of the nineteenth century — at least that part of it (the major part) that grew up under the aegis of the *Cultuurstelsel* — was uniquely situated in regard to

---

[406] Tomich, *Slavery in the Circuit of Sugar*, p. 76.

[407] Jock Galloway's remarks ('The Modernisation of Sugar Production in Southeast Asia', pp. 3-5) about the 'rise' of the 'centralised factory' in Java betrays his unfamiliarity with the literature, especially the literature written in Dutch. In reality, Java did *not* (for the most part) develop a central factory system such as existed in the Caribbean, notably Cuba, by the early twentieth century. Instead, it continued to rely predominantly on factories that were, on average, rather small by international standards, and on whose *rayon* or *areaal* [i.e. the area officially accorded to the sugar factories for the rental of land for cane planting] cane was raised by direct farming organised and supervised by the personnel of each factory. See e.g. Knight, *Commodities*, pp. 54-8.

its access to land. As we saw in a previous chapter, each of the 100 or so 'contract' factories set up under the *Stelsel* between the 1830s and 1850s was assigned a so-called *beschikkingskring* or *kring*. From fields within the *kring*, the factories contracted to the Indies Government obtained their raw material and drew much of their labour. The essential point about the *kring*, however, was that it proved — unlike the legally delineated unit of the estate or plantation — to be a flexible basis for expanding future production. With the phasing-out of the *Cultuurstelsel*, as far as the production of cane was concerned during the course of the 1880s, the *kring* became what was usually designated as the factory's *rayon* or 'procurement zone'. It could be increased in size (albeit within limits imposed by the Indies Government), and within it cane could be raised in innovative and highly productive ways.

In consequence, the Java industry was not hamstrung by an agrarian-cum-agricultural matrix that confined its future growth. Almost fortuitously (as it would appear), the *Cultuurstelsel* had created a basis for the industry in the lowlands of rural Java that allowed ongoing modernisation without the need for radical reconstruction. The agrarian matrix, constructed to supply the industry with land and labour under its aegis during the 1830s and 1840s, had the capacity to expand in tandem with the requirements of industrial manufacture. Matching machinery to 'plantation' was vital. Back in the 1820s, for example, the British-colonial firm of Trail & Co, operating with recently updated, imported machinery in the proximity of Batavia, where labour was scarce, lamented that it was largely 'the want of hands' that have 'prevented our carrying on the culture of the sugar cane upon a sufficiently large scale to correspond to the powerful execution our machinery is capable of …'[408] The situation facing the industrial project operating under the aegis of the *Cultuurstelsel* two decades later was substantially different. An inherent degree of flexibility in the agricultural matrix created during the decades of the mid-nineteenth century allowed for a sufficient degree of expansion to sustain an ongoing process of technological-scientific advance without a prior requirement for the reconstruction of the entire unit of production. As was rarely the case elsewhere, the field did not constrain the factory.

The upshot (as we have seen in detail in the preceding pages) was that by the early 1880s — on the eve of the international sugar crisis of 1884 — the Java industry, by virtue of the technologically advanced state of a significant number of its

---

[408] Trail & Co to NHM, quoted in NFB, 11.4.1826/5.

factories, was well placed to survive the major upheaval. By the same token, moreover, the industry had attained a position in respect to both the technology and science of sugar production that placed it well ahead of any of its erstwhile counterparts elsewhere in Asia and the Indian Ocean and — broadly speaking — on par with most other major cane sugar producers worldwide. As such, Java sugar had come to constitute a major industrial project. It is to the future of that project — how it evolved through the crisis years of the mid-1880s and beyond — to which we can now turn by way of conclusion.

Conclusion

The Future of an Industrial Project: The 1880s and Beyond

During the middle decades of the nineteenth century (1830s-1880s), Java became, perhaps somewhat surprisingly, a world leader in the industrialised manufacture of sugar. It thereby laid the foundations for the Dutch colony's transformation into the 'Oriental Cuba', an Asian counterpart of the foremost of the sugar industries in the New World. It did so, as we have seen in the preceding account, on the basis of a number of complementary developments. One was the determination in Dutch colonial circles from the late 1820s onward to develop a proto-command economy in the Indies, with a view to exploiting the agricultural resources of Java, in particular, as the basis for large-scale production of 'world' commodities — the profits from which would flow back to an impoverished Holland. Though not envisaged initially as such, sugar became the centre-piece of the new *Cultuurstelsel* or System of [State] Cultivations (even though coffee continued to supply the greater part of the island's exports until sometime in the 1880s); and the state's largesse, in the form of capital loans, working capital, commandeered access to land and to local, servile labour was absolutely crucial to the establishment of the industrial project.

The Indies Government's achievement was twofold. Its ability to harness to the *Stelsel* — and in so-doing greatly expand — an elaborate labour-service regime that it had inherited from the pre-colonial state combined with a transformative 'peasantisation' of the island's rural social-economic formation. In tandem, these developments created an agrarian basis for sugar production which had few or no parallels elsewhere in the international sugar economy of the period. The upshot was a sugar complex, embedded in a much larger 'peasant' economy based on the cultivation of rice and second crops, which eschewed plantations and slaves and operated instead in the context of the forced labour of peasants and of 'cane-gardens' comprising fields taken from peasant farmers on a rotational basis. Very neatly, though largely contingently, the *Stelsel* exploited peasants without (formally) expropriating them, though its effective operation depended to a degree on a skewed access to resources in 'village' Java which was vital to the supply of labour that the industrial project required.

Even so, many of the state officials who put the *Cultuurstelsel* into place over a couple of decades in the middle of the nineteenth century had only limited time for the high technology and major capital expense of an increasingly developed and ongoing industrial project in sugar. Indeed, some of them suspected that such a project might have a disruptive impact on the order of Javanese rural society. Despite the degree of colonial reconstruction of the rural world under the auspices of the state which took place over the course of the nineteenth century, the conservation of the 'peasantry' was nonetheless a prime concern of what was becoming — from the mid-century onward — an increasingly formalised and self-conscious bureaucracy. In these circumstances, the driving force behind the industrial project was not so much the Indies bureaucracy as the Indies bourgeoisie.

Almost despite itself, the *Cultuurstelsel* fostered the growth of a 'colonial' bourgeoisie whose family ties linked it both to the Indies bureaucracy and, even more importantly, to its metropolitan counterpart. Indeed, it did something to invigorate the latter. As with Cuba and metropolitan Spain at around the same time, it would be possible to make out a case for the 'peripheral' tail wagging the metropolitan dog. Be that as it may, the critical point for the furtherance of the industrial project in sugar was that this emergent bourgeoisie — of sugar manufacturers, merchants, speculators and rent-seekers — came to its support at a vital moment. It did so just when the Indies Government lost interest in the further implementation in Java of the technological revolution in sugar manufacture which was the hallmark of the international sugar economy as beet fought it out with cane during the middle decades of the nineteenth century.

What the bourgeouisie engendered was a Creole industrial enterprise centred on sugar. They imported both the machinery (initially with subventions from the colonial treasury) and the people needed to maintain, repair and rebuild it. In conjunction with a skilled local workforce, they created a nucleus of engineering and scientific know-how which kept the industry moving forward. Backed by the quasi-governmental Netherlands Trading Society (NHM) — which in this matter was closely aligned to bourgeois interests in the colony — and by other major trading concerns and individual capitalists, sugar manufacture was able to generate sufficient profit to finance the continued industrialisation of production.

In the mid-1880s, however, the Indies bourgeoisie ran into difficulties when the world price of sugar suddenly collapsed after a slow decline over a decade or more. At this point, their deep-rooted and constantly renewed connections with Holland came to the rescue of sugar capital (if not of particular capitalists), and it proved possible to reconstruct the financial basis of the industry, albeit on a footing that removed much of the overall control from colony to metropolis. Such was the secular history of finance and management in the industry, however, that the dichotomy is a largely misleading one. From the 1830s onward, a situation had developed in Java in which both state and bourgeois capital came together to finance the ongoing development of the sugar industry. The *Cultuurstelsel*, far from suppressing the growth of mercantile capital in the colony, created rich opportunities for it. The trade in sugar, increasingly in 'private' hands circa 1850 onward, appears to have constituted the largest source of such capital accumulation, though other export commodities also played a role, as did a parallel growth in imports. An equally critical point, however, was that the emergence of an Indies bourgeoisie meant that support for the industrial project in Java sugar was intimately bound up with its long-standing interface with its metropolitan counterpart. A crucial consequence of this association was that the industrial project was able to weather the mid-1880s crisis rather than succumb to it.

A glance at what happened — or rather, did not happen — in the notionally comparable sugar colonies of Mauritius and the Philippines in the late nineteenth century is instructive. Both were seemingly well-placed around the middle of the century to undergo similar developments to those which occurred in Java circa 1850 onward. Subsequent to the crisis, sugar production in the Dutch colony reached its apogee during a period of renewed and ongoing expansion which began in the late 1880s and lasted until the onset of the inter-war depression of the 1930s (an event that reduced the industry, temporarily, to a mere shadow of its former self).[409] During this period, the Java industry, having lost markets in the West which had sustained its

---

[409] For a review of developments in the late nineteenth century, see Knight, *Commodities and Colonialism*, pp. 53-96; Bosma, *Industrial Sugar Plantation*, pp. 130-63; Elson, *Javanese Peasants*, pp. 127-60.

mid-nineteenth growth, developed a vital 'Asia Connection'. In so doing, it became the prime supplier of industrially manufactured sugar to markets in China, India and Japan. The Java industry sustained this connection by building a labour-intensive agro-industry in Java itself which compensated for the island's relative paucity of land. In short, the industrial project in sugar had a great future in Java. In the immediate circumstances in which the Java industry found itself in the mid-1880s, however, it looked as if it might have no future at all.

By this time, the majority of Java's colonial sugar factories were well on the way to making the transition to a fully industrialised mode of operation, predicated on the incorporation into the production line of Multiple Effect apparatus to bring about continuous process manufacture. While this involved manufacturers in considerable financial outlays, it was judged as justified in terms of the improved quality and quantity of the product and, importantly, in terms of substantially reduced fuel costs. The upshot was that it kept the Java industry well abreast of other advanced sectors of the international sugar economy in terms of the technology of manufacture. Elsewhere in Asia itself (with a few exceptions in the Indian subcontinent) there was no parallel until the early twentieth century to what was already taking place in Java two or three decades earlier. In short, nothing could be further from the truth than the old canard (promoted by late colonial industrialists and financiers seeking to boost their own achievements) that in the wake of the crisis of 1884, metropolitan capital moved to take over a moribund 'state enterprise' that was desperately in need of re-capitalisation and modernisation.

Nonetheless, the effects of that crisis — the sudden emergence of what would now be called a 'bear market' in the international sugar economy — threatened to nullify all the manifold advances of the preceding decades. Precipitated by a crisis of overproduction — itself a consequence of the struggle for hegemony in world markets between cane and beet sugar — and by stagnating demand, it saw the industrially manufactured form of the commodity ('centrifugal' sugar) lose between one-third and one-half its value in the course of a few months.[410] Worldwide, industrial sugar producers and their financiers were faced with bankruptcy. The situation of the Java

---

[410] The most richly detailed modern account of the crisis of 1884 and its aftermath (on which I gratefully draw in what follows) is to be found in Claver, *Dutch Commerce and Chinese Merchants*, pp. 109-48.

industry was no exception. By 1885, several locally based firms with a big stake in the industry had gone to the wall, while others teetered on the verge of collapse.

Yet all was not lost. The steep drop in price meant that industrially manufactured sugar was now within the reach of consumers for whom it had previously been, at best, an expensive and rare luxury. This was particularly the case in Asia, where newly modern people in newly modern cities were looking for newly modern commodities — white, factory-made sugar among them. Those industrial sugar manufacturers who were able to accommodate themselves to the much lower price for their product prevailing after 1884 were able to enter expanding markets largely closed to them hitherto by the lower price of (and consumer preference for) artisan-made sugar, some of it locally produced. This transformation of the commodity's Asian market, a transformation that was embryonic in the closing decades of the nineteenth century and was still continuing in and beyond the 1930s, was something from which the industrial project in Java sugar was able to benefit. Indeed, its future lay there.

In the 1880s, however, that future was still some way off, and the industry was saved most immediately, as we have already seen, by timely interventions made possible by the long-nurtured connections between the 'Indies' bourgeoisie, who owned and ran the bulk of the Java industry when the crisis hit, and their metropolitan counterparts. In smoke-filled rooms along the 'grand canals' of the Heerengracht and Keizersgracht, in what was then the commercial heart of Amsterdam, plans were set in motion to rescue a colonial industrial project in which so many friends and relatives had a stake.

By and large, the plans worked. The colony's sugar factories came increasingly into the orbit of Netherlands-based financiers. Under their aegis, metropolitan capital played an important role — albeit only in the short term — in substantial reconstruction of the basis on which the production and sale of the commodity was financed. In the longer term, however, it was not metropolitan finance that underpinned the industry's survival and, crucially, its resumed growth. Rather, it was the industry's ability to finance its expansion on the basis of retained profits. In part, this was predicated on a business culture, in a uniquely financially self-contained industry with few 'outside' investors, which privileged such investment in place of the payment of generous dividends. As a business strategy, however, it also relied on the sheer amount of money that was to be made from a highly sophisticated (not to say ruthless) exploitation of Java's agrarian resources.

As this suggests, finance was only a part of the explanation for the industrial project's salvation. What also mattered — and mattered very substantially — were economic and social conditions in the lowlands of East and Central Java, where the overwhelming majority of the island's sugar factories were located. There, a combination of agrarian circumstances in the 1880s and 1890s proved instrumental in keeping the project afloat. What the industrial project needed to 'get it back on its feet' was an access to land and irrigation water which was not unduly trammelled by considerations of the 'opportunity cost' of growing cane relative to other crops, and a workforce that was numerous enough to keep wages low and workers malleable. By and large, this was what it got.

The old arrangements under which the industry had secured raw material and labourers during the heyday of the *Cultuurstelsel* had been completely phased out by the mid-1880s. Compulsory labour-service in sugar fields and factories was a thing of the past, as was the state's seasonal requisition of land for the growing of cane. These arrangements were replaced, however, by new ones that, in terms of access to land (if not to labour), maintained the industry's hegemony over rural resources. Under the new dispensation, sugar factories rented the land they needed from peasant farmers in quantities and at a price that sometimes owed a great deal to the connivance of local-level state officials and almost invariably to that of suitably bribed village headmen. In some parts of the island, at least, the industry also managed to come to mutually advantageous understandings with better-off, 'big' peasants who might use their influence with their less economically strong clients. The industry was also generally successful in maintaining control over the irrigation water, often in short supply, so vital to the success of the newly planted cane.

Throughout all this, the colonial Government of the day was, on balance, sympathetic to the industry's interests. To be sure, there was plenty of room for clashes with a state bureaucracy that had a paternal view of 'its' peasants — and that regarded the undermining of peasant self-sufficiency as likely to jeopardise its control over the countryside. Even so, the fact was that the Governor-General for much of the 1890s — a crucial decade for the industry's survival — was notoriously partial to the sugar interest. Indeed, his own family owned a large sugar factory and he was a good friend of the ambitious chairman of the newly established sugar industry syndicate. He helped emasculate measures proposed by his own senior officials which might otherwise have circumscribed the industry's activities.

Yet states do not act in a vacuum. A rural recession in the 1880s and 1890s (which caused Dutch officials a decade later to speak of 'declining' or 'diminished' welfare in the countryside of Java), played into the industry's hands — and into those within the state who sought to promote its interests. The prevailing low price of rice, in particular, reduced friction over the opportunity cost of growing cane, while also helping ensure that wages could be cut or held down in conjunction with bringing the cheap labour of women and children into the industry workforce on an apparently totally unprecedented scale. In short, though in a different format that had major implications for the way in which fieldwork in Java sugar subsequently evolved, the industrial project was able to continue to draw on access to rural resources. These resources, in the case of land, might aptly be described as 'privileged'. In the case of labour, they depended both on the island's burgeoning population and on a restructuring of the 'peasantry' which the industry, in tandem with the larger workings of the colonial state in the mid-century decades, had brought in its wake.

The upshot of these several factors, operating in conjunction, was that the industrial project in sugar in rural Java was able to ride the crisis of the mid-1880s in a robust fashion. Between 1885 and the early 1900s, the output of Java's sugar factories increased from under 400 000 to around 1 million MT, and exports increased in a like manner. The 'secret' of the industry — whose achievements in this respect brought international renown — lay in three things: first, its exploitation of locally available labour to create a sophisticated 'agro-industry' in the field, characterised by huge labour inputs organised along quasi-industrial lines; second, intensive supervision that was both informed and informing; and third, a programme of Research and Development which led the world in the international sugar economy of the day. With some notable exceptions, the colonial sugar companies operating in Java in the late nineteenth and early twentieth century were not able to afford the massive factory complexes of their occidental coeval and sometimes rival in far-away Cuba. Nor, given the Lilliputian world of peasant Java in which they were embedded, were such complexes necessarily practical or feasible. What the industrial project in Java sugar could not achieve in terms of economies of scale in the manufacturing sector, however, it more than made up for by levels of productivity in its cane fields which were unmatched globally.

G Roger Knight

The Inter-war Depression and its Aftermath[411]

The way for the industrial project appeared to be ever upward (barring a number of potentially serious problems in the agricultural sector in the 1910s). Then came the inter-war depression. It was not so much the depression per se that impacted so massively on colonial Java's sugar producers, but the realignment of major sectors of the international sugar economy associated with it. To be sure, per capita sugar consumption declined worldwide for a period in the early 1930s. But the real problem for the Java producers was a trend toward economic autarchy in their major overseas sales areas — a trend that the depression exacerbated but did not cause.

---

[411] For an overview, see Bosma, *Industrial Sugar Plantation*, pp. 214-30. The major regional histories of the industry all conclude with the inter-war depression and its immediate aftermath, e.g. Elson, *Javanese Peasants*. Notable among the exceptions is the succinct treatment of the subject by Pierre van der Eng, *Agricultural Growth in Indonesia: Productivity Change and Policy Impact since 1880*, Basingstoke & London, Macmillan Press, 1996, pp. 224-30. His prime focus, however, (as is clear from the title of his book) is on the role of the sugar industry in the history of agricultural growth in Indonesia. Peter Boomgaard, in an essay written some twenty years ago ('Treacherous Cane: the Java Sugar Industry', in Bill Albert & Adrian Graves, *The World Sugar Economy in War and Depression, 1914-1940*, London & New York, Routledge 1992, pp. 157-69) confines his remarks to the inter-war decades, leaving the broader field to the distinguished Indonesian historian, Mubyarto (e.g. 'The Sugar Industry', *Bulletin of Indonesian Economic Studies*, vol. 5, no. 2, 1969, pp. 37-54), who drew valuable attention, albeit in fairly summary fashion, to a number of critical themes. There remain a number of specialist studies of developments in the second half of the twentieth century, but these deal primarily with the rise of 'smallholder' cane production. See in particular Colin Brown, 'The Intensified Smallholder Cane Programme: First Five Years', *Bulletin of Indonesian Economic Studies*, vol. 18, no. 1, 1982, pp. 39-60; Hartveld, 'Raising Cane'; Ernst Spaan & Aard Hartveld, 'Socio-Economic Change and Rural Entrepreneurs in Pre-Crisis East Java, Indonesia: Case Study of a Madurese Upland Community', *Sojourn: Social Issues in Southeast Asia*, vol. 17, no. 2, 2002, pp. 274-300; Mubyarto, 'The Sugar Industry: From Estate to Smallholder Cane', *Bulletin of Indonesian Economic Studies*, vol. 13, no. 2, 1977, pp. 29-44; Frans Hüsken, 'Cycles of Commercialisation and Accumulation in a Central Javanese Village', in G Hart et al. (eds), *Agrarian Transformations: Local Processes and the State in Southeast Asia*, Berkley & Los Angeles, University of California Press, 1989, pp. 303-31; Kano, Husken & Suryo, *Beneath the Smoke of the Sugar Mill*. See also G Roger Knight, 'From *Merdeka* to Massacre: The Politics of Sugar in the Early Years of the Indonesian Republic', *Journal of Southeast Asian Studies*, vol. 43, no. 3, 2012, pp. 402-21. The potentially useful work on Java sugar by the veteren commentator Alec Gordon is ultimately ruled out of court by its author's simplistic level of analysis, his tiresome dogmatism and the patent inadequacy of his 'scholarship'. His best work is his earliest, viz. 'The Collapse of Java's Colonial Sugar System and the Breakdown of Independent Indonesia's Economy', in F Anrooij et al., *Between People and Statistics*, The Hague, Nijhoff, 1979, pp. 251-66.

Java had reigned supreme as a supplier of industrially manufactured sugar in one form or another to markets in East and South Asia for more than a quarter of a century. Beginning in 1930, however, it lost that position to new, industrial sugar producers elsewhere in Asia. These producers were in the Japanese 'sugar empire', which was based in Taiwan and in Japanese-mandated territories in the south Pacific (and which, fatally for Java, began to get a firm grip on the vital China market). They were also in the Indian subcontinent, where a long-established sugar industry took on a wholly new life from the late 1920s onward. Java sugar became, quite suddenly, bereft of customers. Within scarcely two years, around 80 per cent of capacity stood idle, and there were commensurate lay-offs of workers and personnel with a correspondingly huge reduction in the amount of land brought under cane.

It might have been the end, but it wasn't. Indeed, by the time that the Second World War engulfed South-East Asia at the beginning of 1942, Java's factories were turning out rather more than 50 per cent of their pre-depression peak production. Historically, ultra-cheap labour and land-costs had, courtesy of the depression, tempted the sugar companies to renew their operations. The sugar companies made the supposition that their product would be so cheap that it could find a sale on the global 'spot markets', which were all that was left of the global sugar market once it had been carved up by imperial preferences and protective tariffs. Thereafter, the going got increasingly rough. Between 1942 and 1945, the Japanese occupation authorities closed down most factories (since there was no obvious outlet for their output, given that they had sugar enough in Taiwan and the newly conquered Philippines) and wrecked others in an unsuccessful attempt to turn sugar into aviation fuel. More destruction followed between 1945 and 1949, as the Dutch and Indonesian Republicans of a variety of persuasions strove for supremacy in the struggle for Indonesian independence which began in the immediate wake of the Second World War. At times, the struggle became bitter and violent, and sugar factories fell victim to Republican scorched earth tactics and the general mayhem of the period.

Even so, when the Dutch finally conceded defeat at the end of 1949, the new Republic inherited an industrial project that was still important enough — in terms of export potential and a growing domestic market for centrifugal sugar — to be revived once more. By the time that the industry was nationalised (between 1957 and 1959), there were fifty or so sugar factories operating in Java, around two-thirds of the number that had been working prior to the Second World War. Nationalisation placed the industrial project under the de facto control of the Indonesian army, and it became even more a state-run concern when the army took control of the Republic itself in the mid-1960s. Java sugar had by this time totally disappeared from the international market, its output completely absorbed by domestic sales. In fact, it could not satisfy the growing market in the Republic for industrially manufactured sugar, which accordingly began to be imported in significant quantities. Late twentieth-century moves to shift the bulk of the production to the so-called Outer Islands met with some success — and meant that Java ceased to be anything but a minor supplier to the Indonesian market. Some of the island's by-now antiquated factories, relics from the days of steam, became tourist attractions or were closed down for good, while a few others were (partially) re-equipped and kept in production.

As an 'industrial project', however, Java sugar had ceased to have any relevance. It had still been the case in the 1920s and 1930s that those of Java's sugar factories falling into the 'state of the art' category could reasonably be seen as harbingers of the industrial modernity in the Indies/Indonesia for which both Indonesian nationalists and some Dutch colonialists strove. Even as late as the 1950s, the modernising Sultan of Yogyakarta (South-Central Java) included a brand-new, automated sugar factory along with an engineering works in a trio of industrial operations which he got underway there. From then on, however, sugar manufacture could no longer be considered as anywhere near the cutting edge of twentieth-century industrial technology. The new wave of industrial projects established in Indonesia under Suharto's New Order post-1967 pinnacled not in sugar but in aero-space ventures. Sugar remained in Java because it provided work in rural areas where no other work was available, and attempts to perpetuate its production there fused with talk of using it as a 'green fuel' to make ethanol. (During World War Two, the Japanese had been half a century or more ahead of their time.) Meanwhile, big sugar business increasingly relied on production in the Outer Islands or on imports, legitimate or otherwise. Even though, at the time of writing, it still accounted for around 60 per cent of Indonesia's sugar output, the industrial project in Java sugar, after 150 years was well on the way to becoming, in terms of the technology of manufacture, little more than a quaint curiosity.

Archival Sources

ANRI (Arsip Nasional Republik Indonesia, Jakarta)

Pekalongan, 80, Cultuurverslag Pekalongan, 1834, pp. 1-14, ANRI, Arsip Cultuurs, 1624.

'Rapport omtrent de suikermolen te Wonopringgo', in Vitalis to Directeur Cultuurs, 10.3.1834/25, ANRI, Archief Cultuurs, no. 333, Exh. 13.3.1834/761.

AD (Arsip Daerah [Local Archive]) in ANRI

AD, Pekalongan, nos. 1-3.

AD, Pekalongan, no. 100.

Assistant Res. Krawang, 'Verslag omtrent den Toestand der Verkoopte en den Verhuurde Landen in der Afd. Krawang', AD, 16 March 1850, Krawang, no. 9.

AV, Pekalongan, 1831 & 1832 [unpaginated] & Directeur Cultuurs to Resident Pekalongan, 13.3.1832/390.

AV, Pekalongan, 1863 [unpaginated], AD, Pekalongan, no. 6.

AV, Pekalongan, 1831, Bijl. F, AD, Pekalongon, no. 2.

'Bijl. (no. 6) Behoorende tot de Memorie van den Paccalongangsche Resident JA Middelkoop', 1808, AD, Pekalongan, no. 48.

'Brieven Aankomende van de Directeur van Cultuurs 1832', Pekalongan, no. 80.

'Civeel Teregtzetting Landraad Pekalongan, 16.3.1847', in AD, Pekalongan, no. 58.

'Memorie van den Resident Willem Beekman ... 25 Augustus 1803' [unpaginated], in AD, Pekalongan, no. 48.

'PV, Pekalongan, 1858', p. 11, in AD, Pekalongan, no. 1/5.

'Solo is immer de Negari van het land' ['Solo remains the Centre of their realm'], PV, Pekalongan, 1857 [unpaginated], AD, Pekalongan, no. 5.

NA (Nationaal Archief, The Hague)

Collectie Baud, in NA

L Vitalis, 'Rapport Pekalongan 1834', pp. 35-6, NA, Collectie Baud, 460.
'Aantekeningen … Reise GG ad interim [JC Baud] Mei-Augustus 1834' [unpaginated], NA, Collectie Baud, 462.
AV, Pekalongan, 1834 [unpaginated], NA, Collectie Baud, 391.

Collectie Schneither, in NA

'AV Batavia', 1824, vol. 3, p. 23, NA, Collectie Schneither, 84.
Residency Report Semarang 1823 (Domis), pp. 288-9, NA, Collectie Schneither, 91.
'Statistiek Pekalongan 1821', B/2, NA, Collectie Schneither, 90.

MK (Archief Ministerie van Kolonien), in NA

'Stamboeken Indische Ambtenaren', MK.
'Aantoning der op Java gevestigde Suiker Etablissmenten tengevolge van gesloten contracten met het Government', 11.9.1834, MK, 3203.
Exh. (Exhibitum [Agenda item]), in NA, MK
    Exh. 24.6.1840/19, NA, MK.
    Exh. 6.7.1840/20, NA, MK.
    Exh. 16.7.1840/5, NA, MK.
    'Cultuurinrigtingen op Java … tot Ultimo 1844', Exh. 1.2.1847/22, NA, MK.
    'Lijst … Kultuurondernemingen … Ultimo December 1844', in Exh. 1.2.1847/22, NA, MK.
    Marginal comments of the Director of Cultivations in E & L Saportas, 'Rapport over den toestand van het suiker fabriekwezen op Java', in Exh. 24.4.1847/28, NA, MK.
'Kultuurinrigtingen op Java 1852', Exh. 17.3.1854/4, NA, MK.
'Kultuurinrigtingen NI 1852 & 1853', Exh. 17.3.1854/4, NA, MK.
'Kultuurinrigtingen NI 1852 & 1853', Exh. 21.3.1855/15, NA, MK.

Exh. 20.10.1859/17, NA, MK.

Exh. Geheim 29.2.1860/54, NA, MK.

'Kultuurinrigtingen NI 1861', Exh. 29.1.1863/5, NA, MK.

Indische Besluit [Indies Government Decision], in NA, MK

    IB, 29.3.1823/4, MK, 2468.

    IB, 26.8.1823/23, MK, 2779.

    IB, 24.5.1824/2, MK, 2476.

    IB, 28.12.1824/13, MK 2786.

    IB, 13.8.1827/8, MK, 2507.

    IB, 21.4.1828/17, MK, 2515.

    IB, 20.6.1828/9 & 10, MK, 2517.

    IB, 19.3.1832/1, MK, 2545.

    IB, 25.5.1833/3, MK, 2847.

    IB, 5.7.1834/3, MK, 2852.

    IB, 3.10.1834/7, MK, 2853.

    IB, 17.1.1834/9, MK, 2846.

    IB 24.12.1834/10, MK, 2853.

    IB, 12.12.1838/10, MK, 2589.

    IB, 15.8.1840/20, MK, 2609.

    IB, 29.6.1841/5, MK, 2619.

    IB, 9.2.1842/20, MK, 2630.

    IB, 13.9.1842/1, MK, 2637.

    IB, 11.2.1843/4, MK, 2642.

    IB, 1.7.1843/23, MK, 2647.

    IB, 2.11.1846/22, MK, 2688.

VMK (Verbaal Ministerie van Kolonien), in NA, MK

    VMK, 17.11.1826/56.

    VMK, 9.11.1829/46.

    VMK, 19.10.1830/21.

    VMK, 9.12.1841/9.

    VMK, 30.5.1846/21-305.

    VMK, 2.11.1846/411.

    VMK, 8.4.1870/17.

    'Extract uit de Stamboek der Heeren Officieren van het Nederland'sch Oost-Indische Leger', in VMK, 9.12.1841/9.

NHMA (Archief Hoofdkantor [Head Office] Nederlandsche Handel-Maatschappij), in NA

'Aantekeningen uit de Correspondentie Factorij', NHMA, 7999, file 588.
'Beschrijving van de Installatie Kalimatie' [c. 1908], NHMA, 7945.
'[Extract] Kontracten ... vervaardigen en verzending stoomtoestellen tot het kooken van suiker', NHMA, 7999, file 588.
JL van Gennep, 'Cultuurondernemingen op Java, 1870', Reisverslagen en Rapporten no. 70, NHMA.
'Opgave wegens de op Java werkende suikerfabrieken, Juni 1848', in NHMA, 9207.
'Overzicht van de Installatie van Wonopringgo' [c. 1905], File 'Wonopringgo', in NHMA, 7945.
'Particularieten omtrent de Sf. Djombang', 22.11.1884, in NHMA, 7966.
'Poerwodadi voor 1888' in NHMA, 7944.
JVFB (Jaarverslag Factorij Batavia NHM [Batavia Branch Office NHM]), in NA, NHMA
    JVFB, vol. 16, 1840-41, p. 3.
    JVFB, vol. 23, 1847-48, p. 60.
    JVFB, vol. 24, 1848-49, pp. 76-7.
    JVFB, vol. 28, 1852-53, pp. 23-5.
    JVFB, vol. 35, 1859-60, p. 255.
    JVFB, vol. 37, 1861-62, appendix.
    JVFB, vol. 38, 1862-63, pp. 20-5.
    JVFB, vol. 39, 1863-64, pp. 35-45.
    JVFB, vol. 56, 1881, p. 52.
    JVFB, vol. 57, 1882, pp. 55-8.
    JVFB, vol. 58, 1883, pp. 51-2.
    JVFB, vol. 59, 1884, p. 7, 17 & 71.
    JVFB, vol. 60, 1885, p. 14.
NHMR (Registers houdende inschrijjvingen van overeenkomsten met diverse Suikerfabrieken ...), (Registers recording agreements with Sugar Factories ...) 1858-1879, 7 vols, in NA, NHMA
    NHMR, 4796-4797.
    NHMR, 4976.
    NHMR, 4978.

NFB (Notulen [Minutes] Factorij Batavia), in NA, NHMA

    NFB, 11.4.1826/5.

    'Nota betreffende de Fabriek Wono Pringo door den Heer CA Granpré Molière', NFB, 31.12.1844/669.

    'Nota betreffende de Fabriek Wono Pringo door den Heer C.A. Granpré Molière', 23.12.1844, in NFB, 31.12.1844.

    NFB, 4.6.1843/614.

    NFB, 29.8.1844/655.

    NFB, 10.7.1852/67.

    NFB, 1.2.1854/109.

    NFB, 6.3.1858/364.

    NFB, 29.9.1858/409.

    NFB, 1.3.1859/449.

    NFB, 15.3.1859/451.

    NFB, 17.9.1859/512.

    NFB, 17.1.1860/549.

    NFB, 2.3.1860/571.

    NFB, 26.9.1860/627.

    NFB, 5.12.1860/668.

    NFB, 2.3.1860/57.

    NFB, 11.2.1863/827.

    NFB, 12.12.1863/889.

Other Collections, in NA

Archief Ministerie van Justitie, NA, 2.09.01, dossier 4862.

Collectie Van den Bosch, NA, 216.

'Extract Kontracten ... vervaardigen en verzending stoomtoestellen tot het kooken van suiker', NA, NHM, 7999, file 588.

'Gedenkboek Koloniale Bank' [MSS], NA, Archief Koloniale Bank, 2.20.04/883, pp. 91-4.

Jaarverslagen NI Handelsbank, 1865-1884, NA, Archief Nederlandsch-Indische Handelsbank, p. 190.

'Overzigt Tegal', NA, Collectie Umbgrove, pp. 1-5.

Journals

KV (Koloniale Verslag (Bijlage bij de Handelingen van de Tweede Kamer der Staten Generaal)), The Hague, Landsdrukkerij

KV, 1849.
KV, 1850.
KV, 1853.
KV, 1853.
KV, 1858.
KV, 1863.
KV, 1867-68.
KV, 1870.
KV, 1875-82.
KV, 1880.
KV, 1881.
KV, 1878.
KV, 1879.
KV, 1882.
KV, 1886.
KV, 1888.

NP (Nederland's Patriciaat)

NP, vol. 5, 1914.
NP, vol. 9, 1918.
NP, vol. 12, 1921-22.
NP, vol. 21, 1933-34.
NP, vol. 50, 1964.
NP, vol. 53, 1967.

IN (De Indische Navorscher)

IN, vol. 1, 1934.
IN, vol. 2, 1988-89.
IN, vol. 3, 1990.

IN, vol. 7, 1994.
IN, vol. 16, 2003.

DNL (De Nederlandsche Leeuw)

DNL, vol. 29, 1911.
DNL, vol. 32, 1914.
DNL, vol. 41, 1923.
DNL, vol. 50, 1932.

NAB (Nederlands Adelsboek)

NAB, vol. 12, 1914.
NAB, vol. 40, 1942.
NAB, vol. 93, 1995.

SU (Stukken Betreffende het Onderzoek de Benoemde Commissie [Umbgrove Commissie] voor de opname der verschillende suikerfabrieken op Java)

Batavia, 1857, Appendix C to *Handelingen van de Tweede Kamer der Staten-Generaal 1862-1863*.
SU, Bijl D.
SU, Bijl E, G & H.
NA, vol. 40, 1942, pp. 596-7.
JV, NI Handelsbank, 1882, vol. 10, NA Handelsbank

Other Archives

Jaarverslagen Internatio, 1863-1887, Gemeente Archief Rotterdam, Archief van de Internationale Crediet-en-Handelsvereeniging 'Rotterdam' (Internatio), Inventaris no. 76.

Gemeente Archief, Amsterdam

Marriage Certificate of Hubertus Paulus Hoevenaar, 2 June 1813.
Death Certificate of Hubertus Paulus Hoevenaar, 3 January 1814.
Marriage Certificate of Paulus Hubertus Hoevenaar, 3 April 1817.

ASNI (Archief voor de Suikerindustrie in Nederlandsch-Indië)

ASNI, vol. 39, no. 1, 1931, p. 92.

Private Collections

'Knops' Description 1814', Mackenzie Collection (Private), 79, p. 270, India Office Library, London.

'Resident Doornik's Replies …', 28.10.1812, India Office Library, London, Mackenzie Collection (Private), vol. 7, p. 173.

'Rothenbuhler Report 1798', p. 64, Mackenzie Collection (Private), no. 7, India Office Library, London.

Robert Hill Edwards's First Journal (in possession of Elaine Nobbs, Charlottetown, PEI, and kindly transcribed for me by Mr Don Jardine, a direct descendant of Robert Hill Edwards, Tom Edwards's younger brother.

Letters

Letters from the NHM Batavia Factorij to NHM Head-Office in Amsterdam located, unless otherwise stated, in Tweede Afdeeling/B, NA NHMA

    Factorij to A'dam, 5.9.1840/1527.
    Factorij to A'dam, 29.11.1841/1819.
    Factorij to A'dam, 8.1.1842/1858.
    Factorij to A'dam, 1.8.1845/233.
    Factorij to A'dam, 17.9.1845/236.
    Factorij to A'dam, 31.12.1845/246.
    Factorij to A'dam, 29.11.1847/305.
    Factorij to A'dam, 25.4.1848/318.
    Factorij to A'dam, 26.8.1848/325.
    Factorij to A'dam, 28.11.1848/338.
    Factorij to A'dam, 24.6.1850/24.
    Factorij to A'dam, 27.7.1850/27.
    Factorij to A'dam, 25.2.1853/192.
    Factorij to A'dam, 26.4.1854/284.
    Factorij to A'dam, 25.9.1854/316.
    Factorij to A'dam, 11.10.1854/320, appendix.

Factory to A'dam, 10.10.1857/2105.
Factorij to A'dam, 24.10.1857/597.
Factorij to A'dam, 25.3.1858/63.
Factorij to A'dam, 7.6.1858/650.
Factorij to A'dam, 20.6.1859/176.
Factorij to A'dam, 7.5.1859/737.
Factorij to A'dam, 7.9.1860/877.
Factorij to A'dam, 16.3.1861/940.
Factorij to A'dam, 2.5.1861/951.
Edwards to Edwards to Factorij, 2.8.1856/1036, enclosed in Factorij to A'dam, 9.8.1856/480.
Factorij, 2.8.1856/1036, in Factorij to A'dam, 9.8.1856/480.
Edwards to Factorij, 24.12.1860, in Factorij to A'dam, 2.1.1861/915.
Edwards to Factorij, 9.9.1854/826, in Factorij to A'dam, 11.10.1854/320.
Edwards to Factorij, 24.12.1860, in Factorij to A'dam, 2.1.1861/915.
[Extract] Edwards to Factorij, 4.2.1854/742, in Factorij to A'dam, 25.2.1854/271.
Factorij to Directeur Cultuures, 31.1.1857/48 in Factorij to A'dam, 11.3.1857/533.
Heijning to De Directie der Vereeniging van Suikerfabrieken te Passoeroean, 20.12.1863, in Factorij to A'dam, 25.1.1864/1225.
JC Teengs [Report on Wonopringgo], Batavia, 27.6.1850 in Factorij to A'dam, 24.7.1850/29.
Baud to van den Bosch, 29.7.1835, in Westendorp Boerma, *Briefwisseling tussen J van den Bosch en JC Baud*, vol. 2, Utrecht, Kemink en Zoon, 1956, p. 180.
van Blommestein, PA, to Factorij, 4.3.1879 & 6.10.1885, NA, NHM.
van den Bosch to Baud, 15 September 1834 & 15 December 1834, in JJ Westendorp Boerma (ed.), *Briefwisseling tussen J van den Bosch en JC Baud*, vol. 1, Utrecht, Kemink en Zoon, 1956, pp. 182-3, 189.
Bremner, Joseph, to [?], Semarang 4.9.1825, enclosure in J McLachlan [to Hugh MacMaster], London, 16.2.1826.
Edwards to Factorij NHM Batavia, 11.12.1858 & 15.12.1858, in NFB, 18.12.1858/430.
Everts, Steven [Superintendent], to Factorij Batavia, 15.1.1881/30, NHMA, 7936.

Factorij to A'dam, 22.7.1881, 'Dossiers Cultuurzaken ... Wonopringgo & Kalimatie' [Extract], NHMA, 7945.

Fokker to Factorij, 21.2.1881, 'Inspectie Rapporten over Eigen en Andere Ondernemingen, 1879-1900', NHMA.

Governeur-Generaal to MK, 8.2.1872/193/3, Exh. 20.11.1872/27, NA, MK.

van Hogendorp, Willem to GK van Hogendorp, 28.2.1826, NA, Collectie Van Hogendorp, 91.

Lucassen, Th., to Baud, 27.3.1845, NA, Collectie Baud, 723.

Maclaine, Gillian, to John Gregorson, Salatiga, 29.5.1822, Gloucestershire Archives, Osborne-Maclaine, MSS D3330, Box 18.

Maclaine, Gillian, to Marjorie Maclaine, 8.10.1825 [copy], MacMaster MSS (in Private Possession, UK).

Nahuijs to Merkus, 22.6.1830, in VMK, 13.5.1831/25-114.

Palmer, John to William Stavers, 2.5.1825, *Letter Books of John Palmer*, Bodleian Library, Oxford, Eng. Lett. c. 102, p. 68.

Palmer, John to Edward Watson, 13.11.1832, *Letter Books of John Palmer*, Bodleian Library, Oxford, Eng. Lett. c. 122, pp. 398-400.

Palmer, John, to Gillian Maclaine, 6.4.1833, *Letter Books of John Palmer*, Bodleian Library, Oxford, Lett. c. 123, p. 387.

Pitcairn, John (*administrateur*, P&T), to van den Bosch, 14.8.1830, NA, Collectie Van den Bosch, 426.

Resident Praetorius to Governeur-Generaal, 28.8.1835/946, ANRI, Asip Cultuurs, no. 46.

Resident Pekalongan to Director Binnenlands Bestur, 20.2.1867/674. Exh. 11.4.1868/91, NA, MK.

Rochussen to Baud, 26.6.1847 & Rochussen to Baud, 29.10.1847, in Jhr. Mr WA Baud, *De Semi-Officiele en Particuliere Briefwisseling tussen JC Baud en JJ Rochussen, 1845-1851*, vol. 2, Assen, Van Gorkom, 1983, pp. 262, 304, no. 3.

Stavers to Nahuijs, 17.10.1823, Nahuijs Papers, vol. 8, no. 3, Leiden Universiteits Bibliotheek, MSS 616.

de Sturler, JE [Secretaris Pekalongan], to Van den Bosch, 2.9.1830.

de Sturler, JE, to Governor-General, 7.3.1832 (extract), in Directeur Cultuurs to Resident Pekalongan, 13.3.1832/390.

Newspapers

Bataviasche Courant

23 February 1826.
22 June 1822/25.
13 November 1824/11.
24 January 1824/4.
30 September 1820/40.
19 June 1824/25.
11 December 1824/50.

Javasche Courant

13 August 1842.
20 October 1827/99.

Websites

http://www.steamindex.com/manlocos/manulist.htm (accessed 12 January 2009).
http://www.encyclopedie.picardie.fr (accessed 15 August 2014).
http://www.enginemuseum.org/sor.html (accessed 15 August 2014).
http://www.du.edu/~ttyler/ploughboy/trstaversjournal.htm (accessed 15 August 2014).
http://www.eugenefranken.nl/hoevenaar.htm (accessed 15 August 2014).
http://www.en.wikipedia.org/wiki/Manlove,_Alliott_%26_Co._Ltd. (accessed 15 August 2014).
http://www.vintagemachinery.org (accessed 15 August 2014).
http://www.myheritage.nl/.../djatiwangi-suikerfabriek-djatiw (accessed 15 August 2014).

Bibliography

Adamson, AH, 1972, *Sugar Without Slaves: The Political Economy of British Guiana, 1838-1904*, New Haven, Yale University Press, 1972.

Adas, Michael, 'The Problem of Paradigms: Patterns of Scientific and Technological Transfer from 1880 to 1950', *Journal of the Japan-Netherlands Institute*, vol. 4, 1996, pp. 277-85.

Aguilar, Filomeno V, Jnr, *Clash of Spirits: The History of Power and Sugar Planter Hegemony on a Visayan Island*, Honolulu, University of Hawai'i Press, 1998.

Akira, Suehiro, *Capital Accumulation in Thailand, 1855-1985*, Tokyo, Centre for East Asian Cultural Studies, 1989.

Albert, Bill & Adrian Graves (eds), *Crisis and Change in the International Sugar Economy, 1860-1914*, Norwich, ISC Press, 1984.

Allen, Richard B, 'The Slender, Sweet Thread: Sugar, Capital and Dependency in Mauritius, 1860-1936', *The Journal of Imperial and Commonwealth History*, vol. 16, 1981, pp. 177-200.

——, *Slaves, Freedmen and Indentured Labourers in Colonial Mauritius*, Cambridge, Cambridge University Press, 1999.

Almanak en Naamregister van Nederlandsch-Indië, Batavia, 1827-64.

d'Almeida, WB, *Life in Java: With Sketches of the Javanese*, vol. 2, London, Hurst & Blackett, 1864.

Amin, Shahid, *Sugar Cane and Sugar in Gorakphur*, Dehli, Oxford University Press, 1984.

——, 'Cataloguing the Countryside: Agricultural Glossaries from Colonial India', *History and Anthropology*, vol. 8, nos. 1-4, 1994, pp. 35-53.

Anderson, BRO'G, 'Old State and New Society: Indonesia's New Order in Comparative Historical Perspective', *Journal of Asian Studies*, vol. 42, no. 3, 1983, pp. 477-96.

van Baardewijk, Frans, *The Cultivation System: Java 1834-1880*, vol. 14 of Peter Boomgaard (ed.), *Changing Economy in Indonesia*, Amsterdam, Royal Tropical Institute (KIT), 1993.

Bakker, Martijn, *Ondernemerschap en Vernieuwing: De Nederlandse Bietsuikerindustrie 1858-1919*, Amsterdam, Stichting Het Nederlandsch Economisch-Historisch Archief, 1989.

Bastin, John, *Raffles' Ideas on the Landrent System in Java*, The Hague, Nijhoff, 1954.

Baud, Jhr Mr WA, *De Semi-Officiele en Particuliere Briefwisseling tussen JC Baud en JJ Rochussen, 1845-1851*, 3 vols, Assen, Van Gorkom, 1983.

Bayly, CA, 'Creating a Colonial Peasantry: India and Java c. 1820-1880', in Mushirul Hasan et al., *India and Indonesia from the 1830s to 1914: The Heyday of Colonial Rule*, Leiden, Brill, 1987, pp. 93-106.

——, *Indian Society and the Making of the British Empire*, Cambridge, Cambridge University Press, 1988.

Beekman, EM, 'Introduction' to Rob Nieuwenhuijs, *Mirror of the Indies: A History of Dutch Colonial Literature*, translated by Frans van Roosevelt, Amherst, University of Massachusetts Press, 1982, pp. xiii-xxiii.

——, *Troubled Pleasures: Dutch Colonial Literature from the East Indies, 1600-1950*, New York, Clarendon Press, 1996.

Benda, Harry J, 'The Pattern of Administrative Reforms in the Closing Years of Dutch Rule in Indonesia', *Journal of Asian Studies*, vol. 25, no. 4, 1966, pp. 589-605.

van den Berg, NP, *Munt-, Crediet- en Bankwezen, Handel en Scheepvaart in Nederlandsch Indië: Historisch-statistische Bijdragen*, The Hague, Nijhoff, 1907.

——, 'Uit de Tijd van de Oprichting en de Eerste Jaren van het Bestaan der Nederlandsch-Indische Handelsbank', *Indische Gids*, vol. 35, no. 2, 1913, pp. 987-1003.

Bergad, Laird W, *Cuban Rural Society in the Nineteenth Century: The Social and Economic History of Monoculture in Matanzas*, Princeton, NJ, Princeton University Press, 1990.

Bernstein, H, 'Capitalism and Petty Bourgeois Production: Class Divisions and Divisions of Labour', *Journal of Peasant Studies*, vol. 15, no. 2, 1988, pp. 258-71.

Billig, Michael S, 'The Death and Rebirth of Entrepreneurism on Negros Island, Philippines: A Critique of Cultural Theories of Enterprise', *Journal of Economic Studies*, vol. 28, no. 3, 1994, pp. 659-78.

Bleeker, P, 'Fragmenten eener Reis over Java', *Tijdschrift voor Nederlandsch- Indië*, vol. 2, 1849, pp. 262-70.

Bloys van Treslong Prins, PC, *Genealogische en Heraldische Gedenkwaardigheden Betreffende Europeanen op Java*, vol. 1, Batavia, Albrecht, 1934.

Blusse, Leonard, *Strange Company: Chinese Settlers, Mestizo Women, and the Dutch in VOC Batavia*, Dordrecht, Foris Publications, 1986.

de Boer, MG, *Geschiedenis der Amsterdamsche Stoomvaart*, Amsterdam, Scheltema & Holkema's Boekhandel, 1921.

——, *Leven en Bedrijf van Gerhard Moritz Roentgen, Grondvester van de Nederlandsche Stoomboot-Maatschappij, Thans Maatschappij voor Scheeps- en Werktuigbouw 'Fijenoord', 1823-1923*, Groningen, Noordhoff, 1923.

Boomgaard, Peter, *Children of the Colonial State*, Amsterdam, Free University Press, 1989.

——, 'Treacherous Cane: The Java Sugar Industry', in Bill Albert & Adrian Graves, *The World Sugar Economy in War and Depression, 1914-1940*, London & New York, Routledge, 1992, pp. 157-69.

——, 'A Bird's Eye View of the Economic and Social Development of the District of Comal, 1750-1940', in Hiroyoshi Kano, Frans Hüsken & Djoko Suryo (eds), *Beneath the Smoke of the Sugar Mill*, Yogyakarta, AKATIGA/Gadjah Mada University Press, 2001, pp. 9-37.

Boomgaard, Peter, Dick Kooiman & Henk Schulte Nordholt (eds), *Linking Destinies: Trade, Towns and Kin in Asian History*, Leiden, KITLV Press, 2008.

Bosma, Ulbe, 'Het Cultuurstelsel en zijn Buitenlandse Ondernemers: Java tussen Oud en Nieuw Kolonialisme', *Tijdschrift voor Sociale en Economische Geschiedenis*, vol. 2, no. 2, 2005, pp. 3-28.

——, 'Sailing through Suez from the South: The Emergence of an Indies-Dutch Migration Circuit, 1815-1940', *International Migration Review*, vol. 41, no. 2, 2007, pp. 511-36.

——, 'Sugar & Dynasty in Yogyakarta', in Ulbe Bosma, Juan A Guisti-Cordero & G Roger Knight (eds), *Sugarlandia Revisited*, New York & Oxford, Berghahn Books, 2007, pp. 73-94.

―, *Koloniaal Circuit: De Migratie tussen Nederland en Indië 1816-1962*, Amsterdam, IISG, 2009.

―, *Indiëgangers: Verhalen van Nederlanders die naar Indië Trokken*, Amsterdam, Bert Bakker, 2010.

―, *The Asian Sugar Plantation in India and Indonesia: Industrial Production 1770-2010*, Cambridge, Cambridge University Press, 2013.

Bosma, Ulbe & G Roger Knight, 'Global Factory and Local Field: Convergence and Divergence in the International Cane-Sugar Industry, 1850-1940', *International Review of Social History*, vol. 49, no. 1, April 2004, pp. 1-26.

Bosma, Ulbe, Juan A Guisti-Cordero & G Roger Knight (eds), *Sugarlandia Revisited: Sugar and Colonialism in Asia and the Americas, 1800 to 1940*, with a preface by Sydney W Mintz, London & New York, Berghahn Publishers, 2007.

Bosma, Ulbe & Remco Raben, *Being 'Dutch' in the Indies: A History of Creolisation and Empire, 1500-1920*, translated by Wendie Shaffer, Athens, Ohio & Singapore, Ohio University Press & Singapore University Press, 2008.

Brass, Tom & Henry Bernstein, 'Introduction: Proletarianisation and Deproletarianisation on the Colonial Plantation', in E Valentine Daniel, Henry Bernstein & Tom Brass (eds), *Plantations, Peasants and Proletarians in Colonial Asia*, London, Frank Cass, 1992, pp. 1-40.

de Bree, L, *Gedenkboek van de Javasche Bank*, vol. 2, Wetevreden, Kolff, 1928.

Breman, Jan, 'Village Java and the Early Colonial State', *Journal of Peasant Studies*, vol. 9, no. 4, 1982, pp. 189-240.

―, *Control of Land and Labour in Colonial Java*, Dordrecht, Foris Publications, 1983.

Breton de Nijs, E [aka Rob Nieuwenhuijs], *Tempo Doeloe: Fotografische Documenten uit het Oude Indië, 1870-1914*, Amsterdam, Querido, 1961.

Broeze, Frank, 'The Merchant Fleet of Java, 1820-1850', *Archipel*, vol. 18, 1979, pp. 251-69.

Brown, Colin 'The Intensified Smallholder Cane Programme: First Five Years', *Bulletin of Indonesian Economic Studies*, vol. 18, no. 1, 1982, pp. 39-60.

Budding, SA, *Neêrlands-Oost-Indië: Reizen over Java, Madura, Makassar [...]: Gedaan Gedurende het Tijdvak van 1852-1857*, vol. 1, Rotterdam, Wijt, 1859.

Buettner, Elizabeth, *Empire Families: Britons and Late Imperial India*, Oxford &

New York, Oxford University Press, 2004.

à Campo, JNFM, *Engines of Empire: Steam Shipping and State Formation in Colonial Indonesia*, Hilversum, Verloren, 2005.

Carey, PBR, 'Changing Javanese Perceptions of the Chinese Communities in Central Java', *Indonesia*, vol. 37, 1984, pp. 1-47.

——, 'Review of J van Goor, Kooplieden, Predikanten en Bestuurders Overzee: Beeldvorming en Plaatsbepaling in een Andere Wereld', *Itinerario*, vol. 8, no. 1, 1984, pp. 162-3.

——, 'Waiting for the "Just King": The Agrarian World of South-Central Java from Giyanti (1755) to the Java War (1825)', *Modern Asian Studies*, vol. 20, no. 1, 1986, pp. 59-137.

——, *The Power of Prophecy: Prince Dipanagara and the End of the Old Order in Java, 1785-1855*, Leiden, KITLV Press, 2008.

Chalmin, PhG, 'Important Trends in Sugar Diplomacy before 1914', in Bill Albert & Adrian Graves (eds), *Crisis and Change in the International Sugar Economy, 1860-1914*, Norwich, ISC Press, 1984.

Christiaans, Peter, 'Vincent (Van der Parra Breton)', in *De Indische Navorscher*, vol. 2, 1986, p. 50.

——, 'Van Beusechem', *De Indische Navorscher*, vol. 16, 2003, pp. 1-7.

——, 'Leading Personnel of the NHM Factorij Batavia, 1826-1884', (forthcoming), MSS copy in possession of the author.

Clarence-Smith, William G, 'The Rise and Fall of Hadhrami Shipping in the Indian Ocean, c1750-c1940', in David Parkin & Ruth Barnes (eds), *Ships and the Development of Maritime Technology in the Indian Ocean*, London, Routledge Curzon, 2002, pp. 227-58.

Claver, Alexander, 'The Colonial Flow of Trade, Credit and Information: The Chinese-Arab Clientele System of Van Beek, Reineke and Co/HVA (1870s-1880s)', *Itinerario*, vol. 26, no. 2, 2012, pp. 113-21.

——, *Dutch Commerce and Chinese Merchants in Java: Colonial Relationships in Trade and Finance, 1800-1942*, Leiden and Boston, Brill, 2014.

Coombes, A North, *The Evolution of Sugarcane Culture in Mauritius with a Chapter on The Evolution of the Mauritian Sugar Factory*, Mauritius, Department of Agriculture, 1937.

Cooper, Frederick, 'Peasants, Capitalists and Historians: A Review Article', *Journal of Southern African Studies*, vol. 7, no. 2, 1981, pp. 284-314.

———, *Colonialism in Question: Theory, Knowledge, History*, Berkeley, University of California Press, 2005.

Cote, Joost, 'Romancing the Indies: The Literary Construction of *Tempo Doeloe*', in Joost Cote & Loes Westerbeek (eds), *Recalling the Indies: Colonial Culture & Postcolonial Identities*, Amsterdam, Aksant, 2005, pp. 133-72.

Creutzberg, Peter, *Indonesia's Export Crops*, vol. 1 of Peter Boomgaard (ed.), *Changing Economy in Indonesia*, The Hague, Nijhoff, 1975.

Curry-Machado, Jon, '"Rich Flames and Hired Tears": Sugar, Sub-Imperial Agents and the Cuban Phoenix of Empire', *Journal of Global History*, vol. 4, no. 1, 2009, pp. 33-56.

———, *Cuban Sugar Industry: Transnational Networks and Engineering Migrants in Mid-Nineteenth Century Cuba*, New York, Palgrave Macmillan, 2011.

Daniels, J & C, 'The Origin of the Sugar Cane Roller Mill', *Technology and Culture*, vol. 29, no. 3, 1988, pp. 493-535.

Deerr, Noel, *The History of Sugar*, vol. 2, London, Chapman and Hall, 1950.

Deinum, H, 'Bevolkingssuiker', in CJJ van Hall & C van de Koppel, *De Landbouw in de Indische Archipel*, vol. 2A, The Hague, Van Hoeve, 1948.

Dekker, W, 'Tussen Zelfvoorziening en Commerciele Landbouw', Docteraalscriptie, Vrije Universitiet, Amsterdam, 1978.

van Deventer, S, *Bijdragen tot de Kennis van het Landelijk Stelsel op Java*, Zaltbommel, Joh. Noman & Zoon, 3 vols, 1865-66.

De Zaken van het Land Simbang Nader Toegelicht (uitegeven door de Kommissie van Liquidatie des Boedels van wijlen den Heer JE Herderschee), The Hague, Nijhoff, 1866.

Dick, Howard W, 'Nineteenth Century Industrialisation: A Missed Opportunity?', in J Thomas Lindblad (ed.), *New Challenges in the Modern Economic History of Indonesia*, Leiden, Programme of Indonesian Studies, Leiden University, 1993, pp. 123-49.

———, *Surabaya: City of Work*, Athens, Ohio, Ohio University Press, 2002.

Dirkzwager, Jan M, 'A Case of Transfer of Technology: Ship Design and Construction in Nineteenth-Century Netherlands', in Gordon Jackson & David M Williams (eds), *Shipping, Technology, and Imperialism: Papers Presented to the Third British-Dutch Maritime History Conference*, Farnham, Ashgate, 1996, pp. 189-210.

Dixon, Conrad, 'The Rise of the Engineer in the Nineteenth Century', in Gordon Jackson & David M Williams (eds), *Shipping, Technology, and Imperialism: Papers Presented to the third British-Dutch Maritime History Conference*, Farnham, Ashgate, 1996, pp. 231-41.

van den Doel, HW, *De Stille Macht: De Europese Binnenlands Bestuur op Java en Madoera, 1808-1942*, Amsterdam, Bert Bakker, 1994.

Echauz, Robustiano, *Sketches of the Island of Negros*, 1894, translated and annotated by DV Hart, with an Introduction by John Larkin, Ohio, Ohio University, Centre for International Studies, Papers in International Studies, Southeast Asia Series, no. 50, 1978.

Elson, RE, 'The Cultivation System and "Agricultural Involution"', Working Paper no. 14, Centre of Southeast Asian Studies, Monash University, Melbourne, 1978.

——, *Javanese Peasants and the Colonial Sugar Industry: Impact and Change in an East Java Residency, 1830-1940*, Singapore, Oxford University Press, 1984.

——, *Village Java under the Cultivation System 1830-1870*, Sydney, Allen & Unwin, 1994.

——, 'Clifford Geertz, 1926-2006: Meaning, Method and Indonesian Economic History, *Bulletin of Indonesian Economic Studies*, vol. 43, no. 2, 2007, pp. 251-63.

Emmen, QAD, *Rietsuikerfabrieken op Java en hare Machinerieën*, 4th ed., vol. 2, Tegal, De Boer, 1930.

van der Eng, Pierre, *Agricultural Growth in Indonesia: Productivity Change and Policy Impact since 1880*, Basingstoke & London, Macmillan Press, 1996.

van Enk, EMC, 'Britse Kooplieden en de Cultures op Java: Harvey Thompson (1790-1837), en zijn Financiers', Proefschrift, Vrije Universiteit Amsterdam, 1999.

Evans, EW, *The Sugar-Planter's Manual: Being a Treatise on the Art of Obtaining Sugar from the Sugar-Cane*, London, Longman, Brown, Green and Longmans, 1847.

von Faber, GH, *Oud Soerabaia*, Soerabaia, Gemeente Soerabaia, 1931.

Fasseur, C, *Kultuurstelsel en Koloniale Baten*, Leiden, Universitaire Pers, 1975.

——, 'Purse or Principle: Dutch Colonial Policy in the 1860s and the Decline of the Cultivation System', *Modern Asian Studies*, vol. 25, no. 1, 1991, pp. 33-52.

———, *The Politics of Colonial Exploitation*, translated and edited by RE Elson & Ary Kraal, Southeast Asia Program, Cornell University, Ithaca, NY, 1992.

———, *De Indologen: Ambtenaren voor de Oost, 1825-1950*, Amsterdam, Bert Bakker, 1993.

———, Indischgasten, Amsterdam, Ooievaar, 1996.

Fernando, MR, 'Peasants and Plantation: The Social Impact of the European Plantation Economy in Cirebon Residency from the Cultivation System to the End of the First Decade of the Twentieth Century', PhD diss, Monash University, Melbourne, 1982.

Franken, Eugene, *Hubertus Paulus Hoevenaar: Kasteelheer en Ondernemer*, (forthcoming).

Furnivall, JS, *Netherlands India: A Study of Plural Economy*, Cambridge, Cambridge University Press, 1939.

Galloway, Jock H, *The Cane Sugar Industry: An Historical Geography from its Origins to 1914*, Cambridge, Cambridge University Press, 1989.

———, 'The Modernisation of Sugar Production in Southeast Asia, 1880-1940', *The Geographical Review*, vol. 95, no. 1, January 2005, pp. 1-24.

Gastra, Femme, 'The Experience of Travelling to the Dutch East Indies by the Overland Route, 1844-1869', in Gordon Jackson & David M Williams (eds), *Shipping, Technology, and Imperialism: Papers Presented to the Third British-Dutch Maritime History Conference*, Farnham, Ashgate, 1996, pp. 120-37.

Geertz, Clifford, *Agricultural Involution: The Process of Ecological Change in Indonesia*, Berkeley & Los Angeles, University of California Press, 1963.

Gevers Deynoot, Jhr Mr WT, *Herinneringen eener Reis naar Nederlandsch-Indië in 1862*, The Hague, Nijhoff, 1864.

Gibson-Hill, CA, 'The Steamers Employed in Asian Water, 1819-39', *Journal of the Malayan Branch of the Royal Asiatic Society*, vol. 27, 1954.

Glamann, K, *Dutch-Asiatic Trade, 1620-1740*, The Hague, Nijhoff, 1958.

Gordon, Alec, 'The Collapse of Java's Colonial Sugar System and the Breakdown of Independent Indonesia's Economy', in F van Anrooij, Dirk HA Kolff, JTM van Laanen & Gerard J Telkamp, *Between People and Statistics*, The Hague, Nijhoff, 1979, pp. 251-66.

de Graaf, Ton, *Voor Handel en Maatschappij: Geschiedenis van de Nederlandsche Handel-Maatschappij, 1824-1964*, Amsterdam, Boom, 2012.

Peter Griggs, *Global Industry, Local Innovation: The History of Cane Sugar Production in Australia, 1820-1995*, Bern, Peter Lang, 2011.

Gunawan, B & D Valenbreder, 'De Kwestie Netscher: De Verhouding Ambtenaar-Particulier op Java in de Periode 1845-1855', Working paper no. 2, Vakgroep Zuid en Zuidoost Azie, Anthropologisch-Sociologische Centrum, University of Amsterdam, 1978.

de Haan, F, *Oud Batavia*, 2nd ed., vol. 1, Bandoeng, AC Nix & Co., 1935.

——, 'Personalia der Periode van het Engelsch Bestuur over Java', *Bijdragen tot de Taal-, Land-en Volkenkunde*, vol. 92, 1935, pp. 477-681.

Halleux, Robert, *Cockerill: Deux Siecles de Technologie*, Alleur-Liege, Belgium, Editions Du Perron, 1992.

Hartveld, Aard J, 'Raising Cane: Linkages, Organisations and Negotiations in Malang's Sugar Industry, East Java', Proefschrift, Landbouw Universitiet Wageningen, 1996.

Headrick, Daniel R, *The Tools of Empire: Technology and European Imperialism in the Nineteenth Century*, New York, Oxford University Press, 1981.

——, *The Tentacles of Progress: Technology Transfer in the Age of Imperialism, 1850-1940*, New York, Oxford University Press, 1988.

Heitmann, JA, *The Modernisation of the Louisiana Sugar Industry, 1830-1910*, Baton Rouge, Louisiana State University Press, 1987.

van Heumen, F, 'Over de Fabricage van Suiker uit Suikerriet', *Tijdscrijft voor Nederlandsch-Indië* (Nieuwe Reeks) vol. 7, no. 2, 1878, pp. 214-38, 289-319.

Hoadley, Mason C, 'Javanese, Peranakan & Chinese Elites in Cirebon: Changing Ethnic Boundaries', *Journal of Asian Studies*, vol. 47, no. 3, 1988, pp. 503-17.

——, *Towards a Feudal Mode of Production: West Java 1680-1800*, Singapore, Institute of Southeast Asian Studies, 1994.

Hooyman, J, 'Verhandelingen over den Tegenwoordigen Staat van den Landbouw in de Ommelanden van Batavia', *Verhandelingen van het Bataviaasch Genootschap van Kunsten en Wetenschappen*, vol. 1, 1779, pp. 173-263.

Houben, Vincent JH, 'Private Estates in Java in the Nineteenth Century: A Reappraisal', in Thomas J Lindblad (ed.), *New Challenges in the Modern Economic History of Indonesia*, Leiden, Programme of Indonesian Studies, 1993, pp. 47-66.

———, *Kraton and Kumpeni, Surakarta and Yogyakarta, 1830-1870*, Leiden, KITLV Press, 1994.

———, 'Java in the Nineteenth Century: Consolidation of a Territorial State', in Howard Dick, Vincent JH Houben, Thomas J Lindblad & Thee Kian Wie, *The Emergence of a National Economy: An Economic History of Indonesia, 1800-2000*, Sydney, Asian Studies Association of Australia in association with Allen & Unwin, 2002, pp. 56-81.

Hudig Dzn, Jan, *Suikerlords*, Amsterdam, PN van Kampen, 1886.

Hugenholtz, WR, 'The Land Rent Question and its Solution, 1850-1920', in Robert Cribb (ed.), *The Late Colonial State in Indonesia: Political and Economic Foundations of the Netherlands Indies 1880-1842*, Leiden, KITLV Press, 1994, pp. 139-72.

———, *Het Geheim van Paleis Kneuterdijk: De Wekelijkse Gesprekken van Koning Willem II met zijn Minister JC Baud over het Koloniale Beleid en de Herziening van de Grondwet 1841-1848*, Leiden, KITLV Press, 2008.

———, 'Landrentbelasting op Java, 1812-1920', Proefschrift, Universitiet Leiden, 2008.

Hüsken, Frans, 'Cycles of Commercialisation and Accumulation in a Central Javanese Village', in G Hart, A Turton & B White, with B Fegan & Teck Ghee (eds), *Agrarian Transformations: Local Processes and the State in Southeast Asia*, Berkley & Los Angeles, University of California Press, 1989, pp. 303-31.

Innes, Robert LeRoy, 'The Door Ajar: Japan's Foreign Trade in the Seventeenth Century', PhD Diss, University of Michigan, 1980.

Isett, Christopher M, 'Sugar Manufacture and the Agrarian Economy of Nineteenth-Century Taiwan', *Modern China*, vol. 21, no. 2, April 1995, pp. 233-59.

Johnson, David Bruce, 'Rural Society and the Rice Economy in Thailand, 1880-1930', Yale University, PhD Diss, 1975.

[Kamer van Nijverheid en Koophandel te Semarang], *Memorie over de Suikerindustrie in de Governments Residentiën van Midden Java*, Semarang, Van Dorp, 1865.

Kennedy, John, *The History of Steam Navigation*, Liverpool, Charles Birchall, 1903.

Ketjen, E, 'Levensbericht van FJ Rothenbuhler', *Verhandelingen Bataviaasche Genootschap van Kunsten en Wetenschappen*, vol. 41, 1881, pp. 71-3.

Knaap, Gerrit, 'Maritime Trade in Small-Town Java around 1775', in Peter Boomgaard, Dick Kooiman & Henk Schulte Nordholt (eds), *Linking Destinies: Trade, Towns and Kin in Asian History*, Leiden, KITLV Press, 2008, pp. 81-98.

Knight, Franklin W, 'Origins of Wealth and the Sugar Revolution in Cuba, 1750-1850', *The Hispanic American Historical Review*, vol. 57, no. 2, 1977, pp. 231-53.

Knight, G Roger, 'From Plantation to Padi Field: The Origins of the Nineteenth Century Transformation of Java's Sugar Industry', *Modern Asian Studies*, vol. 14, no. 2, 1980, pp. 177-204.

——, '"The People's Own Cultivations": Rice and Second Crops in Pekalongan Residency, North Java, 1800-1870', *Review of Malay and Indonesian Affairs*, vol. 19, no. 2, 1985, pp.1-38.

——, 'Peasant Labour and Capitalist Production in Late Colonial Indonesia: The Campaign at a North Java Sugar Factory 1840-1870', *Journal of Southeast Asian Studies*, vol. 19, no. 2, 1988, pp. 245-65.

——, 'The Peasantry and the Cultivation of Cane in Nineteenth Century Java', in A Booth, WJ O'Malley & A Weidemann (eds), *Indonesian Economic History in the Dutch Colonial Era*, New Haven, Yale University Southeast Asian Series, 1990, pp. 49-66.

——, 'A Case of Mistaken Identity? *Suikerlords* and Ladies, *Tempo Doeloe* and the Dutch Colonial Communities in Nineteenth Century Java', *Social Identities*, vol. 7, no. 3, 2001, pp. 379-91.

——, 'The Blind Eye and the Strong Arm: The Colonial Archive and the Imbrication of Knowledge and Power in Mid-Nineteenth Century Java', *Asian Journal of Social Science*, vol. 33, no. 3, 2005, pp. 544-68.

——, 'Sugar and Servility: Themes of Forced Labor, Resistance and Accommodation in Mid-Nineteenth Century Java', in Edward Alpers, Gwyn Campbell & Michael Salman (eds), *Resisting Bondage in Indian Ocean, Africa and Asia*, London & New York, Routledge, 2006, pp. 69-81.

——, 'From *Merdeka* to Massacre: The Politics of Sugar in the Early Years of the Indonesian Republic', *Journal of Southeast Asian Studies*, vol. 43, no. 3, 2012, pp. 402-21.

——, *Commodities and Colonialism: The Story of Big Sugar in Indonesia, 1880-1942*, Leiden and Boston, Brill, 2013.

——, 'Rescued from the Myths of Time: Toward a Reappraisal of European Mercantile Houses in Mid-Nineteenth Century Java, c. 1830-1870', *Bijdragen tot de Taal-, Land- en Volkenkunde*, (forthcoming).

Kortenhorst, J, 'Eduard Douwes Dekker in den Haag', *Jaarboek Die Haghe*, vol. 51, 1969, pp. 69-98.

Korthals Altes, WL, *Changing Economy in Indonesia (12A), General Trade Statistics 1822-1940*, Amsterdam, Royal Tropical Institute, 1991.

——, *Tussen Cultures en Kredieten: Een Institutionele Gescheidenis van de Nederlandsch-Indische Handelsbank en Nationale Handelsbank, 1863-1964*, Amsterdam, Nederlands Instituut voor het Bank, Verzekerings-en-Effectenbedrief, 2004.

Kwee Hui Kian, *The Political Economy of Java's Northeast Coast c. 1740-1800: Elite Synergy*, Leiden & Boston, Brill, 2006.

——, 'Cultural Strategies, Economic Dominance: The Lineage of the Tan Bing in Nineteenth Century Semarang', in Peter Boomgaard, Dick Kooiman & Henk Schulte Nordholt (eds), *Linking Destinies: Trade, Towns and Kin in Asian History*, Leiden, KITLV Press, 2008, pp. 197-218.

Lamousse, Ronald, 'The Economic Development of the Mauritius Sugar Industry', *Revue Agricole et Sucrière de L'île Maurice*, vol. 43, nos. 1, 2 & 4, 1964, pp. 23-38, 113-27, 354-72; and vol. 44, no. 1, 1965, pp. 11-36.

Larkin, John A, *The Pampangans: Colonial Society in a Philippine Province*, Berkeley & Los Angeles, University of California Press, 1972.

——, *Sugar and the Origins of Modern Philippine Society*, Berkeley & Los Angeles, University of California Press, 1993.

Lees, Lynn Hollen, 'International Management in a Free-Standing Company: The Penang Sugar Estates, Ltd., and the Malayan Sugar Industry, 1851-1914', *Business History Review*, vol. 81, spring 2007, pp. 27-57.

Leidelmeijer, Margaret, *Van Suikermolen tot Grootbedrijf: Technische Vernieuwing in de Java-Suikerindustrie in de Negentiende Eeuw*, Amsterdam, NEHA, 1997.

Leon, JA, *On Sugar Cultivation in Louisiana, Cuba &c. and the British Possessions by an European and Colonial Sugar Manufacturer*, London, Ollivier, 1848.

Lewis, Jack, 'The Rise and Fall of the South African Peasantry: A Critique and Reassessment', *Journal of Southern African Studies*, vol. 11, no. 1, 1984, pp. 1-24.

Lock, CGW, GW Wigner & RH Harland, *Sugar Growing and Refining*, London & New York, Spon, 1882.

Lopez-Varga, VB, *The Socio-Politics of Sugar: Wealth, Power Formation and Change in Negros 1899-1985*, Bacolod, University of St La Salle Press, 1989.

Luiten van Zanden, Jan, 'Linking Two Debates: Money Supply, Wage Labour and Economic Development in Java in the Nineteenth Century', in Jan Lucassen (ed.), *Wages and Currency: Global Comparisons from Antiquity to the Twentieth Century*, Bern, Peter Lang, 2007, pp. 169-92.

Luiten van Zanden, Jan & Arthur van Riel, *The Strictures of Inheritance: The Dutch Economy in the Nineteenth Century*, Princeton, NJ & Oxford, Princeton University Press, 2004.

Lythe, SGE, 'Shipbuilding at Dundee Down to 1914', *Scottish Journal of Political Economy*, vol. 11, no. 3, 1964, pp. 219-32.

Maat, Harro, 'Agricultural Sciences in Colonial Indonesia', *Historia Scientiarum*, vol. 16, no. 3, 2007, pp. 244-63.

McCoy, Alfred W, 'A Queen Dies Slowly: The Rise and Decline of Iloilo City', in Alfred W McCoy & Ed C de Jesus, *Philippine Social History*, Quezon City, Ateneo de Manila University Press, 1982, pp. 297-360.

——, 'Sugar Barons: Formation of a Native Planter Class in the Colonial Philippines', *Journal of Peasant Studies*, vol. 19, no. 3, 1992, pp. 106-41.

MacMicking, Robert, *Recollections of Manilla and the Philippines During 1848, 1849, and 1850*, edited and annotated by Morton J Netzorg, with an Appendix, 'Trade in Panay, 1857-67, Four Letters by Nicholas Loney', Manila, Filipiniana Book Guild, Inc., 1967.

McVey, RT, 'The Materialisation of the Southeast Asian Entrepreneur', in RT McVey (ed.), *Southeast Asian Capitalists*, Ithaca, NY, Cornell University, Southeast Asia Program, Studies in Southeast Asian History, 1992.

Mansvelt, WFM, *Geschiedenis van de Nederlandsche Handel-Maatschappij*, vol. 2, Haarlem, [1924-1926].

Marshall, PJ, 'The Bengal Commercial Society of 1775', *Bulletin of the Institute of Historical Research*, vol. 42, 1969, pp. 173-87.

——, *East Indian Fortunes*, Oxford, Oxford University Press, 1976.

——, *Bengal: The British Bridgehead, Eastern India 1740-1828*, The New Cambridge History of India II, vol. 2, Cambridge, Cambridge University Press, 1987.

Martineau, George, *Sugar*, London, Pitman [1910].

Matthew, HCG & Brian Harrison, 'Cockerill', in *Oxford Dictionary of National Biography*, vol. 11, Oxford, Oxford University Press, 2004.

Mazumdar, Sucheta, *Sugar and Society in China: Peasants, Technology, and the World Market*, Cambridge, MA, Harvard University Asia Centre, 1998.

Meilink-Roelofz, MAP, *Asian Trade and European Influence in the Indonesian Archipelago between 1500 and about 1630*, The Hague, Nijhoff, 1962.

Millard, John, *De Suikerindustrie op Java*, The Hague, Nijhoff, 1869.

——, *Riet en Bietsuiker in Verband tot de Suikerindustrie op Java: Voordracht ter Aanprizing van eene Proef met Diffusie op Java*, Gravenhage, Couvee, 1884.

Mommers, ARM, 'Brabant van Generaliteitsland tot Gewest', Proefschrift, Rijksuniversiteit Leiden, 1953.

The Monthly Repository of Theology and General Literature, vol. 20, 1825.

Moore, Gene M (ed.), *Conrad's Cities: Essays for Hans van Marle*, Amsterdam, Rodopi, 1992.

Moreno-Fraginals, M, *The Sugar Mill: The Socio-Economic Complex of Sugar in Cuba, 1780-1860*, New York, Monthly Review Press, 1976.

Mrazek, Rudolph, *Engineers of Happy Land: Technology and Nationalism in a Colony*, Princeton, NJ, Princeton University Press, 2002.

Mubyarto, 'The Sugar Industry', *Bulletin of Indonesian Economic Studies*, vol. 5, no. 2, 1969, pp. 37-54.

——, 'The Sugar Industry: From Estate to Smallholder Cane', *Bulletin of Indonesian Economic Studies*, vol. 13, no. 2, 1977, pp. 29-44.

Munting, Roger & John Perkins, 'The Cane-Beet Sugar Rivalry in the 19th Century', in Roger Munting & Tamas Szmrecsanyi (eds), *Competing for the Sugar Bowl*, St. Katharinen, Scripta Mercaturae Verlag, 2000, pp. 1-15.

Nagtegaal, Luc, *Riding the Dutch Tiger: The Dutch East India Company and the Northeast Coast of Java 1680-1743*, Leiden, KITLV Press, 1996.

Nahuijs van Burgst, HG, *Herinneringen van het Openbare en Bijzondere Leven (1799-1849) van Mr HG Baron Nahuijs van Burgst*, Utrecht, Gebroeders Muller, 1852.

[Nederburgh, SC], *Journal der Reize van Mr SC Nederburgh, Gewezen Commissaris Generaal over Nederlands India, Langs Java's Noordoostkust, in 1798*, Amsterdam, W Holtrop, 1804.

Netscher, FHJ, *Regt en Onregt of de Toestand der Gewestelijke Besturen in Indie tegenover de Particuliere Industrie*, The Hague, HC Susan, 1864.

——, 'The Effect of Export Cultivations in Nineteenth Century Java', *Modern Asian Studies*, vol. 15, no. 1, 1981, pp. 25-58.

——, Robert, *Java under the Cultivation System*, Leiden, KITLV Press, 1992.

——, *Java's Northeast Coast 1740-1840*, Leiden, CNWS Publications, 2005.

Onghokham, 'The Residency of Madiun: Priyayi and Peasant in the Nineteenth Century', PhD Diss, Yale, 1975.

——, 'Chinese Capitalism in Dutch Java', in Onghokham, *The Thugs, the Curtain Thief and the Sugar Lord: Power, Politics and Culture in Colonial Java*, Jakarta, Metafor, 2003.

Ong Tae Hae, *The Chinaman Abroad: An Account of the Malayan Archipelago, Particularly Java*, translated by WH Medhurst, London, John Snow, 1850.

Oosterwijk, Bram, *Koning van de Koopvaart: Anthony van Hoboken (1756-1850)*, Rotterdam, Stichting Historische Publicaties Roterodamum, 1983.

Oostindie, Gert J, 'Cuban Railroads 1830-1868: Origins and Effects of Progressive Enterpreneurialism', *Caribbean Studies*, vol. 20, vols 3-4, 1988, pp. 24-45.

Oostindie, Gert J, 'La Burguesia Cubana y sus Caminos de Hierro, 1830-1868', *Boletin de Estudios Latinoamericanos y del Caribe*, vol. 37, 1984, pp. 99-115.

Northcote Parkinson C, *Trade in the Eastern Seas, 1793-1813*, London, Frank Cass & Co, 1966 [1937].

Pasleau, Suzy, *John Cockerill: Itineraire d'Un Geant Industriel*, Alleur-Liege, Belgium, Editions Du Perron, 1992.

du Perron-de Roos, E, 'Correspondentie tussen Dirk van Hogendorp en Zijn Broeder Gijsbert Karl van Hogendorp', *Bijdragen tot de Taal-, Land en Volkenkunde*, vol. 102, nos. 1 & 2, 1943, pp. 125-273.

Post, Peter, 'Chinese Business Networks and Japanese Capital in Southeast Asia 1880-1940: Some Preliminary Observations', in RA Brown (ed.), *Chinese Business Enterprise in Asia*, London, Routledge, 1995, pp. 154-76.

Prinsen Geerligs HC, *Korte Handleiding tot de Fabrikatie van Suiker uit Suikerriet op Java*, Semarang, Dorp, 1896.

——, HC, *Cane Sugar and the Process of its Manufacture in Java*, Manchester, Roberts, 1898.

——, 'Invoer en Fabrikatie 1904', *ASNI*, vol. 12, no. 2, 1904.

——, *Cane Sugar and its Manufacture*, Altrincham (Manchester), Norman Rodger, 1909.

Raffles, TS, *The History of Java*, vol. 1, London, Black, Parbury and Allen, 1817.

Ratledge, Andrew, *Competing for the British Sugar Bowl: East India Sugar 1792-1865: Politics, Trade and Sugar Consumption*, Saarbrücken, VDM Verlag Dr Müller, 2009.

Reid, Anthony, *Southeast Asia in the Age of Commerce*, vol. 1: *The Lands below the Winds*, New Haven, Yale University Press, 1988.

Reinsma, R, *Het Verval van het Cultuurstelsel*, Den Haag, Van Keulen, 1955.

Ricklefs, Merle C, 'Some Statistical Evidence on Javanese Social, Economic and Demographic History in the Later Seventeenth and Eighteenth Centuries', *Modern Asian Studies*, vol. 20, no. 1, 1986, pp. 1-32.

Ricklefs, Merle C, *Jogjakarta under Sultan Mangkubumi: A History of the Division of Java*, London, Oxford University Press, 1974.

——, *War, Culture and Economy in Java, 1677-1726*, Sydney, Allen & Unwin, 1993.

[Robinson, HO & A], *Description of Robinson's Steam Cane Mill*, London, [no publisher stated], 1845.

Rogge, J, *Het Handelshuis Van Eeghen*, Amsterdam, Van Ditmar, 1949.

Rush, James, *Opium to Java: Revenue Farming and Chinese Enterprise in Colonial Indonesia 1860-1910*, Ithaca, NY, Cornell University Press, 1990.

Rutger van Swet, Jan, 'President in Indie en Nederland: Mr NP van den Berg als Centraal Bankier', PhD Diss, Universitiet Leiden, 2004.

Salmon, Claudine, 'The Han Family of East Java: Entrepreneurship and Politics (18th-19th Centuries)', *Archipel*, vol. 41, 1991, pp. 53-87.

——, 'Ancestral Halls and Funeral Associations, and Attempts at Resinicization in Nineteenth Century Netherlands India', in Anthony Reid (ed.), *Sojourners and Settlers: Histories of Southeast Asia and the Chinese*, Sydney, Allen & Unwin, 1996, pp. 183-214.

Scoffern, John, *The Manufacture of Sugar in the Colonies and at Home*, London, Longman, Brown, Green and Longmans, 1849.

Seed, John, 'Gentlemen Dissenters: The Social and Political Meanings of Rational Dissent in the 1770s and 1780s', *The Historical Journal*, vol. 28, no. 2, 1985, pp. 299-325.

Segers, WAIM, *Manufacturing Industry 1870-1942*, vol. 8 of P Boomgaard (ed.), *Changing Economy in Indonesia*, Amsterdam, Royal Tropical Institute, 1987.

Sluyterman, Keetie E, *Dutch Enterprise in the Twentieth Century*, London & New York, Routledge, 2005.

Smissaert, MP, *Het Geslacht Smissaert*, Utrecht, Kemink en Zoon, 1882.

Soames, Peter, *Treatise on the Manufacture of Sugar from Sugar Cane*, London & New York, Spon, 1872.

van Soest, JWA, *De Suikeronderneming Kalibagor*, Semarang, Bisschop, 1884.

Soetrisno, Lukman, 'The Sugar Industry and Rural Development: The Impact of Cane Cultivation for Export on Rural Java, 1830-1934', PhD Diss, Cornell University, 1980.

Spaan, Ernst & Aard Hartveld, 'Socio-Economic Change and Rural Entrepreneurs in Pre-Crisis East Java, Indonesia: Case Study of a Madurese Upland Community', *Sojourn: Social Issues in Southeast Asia*, vol. 17, no. 2, 2002, pp. 274-300.

Steijn Parve, DC, 'Nieuwe Uitvindingen Betreffende de Koloniale Suikerbereiding', *Tijdschrijft voor Nederlandsch-Indië* (Nieuwe Reeks), vol. 1, no. 2, 1867, pp. 392-408.

Suryo, Djoko, 'Social and Economic Life in Rural Semarang under Colonial Rule in the later Nineteenth Century', PhD Diss, Monash University, Melbourne, 1982.

Sutherland, Heather, 'The Priyayi', *Indonesia*, vol. 19, 1975, pp. 57-79.

——, *The Making of a Bureaucratic Elite*, Singapore, Heinemann, 1979.

Storcy, William Kelleher, *Science and Power in Colonial Mauritius*, Rochester, NY, University of Rochester Press, 1997.

de Sturler, WL, *Handboek voor den Landbouw in Nederlandsch Oost-Indië*, Leiden, Sythoff, 1863.

Tann, Jennifer, 'Steam and Sugar: The Diffusion of the Stationary Steam Engine to the Caribbean Sugar Industry, 1770-1840', *History of Technology*, vol. 19, 1997, pp. 63-84.

Tann, Jennifer & John Aitkin, 'The Diffusion of the Stationary Steam Engine from Britain to India, 1790-1830', *Indian Economic and Social History Review*, vol. 29, no. 2, 1992, pp. 199-214.

Tichelaar, JJ, 'De Exploitatie eener Suikerfabriek, Zestig Jaar Geleden', *ASNI*, vol. 33, no. 2, 1925, pp. 203-21, 248-70.

Tjoa Tjwan Phing & JJ Moolenaar, *125 Jaren Tjandi, 1832-1957*, Surabaja, Fuhri & Co, 1957.

Tomich, Dale W, *Slavery in the Circuit of Sugar: Martinique and the World Economy 1830-1848*, Baltimore, Johns Hopkins University Press, 1990.

Van Niel, Robert, 'The Alfred A Reed Papers', *Bijdragen tot de Taal-, Land- en Volkenkunde*, vol. 120, 1964, pp. 224-30.

Verbong, Geert, 'Opleiding en Beroep', in HW Lintsen (ed.), *Geschiedenis van de Techniek in Nederland: De Wording van een Moderne Samenleving 1800-1890*, Part 5: *Techniek, Beroep en Praktijk*, Zutphen, Walburg Pers, 1994, pp. 21-83.

Viraphol, Sarasin, *Tribute and Profit: Sino-Siamese Trade 1652-1853*, Cambridge, Mass, Council for East Asian Studies, Harvard University, 1977.

Wachlin, Steven, with a contribution by Marianne Fluitsma & Gerrit Knaap, *Woodbury & Page: Photographers Java*, Leiden, KITLV Press, 1994.

Walker, Herbert S, *The Sugar Industry on the Island of Negros*, Manila, Department of the Interior, Bureau of Science, 1910.

Washbrook, DA, 'Progress and Problems: South Asian Economic and Social History c. 1720-1860', *Modern Asian Studies*, vol. 22, no. 1, 1988, pp. 57-96.

Westendorp Boerma, JJ (ed.), *Briefwisseling tussen J van den Bosch en JC Baud*, vol. 1, Utrecht, Kemink en Zoon, 1956.

Wheatley, Paul, *The Golden Khersonese: Studies in the Historical Geography of the Malay Peninsula before A.D. 1500*, Kuala Lumpur, University of Malaya Press, 1961.

White, Ben, '"Agricultural Involution" and its Critics: Twenty Years after', *Bulletin of Concerned Asian Scholars*, vol. 15, 1983, pp. 18-31.

Yoshihara, Kunio (ed.), *Oei Tiong Ham Concern: The First Business Empire of Southeast Asia*, Kyoto, Center for Southeast Asian Studies, Kyoto University, 1989.

This book is available as a free fully-searchable ebook from

www.adelaide.edu.au/press

www.ingramcontent.com/pod-product-compliance
Lightning Source LLC
Chambersburg PA
CBHW042033100526
44587CB00029B/4411